Anime

BLOOMSBURY FILM GENRES SERIES

Edited by Mark Jancovich and Charles Acland

The *Film Genres* series presents accessible books on popular genres for students, scholars and fans alike. Each volume addresses key films, movements and periods by synthesizing existing literature and proposing new assessments.

Forthcoming:

Film Noir: A Critical Introduction

Published:

Historical Film: A Critical Introduction
Documentary Film: A Critical Introduction
Science Fiction Film: A Critical Introduction
Teen Film: A Critical Introduction
Fantasy Film: A Critical Introduction

Anime

A Critical Introduction

RAYNA DENISON

Bloomsbury Academic
An imprint of Bloomsbury Publishing Plc

B L O O M S B U R Y
LONDON · OXFORD · NEW YORK · NEW DELHI · SYDNEY

Bloomsbury Academic

An imprint of Bloomsbury Publishing Plc

50 Bedford Square
London
WC1B 3DP
UK

1385 Broadway
New York
NY 10018
USA

www.bloomsbury.com

BLOOMSBURY and the Diana logo are trademarks of Bloomsbury Publishing Plc

First published 2015
Reprinted by Bloomsbury Academic 2016

British Library Cataloguing-in-Publication Data
A catalogue record for this book is available from the British Library.

ISBN: HB: 978-1-8478-8480-0
PB: 978-1-8478-8479-4
ePub: 978-1-4725-7676-7
ePDF: 978-1-4725-7681-1

Library of Congress Cataloging-in-Publication Data
Denison, Rayna.
Anime: a critical introduction/Rayna Denison.
pages cm. – (Film genres)
Summary: "From mecha robots to shojo anime's hearts and flowers,
Anime: A Critical Introduction investigates the wild, wonderful and often
misunderstood worlds of Japan's animation genres"– Provided by publisher.
Includes bibliographical references and index.
ISBN 978-1-84788-480-0 (hardback) – ISBN 978-1-84788-479-4 (paperback)
1. Animated films–Japan–History and criticism. I. Title.
NC1766.J3D46 2015
791.43'34–dc23
2015016900

Series: Film Genres

Typeset by Integra Software Services Pvt. Ltd.
Printed and bound in Great Britain

Contents

List of Illustrations   vi

Acknowledgments   viii

Introduction   1

1 Approaching Anime: Genre and Subgenres   15

2 Sci Fi Anime: Cyberpunk to Steampunk   31

3 Anime's Bodies   51

4 Early Anime Histories: Japan and America   69

5 Anime, Video and the *Shōjo* and *Shōnen* Genres   85

6 Post-Video Anime: Digital Media and the
      Revelation of Anime's Hidden Genres   101

7 Ghibli Genre: Toshio Suzuki and
      Studio Ghibli's Brand Identity   117

8 Experiencing Japan's Anime: Genres at the
      Tokyo International Anime Fair   133

9 Anime Horror and Genrification   153

Notes   169

Bibliography   171

Index   187

List of Illustrations

Figure 2.1   Ray Steam uses steampowered jet pack to soar above a sepia-toned London in *Steamboy*   47

Figure 3.1   Chibi wrap party from the *Fullmetal Alchemist Premium OVA Collection*   61

Figure 3.2   Demonic imagery from *Urotsukidōji: Legend of the Overfiend*   64

Figure 4.1   *Norakuro, Private Second Class* and war-time propaganda   74

Figure 4.2   *Hakujaden*, Japan's first color feature film   77

Figure 4.3   Tezuka's limited animation   80

Figure 5.1   Comparison of Japanese boys' and girls' genres through texts. Data amalgamated from Yasuo Yamaguchi 2004, 104–106.   89

Figure 5.2   A girl and her *mecha*, Noa Izumi in *Mobile Police Patlabor*   98

Figure 7.1   Representation of the brand hierarchy at Studio Ghibli in Japan   124

Figure 8.1   Astro Boy shows the way to the Osamu Tezuka museum in Kyoto's train station (personal photograph)   135

Figure 8.2   *Pokémon's* Pikachu looks over the shoulder of *Death Note's shinigami* (death god) Ryuk (personal photograph)   140

Figure 8.3   *Case Closed* booth literally attached to one for
                   Detroit Metal City (personal photograph)   141

Figure 8.4   Pierrot's anniversary booth at TAF 2008
                   (personal photograph)   144

Figure 8.5   Gainax's booth for the launch of *Gurren*
                   Lagann at TAF 2008 (personal photograph)   145

Figure 8.6   Madhouse's booth at TAF 2008
                   (personal photograph)   146

Figure 8.7   *Kyōsō Giga* booth, new media anime with
                   exclusive merchandise (personal photograph)   149

Figure 9.1   Abel Nightroad activates the Kresnik and
                   embraces his inner, gothic vampire   164

Acknowledgments

There are many people who made this book possible, the most important of whom are my parents, Raymond and Sheila, who instilled a lifelong love of anime in me just by letting me watch Saturday morning cartoons, and my partner, John Taylor, who continues to watch with me. Without you, this book simply would never have been.

My thanks, too, to my friends in anime, who have helped me out with research—to Phyll Smith, Hugh K. David and Kim Hallam who lent me many useful magazines and regaled me with fantastic anime stories. Thanks, too, to Hiroko Furukawa for her help on the Manga to Movies project, the translations of which make up a large part of Chapter 7 and to Sachiko Shikoda, whose continuing support is invaluable to all of my research. And to Cameron and Lisa Fearing, you were the inspiration for Chapter 5!

I also owe a debt of gratitude to several funding organizations, particularly the UK's Arts and Humanities Research Council, the Great Britain Sasakawa Foundation and the Daiwa Anglo-Japanese Foundation for the funding of several projects that allowed me to get out to Japan to do research.

My thanks, too, to the series editors Charles Acland and Mark Jancovich for their support and to the editors at Bloomsbury, and the brilliant feedback from their external reader for helping me complete this introduction to anime's genres.

Introduction

Anime seems to defy easy definition. It is a shifting, sliding category of media production that refuses attempts to pin it down. Anime is for some the very definition of "Japanese animation," but closer investigation reveals how easy it would be to contest that understanding. Anime is also highly generic, but is only a genre under highly specific conditions, making a book like this one a necessary intervention into debates about how we understand anime's complex relationship with genre concepts. Furthermore, anime is more than a single mode of media production. Its styles and content are found in everything from advertisements, to webisodes and short, five-minute episode television series, through to the more standard production of "half hour" serialized episodes made for television, through to a wide range of theatrical and straight-to-video (and now DVD other digital formats) film productions. This variety in production makes the categories of anime even harder to conceptualize, requiring us to think not just of popular or ciritical categories, but also about industrial understandings of anime's place in Japan's media markets.

Moreover, anime constantly shifts meanings dependent on where we are when watching it; our access to anime is being limited or expanded by the relationships between distribution markets, by our understanding of language and, increasingly, by the flows of texts across the internet, whether generated by legitimate distributors or fans online. Due to this complexity, this introduction to anime focuses its inquiries on the ways anime has been understood by those who have encountered it, and who have attempted to understand and engage with it. In this introductory chapter, I therefore focus on how key individuals within academia have attempted to define anime, presaging this book's deeper mining of the meanings that "anime" holds for a wide range of fans, critics and academics from around the world.

Even as recently as 2013, Ian Condry's ethnography *The Soul of Anime* told his readers that "Anime ('AH-nee-may') refers to Japanese animated film and television," going on to note that "the worlds of anime extend well beyond what appears on the screen."[1] A host of tensions are bound up within Condry's declaration about how to define anime. Condry suggests, for example, that anime still requires explanation even at the level of pronunciation. His definition also tells us that anime is unstable, shifting between media (moving from film or television to "worlds"). He also argues that anime is both a local media format (it is Japanese) and a part of a wider cultural phenomenon that encompasses much of the globe. In these observations, Condry reveals the vastness of a media category and cultural phenomenon that has been, from time to time, radically oversimplified as "Japanese cartoons."

As Condry suggests, making sense of anime presents a series of challenges. The aim of this book is to reflect on attempts by a wide range of commentators to create order out of the shifting global chaos of anime production, translation, dissemination and consumption, something commentators have routinely done by dividing anime into genres or by trying to understand anime as a genre. I take as my subject, therefore, not just anime, but the ways in which anime is talked about by those enabling its creation and watching over its global dispersal—including industry professionals and academics, but also the trade presses, popular presses and fan communities supporting anime's domestic and transnational life.[2] These sources are my primary sources, and I will largely explore them rather than offering my own analyses of specific anime texts. Wherever possible, I make use of voices and sources that have been crucial to shaping our understandings, but which have been little discussed within anime fandom. For this reason, I privilege the sites of popular debate about anime rather than the authoritative voices of figures like directors, whose proclamations have a tendency to curtail debates about the meanings of anime.

As a consequence of using such alternative and varied sources, I do not propose to answer the question "what is anime?," but rather to seek out the range of meanings that have become associated with anime. I aim to show that anime is not *just* a genre any more than it is *simply* a kind of animation, or a product of *only* Japanese culture. Instead, I contend that anime needs to be understood more broadly as a cultural phenomenon whose meanings are dependent on context. In understanding anime this way, this book acts as an introduction to a cultural category perhaps most notable for its mutability: anime's aesthetics, its (re-)production contexts, its distribution and its consumption by different sets of audiences are constantly changing the way it means and to whom.

As an exemplar of anime's shifting meanings, this introduction outlines some of the attempts by high-profile anime scholars (academic and popular) to define anime. The lack of agreement, even among those whose critiques cluster together, suggests the variegation in anime's cultural meanings. It is useful, therefore, to begin with the early transnational life of anime, as it entered US cultural debates, bringing English-speaking scholars into contact with an already mature media phenomenon that was beginning to penetrate the world's media markets. These early exchanges, often centered around university anime societies, led to an early flourishing of scholarship on anime in the mid-1990s.

At that time, academic authors seem to have been primarily interested in accounting for anime through its difference to contemporaneous US animation. For example, Annalee Newitz describes the anime appearing in American video stores as "[o]ften graphically violent and sexual," but containing a variety of genres: "*anime* range from comic romances about high school students to pornographic tales of demons whose penises are larger than skyscrapers" (1995, 2). Within this generic landscape, Newitz reads two threads of attraction. On the one hand, a sense of "specialized knowledge ordinary Americans do not have," while on the other hand, fans' translation work in the age of laser disc and VHS also spoke to the reproduction of "a Japanese product into a uniquely American one" (3). Her initial foray into anime scholarship would be echoed by later scholars like Henry Jenkins, who see in anime's rise to popularity the creation of a "pop cosmopolitanism," or fandom, that unites fans seeking to distinguish themselves through their consumption of culturally distant texts (2006a).

Similarly, Ben Crawford's early academic reading of anime attempts to map anime in relation to violent content, claiming that anime (and manga) is made up of "mass appeal properties and [a] rich vein of niche properties" (1996, 79). Using this guiding logic, Crawford is able to account for the disparities between anime genres and to analyze their engagements with the more violent aspects of Japan's history and culture. For him, though, anime becomes bound up in the legacies of Japan's wartime history. Again, lingering concerns about the content and meanings of Japanese animation appear sporadically throughout its international history, symptomatically responding to wider social and cultural concerns. For example, when Edward Snowden's betrayal of US secrets became known in 2013, a *New York Times* article appeared claiming that "He socialized with a tight circle of people who were enthralled by the Internet and Japanese anime culture" (Broder and Shane 2013, A20). Anime is no stranger to controversy, be it historical or contemporary, and its association with a range of subaltern social groups the world over has led to a seemingly endless split between those recognizing its artistic merits and those who fear its subcultural, controversial tendencies. Early articles, like those by Newitz and Crawford, therefore, understandably began by engaging with anime's more controversial edges. Journalists and fan-scholars like Antonia Levi (1996), Helen McCarthy and Jonathan Clements (1998) and Gilles Poitras (1999) joined the fray explaining anime's difference to other kinds of animation, focusing on some of the more outré and controversial edges of anime's transnational texts.

As early experts in anime, several of these authors paid close attention to the Japanese roots of these texts, using anime's links to Japanese traditional culture to ameliorate its controversies. For example, Levi asserted anime's special links to Japanese history:

> Even its physical appearance requires a lengthy discussion of Japan's postwar popular media. To examine the source of its dramatic techniques, its themes, and its basic assumptions, requires a deeper knowledge of Japan's pre-history, its myths and legends, its religions, artistic traditions, and philosophies. (1996, 16)

Levi connects interest in anime with a desire to promote Japanese cultural heritage as visualized through anime texts. Poitras echoes her work, attending to the representations of Japanese culture found in anime to suggest how anime might be used as a tool for teaching audiences about Japanese cultural forms.

In a later article, Levi re-evaluated the educative potential of anime. Her initial disappointment that anime's popularity did not lead to a concomitant rise in knowledge and understanding about Japan was leavened by her realization that "What I saw as a failure to appreciate the uniquely Japanese aspects of anime and manga can just as easily be seen as an example of the type of negotiated understandings that result from encoding and decoding"(2006, 43). Borrowing from noted cultural theorist Stuart Hall's work, Levi essentially declares that US fans have localized anime, making it their own phenomenon rather than seeing anime texts as a wholly foreign set of objects. Therefore, the issue of anime's connection to Japanese history and culture softened over time into an appreciation of how anime has become a part of world culture. Notable here is that each of these early anime scholars emphasizes distinctive kinds of difference in their readings: for Levi and Newitz, ones of national and generic content and fandom; for McCarthy and Clements, ones of incorporating eroticism into animation; for Crawford, it was the recognition of anime's dual mass and niche facets. These approaches—the industrial, textual and cultural—would go on to inform the debates around anime's meanings in the decades that followed.

History, industry and anime definitions

These debates are made manifest when trying to pin down the texts and history of anime. Jonathan Clements' excellent history of anime asserts that understanding all of Japanese animation as anime oversimplifies Japanese animation production. Instead, he situates anime within a local animation production culture comprised of everything from cel animation through to puppetry, cut-out animation and stop motion (2013a). In this, he chimes with a recent Japanese academic study, *Anime Gaku* (*Anime Studies*), edited by Mitsuteru Takahashi and Noboyuki Tsugata, who argue that calling Japanese animation "anime" is itself too simplistic (2011, 9). Furthermore, the term "anime" does not cover the earliest periods of Japanese animation production. Tsugata notes that the earliest animation in Japan was "cut paper" animation (2005, 71), and Marc Steinberg observes that animation produced by Tōei Animation[3] as late as the 1950s and 1960s was termed *manga eiga* (manga film), while Osamu Tezuka's early animated television works were known locally as *terebi manga* (manga television), and not as anime (2012, 8–10).

Tze-Yue G. Hu takes this further, extending the list of alternative terms to include:

anime-shon [animation], *manga-eiga* [manga films], *dōga* [moving pictures], *anime manga, komikku eiga* [comic book films], *manga fuirumu* [manga films], *bideo gēmu anime* [video game anime], and so on. Furthermore, the average Japanese also addresses the medium of animation as *anime*, be it Turkish anime, Russian anime, or French anime. (2010, loc 2444)

As these histories of Japanese animation suggest, terminology matters. Anime's rise to dominance within Japanese animation culture demonstrates the power of a particular set of Japanese industries, and (sub)cultural gatekeepers around the world, to control how Japanese animation is understood. "Anime" is, as these accounts suggest, a comparatively new term, one that has been retroactively applied to the whole history of cel animation. As this terminological slippage suggests, Japanese animation has continually changed in format and production media across its history. Studying the discussions around anime, therefore, opens up new possibilities for understanding anime's place within a wider industrial animation landscape.

Furthermore, what we think of as anime has emerged out of competing Japanese industrial practices of animation production, and the range of terms used to describe it gives voice to the tensions being played out within the Japanese animation industry. Hu and Steinberg's lists of terms suggest as much. Their lists comprise terms that illustrate anime's growing transmedia reach— the difference between film and television production and latterly adaptations involving computer games—with each new medium bringing about change within the animation landscape in Japan. Nor are these distinctions new. Most accounts in Japanese claim that anime "began" with Osamu Tezuka's *Astro Boy* (*Tetsuwan Atomu*, 1963–1966) in the early years of television. Takahashi and Tsugata quote Tezuka as saying of his most famous television animation series: "This [*Astro*] is not animation. It is anime," thereby offering another potential starting point for anime in Japan. Moreover, *Astro Boy* was not just the start of anime in Japan, it was also the beginning of Japanese television anime exports to the USA, where it was also first broadcast in 1963.

However, Takahashi and Tsugata go on to argue that, at this early time, anime was still "a phenomenon only for the special community at Mushi Pro [Tezuka's animation company, founded in 1961]. It was probably in the 1990s that its use was properly clarified by fans" (2011, 9). These recent historically focused accounts of Japan's animation history are, therefore, helping to repeal assumptions about anime's dominance in Japan. Through them, we can see that anime is a category that has emerged out of the erasure of historical complexity. However, these claims are being made with the benefit of hindsight, safe in the knowledge that anime has become the dominant domestic industry and a significant transnational cultural phenomenon.

One of the more remarkable aspects of anime is that there are many types of media hidden under its rubric. Major studios, even ones as high profile as Studio Ghibli, produce not just anime films, but also everything from music videos to television advertising (see Chapter 7). Notably, academic books and articles range across a variety of media all identified as anime, most commonly the film and television texts referred to earlier by Condry. However, other authors are now drawing attention to the scope of anime franchising and to the significant roles played by merchandising in anime's "worlds" (see, for example, Azuma 2001; Steinberg 2012). This is another reason for my focus on discourse analysis hereafter: anime's popularity has grown during a period of rapid media development, making anime's core media increasingly difficult to discern. Domestically, Japanese television has been routinely cited as anime's key medium (Azuma 2001; Masuda 2011), but anime films have been at the forefront of its transnational distribution success. It is for this reason that this book's first case study (Chapter 2) is a consideration of anime's relationship with science fiction films. Thereafter, I expand the media perspective on anime outwards to take in the distinctive Original Video Animation (OVA or OAV) format introduced in the video era (Chapter 3), before considering digital anime (Chapter 6) and anime branding and advertising practices (Chapters 7 and 9).

Home media have been essential to the shaping of anime. VHS, DVD, Blu-ray, LaserDisc and internet streaming and downloading technologies have all helped to disperse anime texts around the world in different periods, and along more and less legal routes. Laurie Cubbison rightly asserts that the distinction between media formats is important because the format "affects the experience of the text…. when works are produced in alternate languages and formatted as different kinds of objects, the textual experience alters" (2005, 45–46). Anime's trasnsmediality is important (see Condry 2013 for more on "transmedia"). While many of the films studied hereafter have enjoyed transnational cinematic exhibition, the norm for fans outside Japan has long been home viewing. As Cubbison argues, unless we pay attention to how anime is being watched, it is difficult to assert any common ground shared between, or to examine hierarchies among, anime's textual networks.

Hiroki Azuma argues against such hierarchies, however, contending that fans access anime from any number of entry points, and that anime texts are just "raw materials for remixing, presenting ... fragments without a unified narrative" (2009, 38). While this may assume too free a media consumption environment, the idea of anime as a "database" (Azuma 2009) that fans construct provides a useful way of thinking about how all consumers, not just anime's extreme *otaku*, connect with anime's transmedia worlds. Marc Steinberg takes this one stage further. Steinberg argues that "anime was constituted and experienced as a medium that referenced and drew on other media formats" from its earliest existence, and that "Anime was an *intermedia*—a medium composed of an assemblage of discrete media, a medium composed of other media forms" (2012, 17). Here, Steinberg refuses to dismiss anime's transmedia borrowing as straightforwardly "postmodern," and engages instead with this borrowing as evidence for the kinds of emphatic "made-ness" that Dani Cavallaro has observed (2007, 1). Woojeong Joo, Rayna Denison and Hiroko Furukawa (2013) have also discussed anime as only one part of Japan's dispersed networks of multimedia adaptation, building on industrial work on the anime industry being undertaken in Japan (Masuda 2011; Masuda and the Japanese Animation Association Database Working Group 2011). This research shows how chains of adaptations are created running from manga through television and on to film, all the while spurring the creation of ever-more dispersed ancillary media networks. Anime, therefore, is not just an intermedia, it also forms part of vast intertextual franchise empires—what Marc Steinberg and others analyze as "Japan's media mix" culture (2012; see also Ito 2003).

Of this culture, Steinberg writes, "anime media mix ... has no single goal or teleological end; the general consumption of any of the media mix's products will grow the entire enterprise. Since each media-commodity is also an advertisement for further products in the same franchise, this is a consumption that produces more consumption" (Steinberg 2012, 141). Recent scholarly interest in anime's media mix accords with current thinking on the importance of "inter-textual relays" within genre filmmaking in the USA. Steve Neale, for example, argues that "the industry's inter-textual relay also provides images of and for genres themselves" (2000, 40). I am taking a broader view of intertextuality than Neale, who considers it in specific relation to the materials circulating around a film's release. Nonetheless, anime's wider franchise intertexts—from manga origins to video game spin-offs to merchandising and advertising—have implications for how we might conceptualize anime as a cultural phenomenon and as a genre. They potentially impact on how we understand the significance of anime in relation to other kinds of Japanese (and international) media. For these reasons, anime is examined here not only as a part of film production, but as part of broader intertextual networks (Kinder, 1993), only parts of which usually travel abroad (see, for example, Chapters 6 and 9).

Textual and technical definitions of anime

The dual specters of cultural and textual distinction continue to inform these debates about anime's definitions. Recently, Hu has called anime a "medium-genre," creating an approach to anime texts that examines both their historical and textual "frames" (2010). Of this Hu writes, "my reading of anime frames is initially literal and later cultural. But circularly, the orientation of my cultural reading of anime is also guided and lured by the literal technical images presented within the frames" (loc. 328). Frames of anime within historical contexts thereby form a palimpsest within Hu's understanding of anime's aesthetics. Dani Cavallaro, one of the more prolific recent authors in anime studies, moves deeper into the texts when looking for the essence of anime. She states that "anime's twin aversion to the naturalistic rendition of mass and to the emulation of the conventions of live-action cinema in the representation of movement" are what give anime a distinctive look (2007, 1). Cavallaro's is, as a result, a less culturally grounded approach, seeking meanings in texts and specifically in the way anime represents a distinctive relationship to onscreen movement.

Thomas LaMarre, an influential voice in the field of anime studies, takes a similar stance to Cavallaro in some respects, arguing that anime needs to be understood as a specific kind of animation with its own aesthetic, one created by what he calls the "animetic machine." LaMarre's "machine" includes the actual technologies used to create anime, as well as the creative personnel and institutional surround of Japanese animation production, which, similar to Cavallaro, he argues have helped to produce a specific approach to on-screen movement (2009, 33–38). Elsewhere, but in a similar vein, LaMarre argues for a politics of anime movement and sees anime as offering a "recoding of movement" onscreen that does not rely on depth, but which instead highlights and makes use of "flatness" (2002, 333). LaMarre starts from the literal machine used to produce anime: the multiplane camera of cel animation. However, he sees the flattening of movement and depth in anime as conscious aesthetic choices, arguing that the possibility of depth is introduced and then crushed, so that "no element within the image is more important than any other element" (2006a, 136, and for more on the multiplane animation camera, see Crafton 2005).

Anime is therefore routinely defined as a type of "limited" animation, influenced by US television cartoons similar to those made by Hanna-Barbera and Filmation (Furniss 1998). But, LaMarre notes that Japanese animation, like that seen in Tōei Animation's films had a very different aesthetic to Tezuka's early television "anime," meaning that even early on, Japanese cel animation had no single aesthetic mode. Anime texts, as a consequence, provide another slippery surface upon which it is difficult to gain purchase for definitions.

Nonetheless, in his explorations of anime movement and space, LaMarre's investigations of anime texts open up a useful space in which to consider why anime has become so instantly recognizable to so many. He creates a theory for understanding anime as a unique and culturally specific case of animation. What LaMarre shares with Cavallaro and Hu is an interest in the technical side of Japanese animation production. This is a useful intervention, and one that holds much promise within the burgeoning field of animation studies. Likewise, and regardless of their finer distinctions, these books all deal with anime's ability to be read through specific textual "frames": as a genre, as a medium or as part of an "animetic machine," all the while remaining surprisingly difficult to pin down. The variance in these approaches to anime signals the variety in anime itself, not just over time but also in the distinctions that can be drawn between the styles of different directors, studios and genres. The texts of anime, so recognizable to transnational audiences, seem to stubbornly refuse essentializing or universalizing theoretical forces, instead offering up texts open to a wide range of theoretical approaches and interpretations. In this respect, anime texts suggest similar problems to those encountered by genre theorists, which is why Chapter 1 will propose a method for studying anime using the tools offered by genre theory.

One of the difficulties in analyzing the texts and genres of anime comes from the fact that scholars are not comparing like with like. Anime television programmes are now made on computers, not with multiplane cameras, but anime still normally retains aspects of its limited animation roots. Character design techniques from manga and even aspects of television anime's "limited animation" aesthetics continue to appear within Japan's growing 3D computer-generated animation industry. *Neon Genesis Evangelion* (*Shin Seiki Evangerion*, 1995–1996), one of the most influential anime television series of the 1990s, for example, is now being reimagined in 3D computer-generated animation films (2007, 2009 and 2012 to date), taking its initially "flat" aesthetic and character designs and rendering them within slicker, 3D, but still recognizably "anime," films. Anime is, by such means, on the cusp of another watershed change. With this technological shift comes new challenges to the cultural category of "anime"—what to include under its ever-expanding umbrella, what to consider as its norms and how to analyze its aesthetics.

Anime's relationship to nation and culture

On almost every level, from texts to their cultural consumption, issues of nation and culture continue to play into debates about anime's meanings and definitions. As with Condry and Levi's insistence about anime's links to Japaneseness, most of the authors writing about anime engage with issues of culture, even if their purpose is to deny its importance. Susan J. Napier and Koichi Iwabuchi (2002) at times fall at the latter end of this spectrum, discussing the *mukokuseki* (stateless) nature of anime production. Napier, who wrote one of the first academic books on anime, asserts that anime's statelessness includes the:

> extremely "non-Japanese" depiction of human characters in virtually all anime texts. This is an issue among American audiences new to anime as well, who consistently want to know why the characters look "Western." …To [anime director Mamoru] Oshii and [critic Toshiya] Ueno this deliberate de-Japanicising of the characters is in keeping with their view of anime as offering an alternative world to its Japanese audience. (2001, 25)

Iwabuchi, citing Eiji Ōtsuka, another prominent Japanese critic, asks a fundamental question:

> If it is indeed the case that the Japaneseness of Japanese animation derives, consciously or unconsciously, from its erasure of physical signs of Japaneseness, is not the Japan that Western audiences are at long last coming to appreciate, and even yearn for, an animated, race-less and culture-less, virtual version of "Japan"? (2002, 33)

Here, Iwabuchi echoes Levi's initial disappointment that anime's connections to Japanese culture have not resulted in deep understandings of its originating society (though his theory, which considers how anime texts might "smell" to other cultures, is less pessimistic). What is evident in these analyses is a level of concern about the "right" way for anime to represent Japanese culture abroad. For Napier, via Oshii and Ueno, the *mukokuseki* is actually inward looking, for Iwabuchi and Ōtsuka, it is an outbound projection of a sanitized form of Japanese culture. In these discussions, anime's definitions become burdened by the weight of national representation, even when anime fails to be recognizably Japanese.

However, at the other end of the spectrum, academic work is examining deep levels of cultural specificity and even nationalism within anime. One volume of the influential *Mechademia* book series titled *War/Time*, for example, contains a range of articles about Japanese nationalism within anime (Lunning 2009). In particular, Wendy Goldberg's article on Isao Takahata's *Grave of the Fireflies* (*Hotaru no Haka*, 1988) provides a compelling argument for rethinking Japan's postwar revisionist victim's history. In other volumes, too, Thomas LaMarre has examined Japan's World War II era propaganda animation, linking its depictions of specific animal species to nationalist (and racist) vilifications of Japan's wartime enemies (2008). Michael Dylan Foster has also examined the important links between Shigeru Mizuki's war time experiences and his creation of the ghost and ghoul-filled world of *Graveyard Kitarō* (*Hakaba no Kitarō* 1960–1969), a manga series later adapted into anime and live-action films that frequently explore issues of trauma and loss (2009a and 2009b). In doing so, these articles illustrate a wide range of the darker aspects of Japanese nationalism represented within anime texts that shape understandings of anime content.

More positive representations are also studied, most commonly examining traditional or historical aspects of Japanese culture in anime. Within such discussions, Hayao Miyazaki's *Spirited Away* (*Sen to Chihiro no Kamikakushi*, 2001) has become a canonical film text. For example, Shiro Yoshioka goes as far as to seek the "heart of Japaneseness" in his article on Miyazaki's *Spirited Away*, in which he argues that the director believes that Japaneseness is retained in protagonist Chihiro/Sen's "metaphysical connection with Japanese tradition" (2008, 271). Likewise, Napier has investigated Miyazaki's *Spirited Away*, but she argues that

> Although at first glance seeming to celebrate various aspects of "Japaneseness," embodied in the film's primary *mise-en-scène*, a magical bathhouse of the gods, *Spirited Away*'s narrative trajectory revolves around the tension between Japanese cultural identity and otherness and at least implicitly calls into question the viability of "Japaneseness" in a changing world. (2006, 288)

I too have also called into question the idea that *Spirited Away* offers an easily parsed "Japaneseness," arguing in a 2007 article that the explanatory magazines produced for the release of *Spirited Away* in Japan indicate that its Japanese elements had to be explained even to Japanese audiences. Nonetheless, certain films, like Miyazaki's *Spirited Away*, seem to have sparked the imagination of academics, who canonize them in analyses like these. In this instance, with Hayao Miyazaki and Studio Ghibli, academics have drawn links between a national culture and its films. Chapter 6 therefore takes Ghibli's films as a case study, examining how such canons, in the form of branded-subgenres, are formed across national and linguistic borders.

Being mindful of both sides of the equation—the domestic and the global of anime—enables new frames of analysis to be applied to anime texts within this book, and new debates to emerge. In this book, I am particularly interested in how anime has been understood in relation to local and transnational genres, which are themselves culturally complex concepts, with their own national and transnational debates. I focus on anime genres because of the way genres are often seen, like anime, to operate as cultural categories or phenomena. Moreover, anime is a genre in some constructs (for example, in Hu's "medium-genre"), but is elsewhere an umbrella category providing shelter to a plethora of mutating and mixing genres. Anime, in this instance, provides a set of exemplary case studies through which we can better understand how genres become newly inflected when media cultures collide (for more, see Chapters 1 and 9).

Therefore, I tackle the task of introducing and understanding anime by examining it in relation to emerging methods from media genre studies. In recent years, these methods have been commingling with those of discourse analysis (Mittell 2001 and 2004) and historical materialist reception studies (Staiger 1992 and 2000) to create the kinds of methods that should help to investigate the changing ways in which anime has been conceptualized and categorized by differing groups of people in different places and times (for more on method, see Chapter 1). Genre studies already informs much of the existing work on anime (see, for example, Napier 2005). However, it is most common for discussions of anime's genres to be embedded within explorations of directors' or companies' oeuvres. This is as true in Japan as it is in the West, with myriad Studio Ghibli studies and several "official" histories for other studios that organize the debates around proprietary technologies and content creators rather than around genres (Cavallaro 2006 and 2009; McCarthy 1999; Odell and Le Blanc 2009). To understand the relationship between anime and genre better, I have selected a series of case studies that form the basis of the chapters in this book including high-profile films, and some of the studios that produce them, but I examine each in relation to their reception in specific contexts.

In the first section, I consider some of the biggest debates and issues arising around international understandings of anime. Science fiction has been a dominant organizing frame of reference for anime. Christopher Bolton, Istvan Csicsery-Ronay, Jr. and Takayuki Tatsumi's *Robot Ghosts and Wired Dreams* (2007), for example, investigates the importance of science fiction to contemporary Japanese popular culture and anime production more specifically. They state that "Japanese science fiction has been distributed throughout the world in the most popular new communications technologies—television, videocassettes, arcade games, personal computers, and game consoles" (2007, vii). In this way, science fiction was at the historical forefront of anime's first and second waves of transnational distribution, and has come subsequently to account for a large proportion of the genre discussions around anime. Genre, therefore, has long been at the core of the most significant debates about anime. For this reason, this section of the book begins by mapping the emergence of anime's genres and categories, before moving on to two chapters that trace the importance of two of anime's more controversial genres. Chapter 1 will clarify the discursive method used to analyze anime's interactions with genre, while exploring how anime has been categorized up to now. Chapter 2 looks specifically at academic discourses about two of the more high-profile science fiction anime, while Chapter 3 investigates the emergence of video technologies and how they shaped our understanding of anime's bodies.

The second section offers an historical account of anime's genres, focusing on anime's shifting media platforms. Its three chapters utilize academic, industrial, fan and press discourses to map the emergence of particular kinds of anime media as popular sources for dissemination. Chapter 4 starts with the filmic prehistory of anime before discussing early televisual history of anime and anime's growing transnational reach, whereas, Chapter 5 investigates how fans made use of VHS tapes to begin a transnational grassroots community of anime fandom, responding to a bifurcation of anime into gendered genres in Japan. The last chapter in this section then opens up the debates to see how digital technologies have shaped subsequent understandings of anime. Additionally, Chapter 6 examines how digital technologies have brought fans into conflict with industry, reshaping the relationships between the two. In this way, anime's genres will be shown to have gradually expanded for (trans) national audiences, as ever-more open technological pathways have enabled increases in fan numbers and consumption. In doing so, this section contains within it many of the most significant debates about anime to have taken place in recent years.

By contrast, the final section of this book attempts to shine a light on some of the less theorized and contemplated of anime's engagements with genre. Chapter 7 will chart Studio Ghibli's rise as a local and global brandname, investigating how this brand has related to ideas of genre and animation. Chapter 8 examines how significant "Expos" have become to understanding how anime genres are produced and sold. Using the Tokyo International Anime Fair as a case study, participant observation is used to produce an ethnographically informed study of how genre has recently impacted on Japan's anime markets. I conclude this book by focusing on a popular, but under-investigated anime genre, to attempt to better understand the differences in anime's contemporaneous global meanings. By studying "horror" anime, I investigate how the time lag between releases and the differences between fan cultures and different industrial promotion strategies work to shape culturally specific understandings of anime's genres.

By showing the breadth and variety of anime's interactions with genre, and by moving between academic, industry, press accounts and beyond into a range of marketing and fan discourses, I hope to show just how distinct anime's different global markets have become. I also demonstrate why it is important to view anime within wider contextual frames, specific to particular cultures, times and gatekeepers. While my investigations will not reveal the whole of anime, they do attempt to explore, and where necessary, redress some of the emergent myths about anime's history and its global significance.

Anime has been at the forefront of recent claims about Japan's new "soft power" (McGray 2002; METI 2012; Yasumoto 2011), but what shared cultures, ideas or markets are enabling this cultural strength have been, as yet, little investigated. This introduction to anime responds to this debate by looking at concrete instances of cultural production, reproduction, exchange and markets. In this way, while I do not seek to find one single answer to the question "what is anime?," this book reveals many possible ways of conceptualizing anime's meanings.

1

Approaching Anime: Genre and Subgenres

As a cultural category, anime manifests in ways that are often analogous to, or which echo, academic studies of genre. As shown in the Introduction, anime's cultural meanings have proven difficult to critically map, just as genres have defied easy definition—shifting, growing and spreading even as scholars and fans have attempted to identify canons of texts and group them into meaningful categories. Like the most popular of Hollywood's film genres, anime also acts as an umbrella term for a broad spectrum of productions, and, like Hollywood's genre films, anime texts are continually translated and reproduced when they enter new linguistic and cultural markets. Anime thereby functions similarly to such media genres while not exactly replicating them. This chapter works through these similarities and differences in order to outline a method for dealing with anime's constantly shifting landscape. While attempting not to elide the distinctions between anime and other kinds of generic media, their common ground will be used to build a framework through which anime might be usefully investigated. Using such a method is doubly important to the aims of this book, because I am interested in investigating the myriad genres sheltering under anime's umbrella. In this chapter, therefore, I ask how we might conceptualize a study of anime using the tools provided by genre theory, before going on to outline some of the debates around cross-cultural exchanges in anime genres.

Analyzing anime in context: From genre to anime and from theory to method

There is a long history of genre theory out of which an approach to anime could be constructed. Genre theories gained popularity in the 1960s as a means to account for the cultural significance of popular films. Over the proceeding decades, academic studies of genre have developed a complicated and divergent collection of analytical tools. For example, early forms of genre studies tended to utilize media texts as primary sources, analyzing them from a range of perspectives while arguing for their exemplary status within a particular genre (for more on this, see Altman 1984 and Neale 2000). Most famously, US film genres like the Western, gangster film, musicals and film noir have been treated to in-depth textual analyses of these kinds. One influential example from this tradition is Jim Kitses' study *Horizons West* (1969 [2007]),[1] which examines the Western film genre. *Horizons West* has become a touchstone for much of the "structuralist" work which has followed (see Schatz 1981). Kitses' use of antinomies inspired much subsequent genre work (including work on Japanese film genres: Desser 1992), creating an approach formulated around thematic structural oppositions onto which analyses of a wide range of genre films could be overlaid.

Other early work borrowed from semiotics, linguistics and the Russian formalists, seeking generic meaning in contrasting places within the texts of films. For some scholars, it was the surface elements of films—their *mise-en-scène*, camerawork and other technical elements—that informed their wider significance, while for others it was the repetitions shared across film narratives and iconography that made genre legible (for examples, see Buscombe 1970; McArthur 1972). For several prominent authors of this period, it was iconography that made genre discernible. For example, art and film critic Lawrence Alloway (1963) has claimed that it was a genre's iconography—the props, costumes and other surface elements shared by films—which made genre recognizable to audiences. Alloway also suggested that aspects of these shared visual elements were familiar from audiences' everyday lives, helping them to make sense of generic meanings. Through such analyses, these early authors created a range of tools for analyzing the meanings of film texts, borrowing from traditions in literary and ethnographic work to produce complex definitions of film genres.

For anime, such attention to surface elements of texts may help to explain how audiences come to recognize the styles of various creators and studios, but this cannot be assumed to be coterminous with the idea of anime as a cultural category. Being drawn, anime is always a step removed from the iconography of everyday life, offering a representation of reality, rather than its presentation, to audiences. Anime encompasses a variety of preexisting media genres within its representational lexicon, and it ostentatiously mixes and hybridizes its categories, all the while creating new local subcategories, all of which makes studying anime's iconography or themes an unlikely choice for those attempting to map its cultural meanings. Susan J. Napier's account of the three modes of anime comes closest so far to achieving such an aim, in what she terms the apocalyptic, festival and elegiac types of anime (2001 and 2005). While Napier's reading creates a set of helpful categories through which we might study anime, it also radically simplifies the scope of anime's connections to genre. Take, for example, Shinichirō Watanabe's *Cowboy Bebop* (1998–1999 with a film in 2001), which deliberately mixes elements of space opera with gangster, Western and film noir stylistics, even making occasional comedic forays into horror. *Cowboy Bebop*'s ending may well be elegiac or even, for its characters, apocalyptic, but its mixing of genres means that it also contains moments of the festival. As a result, *Cowboy Bebop* crosses between, and at times exceeds, all of Napier's modes of anime. Moreover, it does so using elements of genres made famous outside of its nation of origin and in other media (particularly, live-action filmmaking). A method is needed, therefore, that can work through anime's nationally and industrially shifting frames of reference.

From these early text-led theories, genre studies has rapidly grown and diversified. There is little agreement about which strands of theory are most effective, however, and considerable differences in approach have emerged. Genealogies of genre studies have become an increasingly popular means by which critics delineate theoretical shifts and assert the need for new approaches. Rick Altman's book *Film/Genre* (1999), for example, reflects on two major traditions before exploring his own new approach to genre theory. Altman names these traditions the *ritual* and *ideological* approaches to genre. Citing literary theorist Vladamir Propp and French structuralist Claude Levi-Strauss (for more on structuralism, see Bordwell 1985, 276–278; Schatz 2003), Altman argues that:

> the ritual approach considers that audiences are the ultimate creators of genres, which function to justify and organize a virtually timeless society. According to this approach, the narrative patterns of generic texts grow out of existing social practices, imaginatively overcoming contradictions within those very practices. (1999, 27)

In essence, the ritual approach is a feedback loop in which audiences create genres by going repeatedly to the cinema to watch similar stories, thus influencing the production of more similar films, something Altman originally cited as a kind of "religious practice" (1984, 9) on the part of audiences. This feedback loop has a high profile in Japan, where fans of anime are courted by industry at annual Expo events (such as the Tokyo International Anime Fair and the Anime Contents Expo, see Chapter 8), and where the work of fans as *dōjinshi* (amateur manga authors, who often produce amateur works that borrow from existing anime), is sometimes monitored by industry at the biannual ComiKet (Comic Market) in Tokyo. There is now even a transnational notion of anime pilgrimage evident in the Japan National Tourism Organization's website (www.jnto.go.jp), extending the religious metaphor of the ritual approach to genre into new kinds of cultural practice.

By comparison, the ideological approach can be found in studies seeking to analyze the hidden and overt rhetoric within films. Altman writes that:

> Imaging narrative texts as the vehicle for a government's address to its citizens/subjects or an industry's appeal to its clients, [Louis] Althusser's system attributes greater importance to discursive concerns than the ritual approach, more sensitive instead to questions of narrative structure. (1999, 27; for more on ideological genre studies, see Klinger 1984)

A top-down approach, rather than the grassroots approach of the ritual genre theorists, "the ideological approach claims that Hollywood takes advantage of spectator energy and psychic investment in order to lure the audience into Hollywood's own positions" (Altman 1984, 9). This is perhaps the most useful aspect of Altman's analysis: the observation that genre can be studied from radically different perspectives. Genre, as a result, appears to be less a product of the films being analyzed than it is a product of how those films are approached and which sources are deemed relevant by the academics analyzing them.

Altman thereby suggests that we need to pay close attention not just to which texts are being analyzed, but also to how they are selected and what kinds of sources are used to make sense of them. In terms of anime, a good example would be the schism between the local Tokyo Metropolitan Government and Japanese manga and anime producers that took place in 2011 (discussed further in Chapter 8), when the government banned adult manga from convenience stores, accusing the industry of producing pornographic images harmful to children. In this example, viewed from the top-down, genre in manga and anime plays highly politicized roles in its local and transnational markets, with different institutions vying for control over the flow of manga and anime images. These kinds of example make the ideological aspects of genre important to understanding anime's meanings.

Film genre theorists have been relatively quick to adopt reflexive and critical approaches to their subjects, particularly in their attempts to challenge the work emerging out of literary theory and textual analysis. Andrew Tudor, for example, writing in 1974, was among the first to note a central paradox in text-led theories of genre:

> almost all writers using the term *genre*, are caught in a dilemma. They are defining a western on the basis of analyzing a body of films that cannot possibly be said to be westerns until after the analysis . . . . That is, we are

caught in a circle that first requires that the films be isolated, for which purpose a criterion is necessary, but the criterion is, in turn, meant to emerge from the empirically established common characteristics of the films. This "empiricist dilemma" has two solutions. One is to classify films according to *a priori* criteria depending on the critical purpose. This leads back to the earlier position in which the special *genre* term is redundant. The second is to lean on common cultural consensus as to what constitutes a western and go on to analyze it in detail .... Genre notions—except in the case of arbitrary definition—are not critics' classifications made for special purposes. *Genre is what we collectively believe it to be.* (135–139, my emphasis)

Tudor's devastating critique of text-led genre studies has since become the origin point for an important strand in genre theory that informs my own approach to anime. His observation about genre's collective construction has subsequently opened up the field of media genre studies to influences from ethnography, anthropology, reception and audience studies, as scholars debate the constituents of the "collective" and think through how such understandings operate in culture (see, for example, Allen 1989; Jancovich 2000; Klinger 1994).

Jason Mittell (2001 and 2004) has produced one of the most coherent challenges to text-led studies of genre, centering on television genre studies. Mittell argues that a textualist assumption lies at the heart of early genre studies (2001, 5), which began with questions about how to define genres before the emergence of "probably the most widespread and influential approach" which "poses *questions of interpretation*" (2004, 4 emphasis in original). Mittell places both of Altman's ritual and ideological categories into this group, along with several other approaches, arguing that "Although their political goals and theoretical assumptions may differ greatly, each of these paradigms approaches texts and genres as collections of meanings to be decoded, analyzed and potentially critiqued" (4). Mittell sees these approaches standing alongside a further set of questions, ones of genre history. Producing histories of genres, he writes, "necessitates an analysis of the actual cultural life of a genre, not as it is abstractly defined or interpreted to be" (6). But this turn to history has itself been fraught with problems that Mittell acknowledges.

Christine Gledhill, for example, cautions that:

The historicity of the genre system complicates the uses of film history, for though genre production history is never done with; historical research does not provide a true identity we can find once and for all in some past origin but is itself ... an object of appropriation, struggle, and, moreover, still in the making. (2000, 241)

Historians, Gledhill argues, are as subjective in their assessments of genre as those undertaking textual analysis. The central problem for Gledhill remains the search for a "correct" definition of genre. If we accept, as Rick Altman (1999, 62–68), Steve Neale (2000, 56) and Jason Mittell (2004, xii) have suggested, that genres are never definable, because they are always *in process*, then we may be a step closer to a useful method for analyzing anime's relationship to genre. But what tools are worth adopting from a field that has reflexively denied the veracity of all of its preceding efforts?

Mittell is among those who have sought to answer this question, and has done so in a way as applicable to a study of anime as to any US genre. Mittell argues that "We need to look beyond the text as the locus for genre and instead locate genres within the complex interrelations among texts, industries, audiences, and historical contexts" (2001, 7). He continues,

> it is more useful to conceive of genres as discursive practices. By regarding genres as a property and function of discourse, we are able to examine the ways in which various forms of communication work to constitute generic definitions and meanings. (8)

In this way, Mittell argues for an approach to genres that moves beyond texts to examine the traces left behind by genres as they move through culture. Other scholars have, as suggested earlier, been doing similar work since the early 1990s, perhaps most notably Mark Jancovich (2000 and 2010), Barbara Klinger (1994, 1997 and 2006) Steve Neale (1993) and Janet Staiger (1992, 2000 and 2005), all of whom have sought to make specific interventions in genre studies through the production of discourse-led analysis.

There are, inevitably, a range of divergent methods to be found within the work of these scholars. However, a set of principles drawn from this scholarship guides my investigations of anime hereafter, seeking out the links between anime and genre. These principles are listed below, and they form the basis of a method which will be used in all of the chapters of this book:

1   "Immanent meaning in a text is denied" (Staiger 2000, 162) and no single text can exemplify an entire genre. Instead, "we need to ask what a genre means *for specific groups in a particular cultural instance*" (Mittell 2004, 5 emphasis in original).

2   Genre is therefore a product of discursive formations created through a wide range of cultural practices, from industry practice through to audience reception and academic commentary (Mittell 2004, 17; Staiger 2000, 162).

3   While it may have been that in the past, "industrial and journalistic
    labels and terms... offer virtually the only available evidence for a
    historical study of the array of genres in circulation" (Neale 1993, 52),
    contemporary researchers are now often faced with an unmanageably
    large cross-section of discourses from which to choose. Moreover,
    those sources are now multinational and come in multiple languages.
    While holism remains a desirable aim (Klinger 1997), and indeed
    is called for by researchers like Mittell (2004) and Staiger (1992),
    in practice the new information glut leads to a stark choice: either
    the researcher must ask a very narrowly defined question or the
    researcher must consider which source type might best help to
    answer the question being asked. In practice, it would be almost
    impossible for a discourse-led study to account for every language
    or every possible source of discourse, so it is vital to be clear
    about which sources have been selected and what motivates the
    researcher's decisions.

4   "Genres are not neutral categories but are situated within larger
    systems of power" (Mittell 2001, 19; see also Jancovich 2010) and
    thus, we must attend to the relative cultural positions of those
    speaking and to their potential agendas. In this, discourse-led
    methods share much with those of earlier ideological studies.

5   Mittell argues that "Much literary and film genre theory, however,
    does not account for... the industry and audience practices unique
    to television" (2001, 3). He goes on to state: "We need to consider
    the medium's particular features as a component of a larger push
    toward specificities in genre analysis" (16). In agreement with this
    position, the effects of producing texts within a particular medium will
    be considered, and questions will be asked about how the medium
    impacts on discursive formations.

6   As Staiger asserts, it is important also to consider what is not
    said within these discursive formations—questioning underlying
    assumptions, power inequalities and looking for less dominant
    strands of discourse. As she writes, the range of discourse should be
    "surveyed not only for what seems possible at that moment but also
    for what the readings did not consider. That is, structuring absences
    are important as well" (2000, 163).

To these vital considerations, I would add just one more principle that
results from attempting a cross-cultural study of anime. As Altman notes,
genre scholars have been "Most comfortable in the seemingly uncomplicated

world of Hollywood classics" (1984, 6) leaving the genres of other national cinemas to be studied elsewhere. National cinemas have often taken on brand-like qualities, wherein genres and marketing techniques merge. This is perhaps most obvious in the cases of Bollywood, *kung fu* films, J-horror and other transnational categories of cinema. These categories have a tendency to lump together very different kinds of films into brand-genres, creating a perpetual newness within the discourse of world cinema that enables a continual "thrill of discovery for those audiences eagerly consuming the next big thing" (Galt and Schoonover 2010, 13).

The field of anime studies is consequently emerging at a temporal and cultural nexus that expanded with growth in animation studies and a transnational boom in anime's popularity, centered on the distribution of Studio Ghibli's films abroad (Denison 2007) and the phenomenal success of the Pokémon franchise (Tobin 2004) in the late 1990s. In an attempt to think through transnational genre exchanges like these, I therefore add the following principle to the list above:

7 The origins of discourse need to be taken into account. Attention should be paid to the national/cultural origins of sources, and to the way concepts of the nation interact with the discursive formation of transcultural genres.

This principle helps to foreground the importance of national ideologies and power relations in the discursive formation of anime as a cultural category. But, it also suggests a move beyond them. It helps to rethink assumptions about the connectivity anime shares with its home nation, opening up a space in which genre or other attributes of anime may play a more important role than nation in defining its meanings. In this way, my analyses will focus on what makes anime distinctive—it is a medium, and it is multimedia, and it is also part of a range of (trans)national media cultures—at the same time as interrogating how anime connects to the many genres that have emerged out of its production and cultural exchange.

Anime's categories: From meta-genre to subgenre and back again

The histories of particular genres would be quite different across different national and international contexts—for instance, the industry history of television animation … would change radically if considering the cultural operation of cartoons in Japan. (Jason Mittell 2004, xv)

Shifting focus to examine the movement of a category from one culture through into others is likely to have the effect Mittell asserts. More than this, pulling focus from a relatively stable, nationally inflected context to examine a category as it slips and slides across geographic, linguistic and cultural borders is likely to produce stark contrasts in our understandings of what genres mean, and to whom. An holistic study of anime is not, however, just beyond the scope of an introductory book like this one; it would require a mastery of far more cultures and languages than even a polymath might boast.

For this reason, I attend to the vagaries of anime's cultural life in three distinct contexts: Japan, whose production of anime has created its most immediate, varied and vibrant cultural context, but also the USA, often framed by the Japanese industry itself as anime's most significant overseas market (Woo, Denison and Furukawa 2013). Added to these contexts, anime has recently been caught up in debates about the relative global power enjoyed by Japan—its "soft power"—and how this power is enabling new, deeper inroads into overseas markets and minds (McGray 2002). A wide range of other secondary or tertiary markets and contexts for anime might also be worth considering: for example, Australia's position as a close geographic neighbor, China's rampant anime consumption practices (often gray or black market) or France's long-held admiration for Japan's animated film and television artistry would be likely to cast new light on our understanding of anime's cultural meanings. However, I want to examine a market often overlooked, in line with Staiger's admonition that we should ensure a voice to audiences less strident in their discourse or global representation.

Therefore, the UK has been selected as a third point of comparison, because its anime culture has often been reliant upon the cultural exchanges taking place between Japan and the USA, while also producing a unique and highly active local industry and fan culture. The UK has developed an anime distribution network that includes independent agents, such as MVM, but which also includes sister organizations of US companies such as Manga Entertainment UK and the now semi-defunct ADVision. As a sometimes tertiary site of anime distribution, the UK's anime discourse offers feedback and commentary on US reproductions of anime, as well as a homegrown set of anime debates. Additionally, the UK has been one of the sites most affected by anime's surge in popularity around the turn of the new millennium.

From a small grassroots movement to numerous but relatively small conventions (often, like AyaCon, taking place at UK university campuses), anime fandom in the UK has grown rapidly across the 1990s, and the UK now boasts a network of annual conventions, retail outlets and online communities that serve the needs of a growing and diverse fanbase. The UK also has multiple magazines that focus on anime, including *Neo* and *MyM*.

The size of anime fandom is perhaps best captured through a consideration of London MCM Expo, held biannually, which features a mix of science fiction, gaming and anime, and which now boasts over 100,000 attendees per event. Anime may still be a subcultural phenomenon in the UK, therefore, but it is one moving ever-closer to the center of the UK's media cultures. The UK consequently provides a valuable site for considering anime's shifting global meanings—in part tertiary market, in part secondary, but one with its own local traditions in anime consumption and reception.

It remains, therefore, to quickly sketch the landscape of anime's shifting presence in global culture. Anime is, as shown in the Introduction, becoming a more and more complex proposition within its Japanese context. The use of the term "meta-genre" might help to explain the difference between how anime is understood in Japan by comparison to the rest of the world. Anime is for everyone in Japan, but not every show is aimed at everyone— there are genres for most age groups, genders and sexual orientations, and anime's genres often reflect industrial categories like the shōnen (boys) and seinen (young adult) that target specific demographics. Thinking of anime as a Japanese "meta-genre" showcases the difference between the media empires built around anime in Japan, and the shadows that those franchises cast through partial distribution to the rest of the world. This suprageneric term is necessary, therefore, because anime in Japan is not just texts or a subculture built around them: it is a complex system of industrially and culturally understood genres and audiences that crosses back and forth between everyday culture and extreme kinds of fandom. At its point of origin in Japan, anime offers an exceptionally broad generic set of possibilities, which could be considered together as forming a "meta-genre" of production and consumption.

Anime's genres have developed historically and cross-culturally even from the earliest points at which "anime" itself came into usage (see Introduction). The terms most frequently used to divide up anime in Japan, however, do not originate with anime, but are borrowed from the language used to describe manga's market niches. Hence, in Japan, the most frequently (and confusingly) applied categories of anime map its intended audiences. Shōnen (young boys) and shōjo (young girls) are the two terms seen most often across discussions of anime, and both emerge out of manga (Berndt 2010; MacWilliams 2008). In Japan, shōnen and shōjo are themselves, therefore, sprawling transmedia categories whose meanings can seem confusing or seemingly arbitrary (for more, see Chapter 6).

The same is true for their adult variations, the seinen (aimed at adult men) and josei (adult women) titles. Take, for example, the all-female manga group Clamp's xxxHolic (2003–2011), which was anthologized in a powerful publisher, Kadokawa's Seinen Young Magazine (1980–), before being adapted into anime television, films and a live-action *dorama* (Japanese television drama). The adaptation into anime, and particularly into *dorama*, suggests a local and transnational repositioning of this franchise toward a female market. For example, by the time it was marketed to UK audiences, the anime version of *xxxHolic* was described with the strap line, "The Choice is Yours ... Beware Your Desires" placing it within an erotic generic discourse, which was compounded by the phrasing used to describe its second DVD collection. The description of the second part begins by announcing that "The hearts of holics interact with every being they encounter, sometimes willingly, sometimes unaware" (Manga Entertainment 2009), which helps to shift the discourse again into one of romance and mystery.

The same sorts of shifts and unexpected audiences can also be found in relation to the *shōnen* and *shōjo* categories, as when *Fullmetal Alchemist* (*Hagane no Renkinjutsushi*, unusually two separate series were produced, first in 2003–2004 and then a remake in 2009–2010, with associated films in 2005 and 2011, created by Hiromu Arakawa) became a female fan favorite in Japan and beyond. *Fullmetal Alchemist*'s anime producer, Masahiko Minami, has commented:

> It wasn't made specifically for female fans, of course, but I am glad they like it in their own way. The ideal shows are ones with a broad reach that will be loved for years to come ... rather than simply creating something targeting female fans to begin with. (quoted in Kemps and Lamb 2013)

Already the tensions within the gendered categories used by the Japanese industry are visible. However, these terms have been exported to describe anime texts abroad, despite the fact that the distinctions between these categories are continually being broken down by fans and international distributors who seemingly want to sell and consume anime in contradistinction to the original marketing and framing of texts. In these ways, anime's traditional generic borrowings from the manga industry are being diluted and mutated in intriguing ways.

However, what is perhaps most intriguing about Japanese anime genre terms is the way they are used as markers of distinction and cultural difference by overseas fans and commentators (for more on distinction and fan hierarchies, see Jancovich 2000). Whereas Altman argues that Hollywood genres are created when hybridized terminology becomes able to stand alone (for example, when the musical comedy becomes the musical), it seems that anime's genres have been adopted in a slightly different way. For anime, there is a complex interplay between Japanese and English language genre terminology (explored further in Chapter 9). For example, the UK's *Neo* magazine will occasionally forego translations using a localized version of the

Japanese *shōnen* as a subgenre of action anime, as when it says, "Shonen action fans—we know you're out there, and so does Manga [Entertainment]!" (Kamen 2014, 18). This commentator then goes on to list a range of anime titles first popularized in Japan's premiere manga anthology magazine, *Weekly Shōnen Jump*. Similarly, while stand-ins or analogous genres like romantic comedy are more commonly used in the place of *shōjo* in both US and UK magazines, the use of the term without translation does frequently appear in journalistic and fan-scholar coverage of anime. For example, more than a decade ago, Helen McCarthy used the term "shojo" in her essay on the maturation of the "magical girl" genre of anime (1998), describing a wealth of generic attributes that might be found within this category, from love to melodrama and even, sometimes, sex (see Chapter 5 for early fan debates about gendered anime genre categories).

Beyond such market-based categories, anime has also developed a series of content-based generic terms. Perhaps most notoriously, and incorrectly, the term *hentai* (perverse) has been used to describe pornographic anime. For example, in 1997, a *Washington Post* article on anime fandom noted that anime "can be sexual or grotesque—the rape of female characters by tentacled demons is a favorite theme—and it can be vividly violent" naming this kind of sexualized violence '*hentai*' (Span 1997, B01; for a more recent use, see the BBFC's recent podcast on anime). The misappropriation of *hentai* as a generic category seems to have been linked to the VHS distribution of one particular anime text, *Urotsukidōji: Legend of the Overfiend*, which is why this distribution medium and this series of short films are the focus of Chapter 3. Since the 1990s, there has also been a gradual shift in pornographic terminology from the "extreme" of *hentai* to *shōnen ai* (boys love) to *yaoi* (derived from the amateur manga movement, see Levi, McHarry and Pagliossotti 2008) as the internet has enabled greater exchanges in pornographic manga and anime content. Latterly, these debates have been reshaped by discussions of pornography aimed at a female audience and produced by amateurs, rather than focusing on the extremes of *hentai*'s violence against women (Zanghellini 2009). If any genre has altered since the "digital turn" it is anime pornography, and with its shifts in markets and production has come a concomitant ambiguity in terminology.

Less ambiguous, but no less ambivalent early on, has been the transnational exportation of the Japanese-derived *mecha* (mechanical) category. Often linked to the science fiction and *shōnen* genres, *mecha* became popularized as a transnational genre between the 1980s and 2000s, thanks to the exportation popular "giant robot" series such as *Robotech* (1986), *Voltron* (a series reedited for transnational distribution from the Japanese *King of the Beasts GoLion*, 1981–1982, and *Armoured Fleet Dairugger XV*, 1982–1983, shown in the USA from 1984) and, perhaps most significantly, *Gundam* (with

Gundam Wing broadcast in 2000). Early *mecha* series were not without their controversies, now investigated by Brian Ruh, who explains how three separate anime series were grafted together for the 85-episode run of the series *Robotech* (1985) (*Super-dimensional Fortress Macross*, 1982–1983; *Genesis Climber Mospeada*, 1983–1984; and *Superdimensional Cavalry Southern Cross*, 1984). As anime fandom developed across this period, even the idea of *mecha* anime became caught up in controversy: "a number of fans have decried *Robotech* as a butchery of the original Japanese programs" (Ruh 2010, 37, for more, see Chapters 2 and 5).

Despite these rocky beginnings, *mecha* shows continue to be popular at home in Japan and abroad in the USA and UK, and the term has had a sustained life. Matt Kamen, writing about the history of the genre in the UK's *Neo* magazine, traces the history of contemporary *mecha* shows to a shift in the genre: "That change was pronounced '*Gundam*' and to be unaware of its atomic impact on pop-culture worldwide is to have been living under a very large, dark, soundproof rock" (2009, 8). In Japan, the impact of this franchise has moved beyond anime texts into the realms of fully fledged cultural phenomenon. When Bandai, a major Japanese toy producer responsible for generations of Gundam toys, opened its museum in Chiba (now reopened in Omocha-no-machi) a Gundam café nestled at the heart of the complex. Such cafés have now been launched as a hugely popular franchise in and around Tokyo. The influence of the *Gundam* franchise on Bandai is still potent, with a life-sized giant Gundam head greeting visitors to Bandai's new toy museum. But more than this, the 30th anniversary of the series in 2009 was celebrated by the production of a full-sized giant robot statue in Odaiba, Tokyo, which now features as part of the "Gundam Front" outside Odaiba's DiversCity shopping mall. As anime, cultural experience, food culture and toys, *Gundam* has taken the *mecha* genre beyond anime texts and into the realms of more tangible popular culture in Japan (see Chapter 5).

However, the *mecha* "genre" is also, potentially, only a subgenre of a wider science fiction category of anime. As an imported concept, science fiction's influence on anime is visible from the beginning of its life as television, and its impact will be discussed further in Chapters 2 and 5. However, science fiction's overarching hold on much of anime production, from Osamu Tezuka's *Astro Boy* and beyond, is worth considering here for the way it has filtered through so much of the discourse around anime in Japan and beyond. Science fiction has become so bound up within Japanese media production that now it is normal for the romanized phrase "SF" to stand in for the term. For example, discussing the novel upon which his film *The Girl Who Leapt Through Time* (*Toki o Kakeru Shōjo*, 2006) is based, Mamoru Hosoda says, "But the original, its depiction of the future, which is viewed from the period in which the book was written, is interesting but is more about time slips than being an SF thing" (Hosoda 2006, 82). This truncated deployment of a transnational genre term suggests its localization within Japan, and the way it has come to be translated for Japanese sensibilities.

However, SF is not always used in Japan. To return the director of *Cowboy Bebop* for a moment, Watanabe's new anime, *Space Dandy* (2014), has an official website that bristles with references to space, but which never names the show as science fiction. For example, the main introductory page alone mentions that its main character, Dandy, is a hunter of "aliens" no fewer than five times (http://space-dandy.com/intro/). Science fiction is also raised as a spectral presence in the geneaologies of texts produced by industry, as when animation director Hirotoshi Sano introduces *Rahxephon* (2002, quoted in Hikawa, 2001) in Japan's *Animage* magazine. He begins by saying that he asked the director Yutaka Izubuchi which anime he thought had interesting stories, and Izubuchi named *Space Battleship Yamato* (1975), *The Adventures of Ganba* (1977) and *Super Machine Zambot 3* (1977) (Hikawa 2001: 122). Each of these anime texts, particularly the first example, is viewed as classic science fiction anime, and by invoking such comparators, Sano reveals the generic associations desired for *Rahxephon*. While neither example directly invokes science fiction, nevertheless, each borrows from science fiction, or SF, to create associations to an anime genre that will help audiences to identify texts. In these ways, science fiction is further localized into anime's industrial landscape, making it as much a Japanese genre as an imported one (see Chapter 2).

As I argue in Chapters 6 and 9, moreover, one of the most important ways anime franchises stay alive is by mixing their genres. For example, with long-running franchise *Case Closed* (*Meitantei Konan*), the boy detective is kept interesting by dropping him into differently inflected genre narratives over time. Even a brief glance at the cinema *pamfuretto* (pamphlets or brochures) produced for each of the *Case Closed* films shows how often boy-detective Conan Edogawa finds himself shifting between genres. While always maintaining a mystery narrative, the eighteen films in this series intersect with everything from the popular sports genre of anime (in *The Eleventh Striker, Meitantei Conan Jūichi Ninme no Sutoraikā*, 2012) and historical legends about pirate Anne Bonny (*Jolly Roger in the Deep Azure, Meitantei Conan Konpeki no Jorī Rojā*, 2007). These annual *gekijōban* (theatrical versions) of the long-running *Case Closed* series thereby work to drop the well-known characters into new generic settings as a means to periodically refresh the series.

Likewise, other kinds of anime begin from mixed generic premises, as when an anime like *Spice and Wolf* (*Ōkami to Kōshinryō*, 2008) unites the imagery of Japanese folklore with an economics-based narrative; or when vampires become teen idols in school-set *Vampire Knight* (2008); or when the worlds of *oshare-kei* light pop and the death metal music subcultures collide to comic effect in *Detroit Metal City* (2008). There are many such generic remixings and inventions in anime, which is why it is so vital to investigate what anime means to particular groups of people at specific moments in time. As a consequence of these choices, anime moves from being a massive transmedia meta-genre at one end of a spectrum to a subcultural collection of genres (or even subgenres) at the other.

Moreover, the attendant genres comprising anime are often argued over by fans from different places and different generations, even while producers and distributors attempt to clarify their meanings. The chapters that follow try to examine some of the greatest discordant moments in anime's transnational travels. In doing so, I fully recognize that many potential genres and subgenres of anime will be left out. Moreover, I have specifically tried to target the cultural gatekeepers that we hear least from within anime fandom, which is perhaps over-influenced by what animators themselves say about their work. The aim is to map some of the highest profile international debates around anime and genre in this first section, before moving on to consider some of the more overlooked aspects of anime's genre history and thinking about anime's connection to genre in new ways, for example, through issues of branding, cultural geography and comparative genre meanings. While this book is not, therefore, a comprehensive history of anime and genre, it is intended to provide the tools needed for future studies of anime's generic meanings. From meta-genre, to genre, to subgenres, anime moves through cultures in ways that speak to local as well as transnational groups of people. In the exchanges, borrowings, reinterpretations and temporal shifts, we can see a phenomenon slowly being worked and reworked by the industries producing it and the audiences who consume it. In this regard, anime is an ever-expanding phenomenon, one that has the potential to help us rethink the way genres function in culture.

2

Sci Fi Anime: Cyberpunk to Steampunk

Anime has long been shaped by science fiction. Some of anime's earliest and biggest transnational hits, especially in film, have been understood in relation to science fiction and its myriad subgenres. This relationship is visible from *Astro Boy* (*Tetsuwan Atomu*, Tezuka Osamu 1963–1966) right through to newer anime like the digitally produced *5 Centimeters Per Second* (*Byōsoku Go Senchimētoru*, Makoto Shinkai, 2007), anime has often made use of "sci fi" tropes and themes to explore the most complex aspects of human existence (Bolton et al. 2007). Daisuke Miyao sees the connection between anime and science fiction as so dominant that discussions of sci fi anime threaten to overwhelm other debates. Miyao cautions against reading the whole of anime as "SF animation for children" because this view of anime's history has been shaped specifically by the context of postwar Japanese anime television, ignoring Japanese animation's long prewar history (2002, 193; see Chapter 4 for more on anime's early history). With Miyao's caveat in mind, however, it is worth considering how science fiction has come to be so important to anime, to the extent that commentators like Simon Richmond feel confident arguing that science fiction is anime's "most popular genre" (2009, 200).

Science fiction anime films are consequently an excellent place to begin an investigation of the relationship between anime and genre. In this chapter, I use the discourse analysis method outlined in Chapter 1 to investigate how two of the most famous "sci fi" anime films—*Akira* (Katsuhiro Ōtomo 1998) and *Ghost in the Shell* (*Kōkaku kidōtai*, Mamoru Oshii, 1995)—came to be understood outside Japan, and how that understanding shaped the discourse on subsequent anime. I start with a transnational view of anime from outside of Japanese culture in order to investigate how the transnational genre of science fiction came to inflect so much of anime reception.

I have chosen these two films because they are frequently credited with popularizing anime in the USA, making them part of a global debate about science fiction and anime (Tsugata 2011b, 10; Yamaguchi 2004, 124–125). In the case studies that follow, I use newspaper reviews and commentary contemporaneous with the releases of *Akira* and *Ghost in the Shell* to reflect upon the roles of genre in transnational criticism. In doing so, I chart the frames that a general audience of film journalists—not fans, not academics—used in assessing anime's cultural significance in these moments. Moreover, I analyze the transnational genre concepts they used to localize, or domesticate, Japanese anime films. Studying this group of commentators helps to reveal some of the cultural tensions around "sci fi" anime and exposes a critical struggle around how to interpret and showcase anime films.

Akira and *Ghost in the Shell* are very difficult to reduce to a quick synopsis—a description is needed to make some sense of the journalistic accounts that follow. *Akira* is the story of friends Tetsuo and Kaneda who live in a dystopic future version of Tokyo, and it follows the disintegration of their lives as Tetsuo begins to develop uncontrollable psychic powers. *Ghost in the Shell*, by contrast, is about a female protagonist, Major Motoko Kusanagi, and her search for the mysterious Puppet Master in another dystopic future, this time questioning the locus and nature of humanity. I argue that despite their obvious differences, both of these films became caught up in a broader discourse about Japanese animation and the cyberpunk subgenre of science fiction. Further, I contend that cyberpunk was particularly useful to critics because of its routine transgression of the boundaries between different media platforms in a period when the idea of "anime films" was itself new.

Thereafter, I compare this period of early transnational anime with reviews for two more films by the same directors, Ōtomo and Oshii. The aim will be to assess how reviewers make sense of broader shifts in the science fiction film genre in relation to high-profile anime releases. *Steamboy* (Ōtomo, 2004) follows the adventures of the young Ray Steam through an alternative historical version of England in which "steam technologies are [used] as the basis for high-tech weaponry" (LaMarre 2009, 6), whereas, as Andrea Horbinski explains, "Set in an alternate modern Europe, *The Sky Crawlers* [Oshii, 2008] follows several Kildren, eternal adolescents … fighter pilots for the Rostock company, which is under contract to Europe to fight a 'war as entertainment'" (2011, 304). These two sets of films allow us to view science fiction and anime through the lens of genre discourse, as journalists attempted to concomitantly make sense of a globalizing genre and a new medium.

In particular, I examine the way these two films interacted with new and emerging subgenres of science fiction, including cyberpunk and steampunk.

Throughout this chapter, I argue that there is a reciprocal set of influences at work. Transnational genre filters are often used to position anime films as they travel the world, while, at the same time, anime films become caught up in wider cultural moments out of which new subgenres emerge. In this respect, anime plays an important role in defining and creating new global media genres.

Japanese sci fi anime: Academic frames from postmodern disaster to *mecha* anime

Another reason to begin with science fiction anime is that like popular discourse, academic writing on anime has long been influenced by this genre. Most academic collections and books on anime contain at least one or two chapters on science fiction anime. For example, almost half of Christopher Bolton et al.'s edited collection on Japanese science fiction is given over to analyses of science fiction anime. They write that due to the lack of translated Japanese science fiction literature, the "dominance of Japanese visual science fiction has eclipsed the fact that Japan has a vibrant tradition of prose science fiction" (2007, x). Susan J. Napier has also suggested that "the enormity of the whole science fiction phenomenon in Japan itself, including novels, fan magazines and comics for both adults and children, is well worthy of scholarly attention" (1996, 237). In seeking to contextualize discussions of anime as part of a *Japanese* science fiction genre, these scholars accord importance to Japanese localizations of an already popular transnational genre.

In her reflections on Japanese films within the science fiction genre, including *Akira*, Napier suggests that Japan's own versions of science fiction have been rapidly changing, principally in their approach to history. For *Akira*, Napier uses the concept of the postmodern to explain the tapestry of texts and cultural reference points alluded to within the body of the film. Napier asserts that "*Akira*'s nihilism has much in common with contemporary American films which can be classified as part of the post modern genre" (247). Napier is joined in her assessment by other academics, including Isolde Standish, who explains that:

Akira is a text which simultaneously displays two distinct characteristics of the postmodern which Frederic Jameson (1983) discussed: an effacement of boundaries, for instance between the previously defined stylistic norms (Eastern and Western) and between past and present, resulting in pastiche and parody; and a schizophrenic treatment of time as "perpetual present." (1998, 62)

For Napier, these moments of parody and pastiche are located in *Akira*'s "fascination with fluctuating identity, as evidenced in Tetsuo's metamorphoses; its use of pastiche in relation to Japanese history and cinematic styles; and its ambivalent attitude toward history" (2005, 260). *Akira*, therefore, has become part of a debate about where and how to situate Japanese "science fiction" in relation to Western-originated academic theories. In using postmodern theories, the layering of nationally inflected genre signifiers within *Akira* (the film references US war films and science fiction as well as borrowing widely from Japanese culture) can be explained as symptomatic of Ōtomo's postmodern approach to storytelling. However, the idea that *Akira* collapses or erases boundaries between nations denies some of the film's complexity and cultural specificity. Doing so suggests that there is only one way to understand the film: as a postmodern work. I want to argue here that postmodern or not, *Akira* was open to a range of interpretations and, consequently, to potentially metamorphic reading strategies.

The academic reception of *Ghost in the Shell* has been similarly limited in its focus. The film has almost uniformly been read in relation to issues of sexuality, gender and what Sharalyn Orbaugh calls "cyborg narratives" (2002). Through these investigations, Major Kusanagi comes to define *Ghost in the Shell*'s meanings. Joseph Christopher Schaub writes that *Ghost in the Shell* "presents a protagonist whose body serves as a battleground for conflicting representations of power in an era of global capitalism" (2001, 8). In her much-reprinted article, Orbaugh extends this reading to argue that in *Ghost in the Shell*, "the interest is not focused on the infinite replicability of cyborgs, but rather the *limits* imposed on subjectivity by such perfect control [of the body] and how these limits may be transcended, moving to the *next* step of evolution" (2002, 446). Even the later television series *Ghost in the Shell: Standalone Complex* (*Kōkaku Kidōtai Stand Alone Complex*, 2002–2003) is analyzed in these terms: "As a full cyborg, [Kusanagi] continually wrestles with the possibility that her entire identity may be fabricated, a position that seems to draw her closer to other full cyborgs" (Corbett 2009, 47). Through her liminal cultural status as a cyborg, somewhere between human and robot, Kusanagi has become the locus for academic discussions of technological change in society and for discussions of human subjectivity in a highly mediated world. The consistency in this discourse is both unusual and somewhat overdetermining; while Kusanagi's character sits at the heart of *Ghost in the Shell*'s philosophical narrative, it seems more that she connected to a broader zeitgeist in which discussions of cyborgs were being explored in relation to emerging digital technologies than that these were the only possible concepts of interest to be found in Oshii's film.

However, within these debates about subjectivity, sex and cyborgs in *Ghost in the Shell*, there are also interesting debates about genre and nation. Schaub and Napier, for example, work through the issue of *Ghost in the Shell*'s genre, deploying similar terms but coming to divergent conclusions. Schaub places the film within the "mecha-anime" genre, which he defines very broadly as mechanical animation, which he states "explicitly take on technology, power, and gender as subject matter." He goes on to claim that "the literary equivalent of mecha-anime is the genre known as cyberpunk" (2001, 80). Although he then goes on to analyze the distinctions between these genres, and the ways they are taken up in *Ghost in the Shell*, it remains that Schaub sees the film as part of a Japanese genre before all else.

By contrast, Napier argues that "Although part of the *mecha* genre, [*Ghost in the Shell*] manipulates traditional *mecha* tropes such as the cyborg and urban high-tech settings to explore more inward states of consciousness" (2005, 104). She continues, "Rather than categorizing *Ghost in the Shell* as a purely *mecha* film, therefore, it might be at least as accurate to call it a 'cyberpunk-noir film' with elegiac, gothic, and even apocalyptic overtones" (105). Where Schaub is definite about how to generically position *Ghost in the Shell*, Napier's reading is far more fluid and appends the text with a wider set of genre descriptors. As a consequence, Napier directly links *Ghost in the Shell* to an historically and culturally American set of genres.

Already, therefore, we can see how *Akira* and *Ghost in the Shell* have become associated with a transnational and local set of science fiction subgenres. However, these academic accounts have the benefit of working with hindsight—of being able to position these films retrospectively into genre categories. In the analysis that follows, I investigate the "genre trouble" suffered by journalists from around the English-speaking world as they attempted to place anime into categories without the benefit of this kind of hindsight.

Anime films or something else?

It is important to note that when *Akira* was released around the world between 1989 and 1991, the idea of "anime" was in its transnational infancy. The reviews and coverage of *Akira* by critics from around the English-speaking world (Australia, the USA, Canada and the UK in particular) hardly used the term "anime" at all.

Instead, they were much more likely to use more generalized descriptions like "Japanese animated feature" to explain *Akira*. For example, Charles

Solomon of the *LA Times* explains that *Akira* is "a Japanese animated feature based on Katsuhiro Otomo's popular comic books about a teen-aged motorcycle gang" and that it "is a compilation of the worst clichés of Japanese animation—two hours of chases, laser attacks, machine-gun battles, spilled stage blood, computer-animated backgrounds and hokey dialogue" (1990). Solomon's assessment, in part because of its scathing tone, is useful in interpreting US understanding of anime. The difficulties Solomon has in placing the film manifest in the language he uses: "stage blood" in particular signaling a conceptual link to live-action cinema, while his list of action and conflict-oriented phrases implies genres that he perceived as lowbrow, an observation confirmed by his assertion that *Akira* is filled with "hokey dialogue." Whether this is a general bias against science fiction and action films, or a more specific dislike of Japanese animated features, is unclear. However, it is clear from Solomon's reading of the film that *Akira* was at the crest in a wave of "Japanese animated features" to have been pouring into the USA. His listing of concepts demonstrates an emergent generic understanding of Japanese animation that would later be reflected in the critical conceptualizations of "anime."

Sheila Johnston, writing for the *Independent* in the UK, offers a similar précis of *Akira*. She claims that

> *Akira* is a Japanese animated feature, set in "Neo-Tokyo, 2019" which the creator, Katsuhiro Otomo, imagines as a nightmare megapolis peopled by gangs of delinquent motorcycle kids .... *Akira* comes badly unstuck (perhaps because of Katsuhiro's background in comic-strips) in the later sections where the story-arc collapses into an unfathomable jumble. (1991)

Although these reviews are separated by time and geographic distance, a consistent review category of "Japanese animated features" is apparent. Johnston, however, further extends this category by invoking the specter of manga when she blames Ōtomo's "comic-strip" past for the abstruse ending of *Akira*. Her comments suggest a further elision in the markets for anime and manga in the early 1990s—not just the lack of a specific noun for these animated films, but a wider misrepresentation of their source matter under the generalized rubric of "comic-strips."

In a more extreme conflation of this kind, Janet Maslin at the *New York Times* assesses *Akira* as:

> a phenomenal work of animation with all the hallmarks of an instant cult classic. Its post-apocalyptic mood, high-tech trappings, thrilling artwork and

a wide array of bizarre characters guarantee it a place in the pantheon of *comic-strip science fiction*. (1990, my emphasis)

As comic-strip science fiction, *Akira* becomes part of newly minted hybrid genre that combines two separate media traditions while eliding a third. What Maslin means by the term "comic-strip" becomes clear as she continues: "Based on Mr. Otomo's widely popular comic-book saga, 'Akira' takes its name from a mysterious force that may be afoot in Neo-Tokyo" (Ibid.). Though it would be easy to read this identification of manga as "comic-strips" as a cultural misrecognition, *Akira*'s transnational history suggests a different explanation. The conflation of the terms "comic-strip" and "manga" may well be the result of Marvel Comics' release of Ōtomo's manga as a full-color comic book in the US market in 1988, years *before* the release of the film (Gravett 2004, 155). The manga was thereby imported into, and became a part of, US comic book culture, making the film it inspired all the more difficult to place within national categories.

As an instant "cult classic," too, *Akira* was overtly marked as an "other" to US filmmaking, even where it was accepted as a localized form of comic-strip science fiction. *Akira*'s exceptional status would still be celebrated nearly half a decade later, when *Ghost in the Shell* enjoyed a high-profile release in the USA and UK. Laurence Lerman, writing for the trade journal *Variety*, explains the process of anime's genrification:

Because anime now has a strong global distribution and retailing network and increased name recognition through word of mouth and recent broadcast licensing deals, anime video releases are fast approaching the kind of popularity usually reserved for more mainstream genres. (1996)

Lerman posits that *Akira* was responsible for beginning this distribution pattern, quoting the director of Manga UK, Mike Preece, saying, "The U.K. had never seen anything like 'Akira' and no one was prepared for it to be such a hit" (Preece quoted in Lerman 1996). *Akira* came to act as a benchmark for subsequent anime, setting the bar high and establishing a generic connection between anime and science fiction. "Otomo's Akira featured prominently in Michael Jackson's video for his recent single Scream" proclaims one UK article about *Ghost in the Shell*, as a means of suggesting *Akira*'s stratospheric popularity and multimedia influence (Smith 1995). As a consequence of these kinds of commentaries, *Akira* would become the dominant "Japanese animated feature" to which new anime films could be compared.

Take, for example, the *Washington Post*'s coverage of *Ghost in the Shell*'s video release:

When the Japanese film Akira hit the home video market in 1989, American audiences were blown away by its state-of-the-art animation and outlandish cyberpunk storyline. Since then, the cult of Japanese animation (or anime, pronounced ANNIE-may) has grown, creating a significant presence on American video shelves. Akira's producers, Yoshimasa Mizuo and Ken Iyadomi, headed up the first East/West anime co-production. The resulting project, Ghost in the Shell, is now in video stores. (O'Connell 1996)

Once again, anime becomes part of a "cult" phenomenon, but now Japanese animation has become, at least in parentheses, "anime" (or, rather, "ANNIE-may"). Moreover, an industrial understanding of anime as a transnational product is developed to create associations between the previous "hit" Akira and the newer project from Akira's producers, who are rarely mentioned elsewhere. Ghost in the Shell is thereby imbued with some of Akira's exceptional qualities.

Laura Evenson in the San Francisco Chronicle performs a similar trick:

The [film] sends viewers into an adrenaline-charged thriller that probably is the most eagerly awaited Japanese animation, or anime (pronounced ah-nee-may) movie, since 1989, when Katsuhiro Otomo launched his blisteringly violent cyberpunk epic "Akira," set in post-World War III Neo-Tokyo. (1996)

In this example, we are enjoined once more to connect Akira and Ghost in the Shell. The status of Ghost in the Shell as part of a genre of Japanese animation, this time "ah-nee-may," is likewise significant for the way these ideas become enmeshed in a wider attempt to categorize this new Japanese film. Ghost in the Shell is at one and the same time a thriller, an anime and close kin with Akira's cyberpunk classification. As this layering of genre terms and explanatory notes suggests, anime's meanings were still up for grabs; but, importantly, by the release of Ghost in the Shell, enough Japanese animated films had begun circulating to justify the introduction of a new term: "anime."

This is not to suggest, however, that anime was the only category used to describe Ghost in the Shell. As Evenson's account shows, there were multiple layers of classificatory terminology applied to Ghost in the Shell. Quite apart from other genres, a high degree of inconsistency lingered around how to name these films, placing "anime" in competition with alternative terms. One often favored in the USA at the time was "Japanimation." Joe Leydon calls "Devotees of Japanimation, graphic novels and cyberpunk literature" to see Ghost in the Shell in his film review for Variety (1996). In Leydon's reading, however, the appeal of Ghost in the Shell reaches across media platforms to fans of US cult media as well as "Japanimation." In this way,

Leydon constructs the transnational audience for *Ghost in the Shell* as a hybrid audience of pre-existing fandoms. In this respect, *Ghost in the Shell* retains the "cult" associations of its predecessor, *Akira*.

In other examples, *Ghost in the Shell*'s genrification demonstrates greater understanding of its place within a Japanese media context. The UK's *Daily Mirror* categorizes *Ghost in the Shell* as part of the "Japanese manga cartoon" genre, proclaiming that "Manga deals with sex, violence, intergalactic monsters and superheroes, and is cut as fast as a pop video. Thankfully, they are all dubbed into perfect English." (Hancock 1995) While this distinctive appellation could be a result of Manga Entertainment's high profile as a UK anime distributor, with "manga" here simply borrowed from the company's name, the use of the lowercase suggests that the author is attempting to connect this anime film back to its roots in Shirō Masamune's manga. Nor is he alone in deploying this new category. Sheila Johnston, in the *Independent* also claims that "Japanese Manga animation is sui generis, and commands a cult following. But it has yet to cross over to a wider audience. Touted as a 'major breakthrough,' Ghost in the Shell won't do the trick" (1995) Here, the slippage between Manga Entertainment and "Japanese Manga animation" is even clearer, with the company name capitalized into this new descriptor for Japanese animation.

In these early years of anime's transnational distribution, then, texts were buffeted by the rise and fall of many critical categories. While Japanimation, Japanese manga animation and others may have eventually fallen by the wayside in favor of "anime," these terms remain significant for what they can reveal about the industrial and cultural meanings of Japanese media texts. As "ah-nee-may" emerged, it is important to note that other forms of Japanese culture were likewise beginning to be recognized. The shift from comic-strip science fiction to manga animation implies as much. Over time, too, as more Japanese animation texts entered English-speaking markets, more and more nuanced and specialized classifications for these texts started to emerge, moving from generalized descriptions like Japanese animated feature to the much more specific manga animation and anime. Furthermore, in these terms we can see the rising importance of anime's Japanese origins within their transnational progress. The way *Ghost in the Shell*'s status as a co-production was highlighted tells us that anime was becoming localized within UK–US media production cultures, and that anime's distributors were able and willing to invest in Japanese media production in order to get the kind of texts that they thought would be popular outside of Japan. Even this early set of debates about how to properly name or categorize "anime" therefore has consequences far beyond a simple generic shorthand. The terms used and widely applied had industrial, ideological and political significance, too.

Akira and *Ghost in the Shell* as cyberpunk anime

The idea that anime was "sui generis," that it has no precursors, is brought into question by the wide range of neologisms brought to bear when *Akira* and *Ghost in the Shell* were released outside Japan. Even more so by the repeated assertions that *Akira* and *Ghost in the Shell* both belong to the cyberpunk subgenre of science fiction. In the quotations already cited, O'Connell says that *Akira* has an "outlandish cyberpunk storyline" and Evenson refers to it as a "violent cyberpunk epic." Each contains the hallmarks of what Rick Altman calls the process of genrification (1999), relying on a more stable category—storyline and the epic, respectively—to legitimize *Akira*'s status within the cyberpunk genre. As both of these claims are made in reviews for *Ghost in the Shell*'s 1996 release, and because academic criticism has already been shown to place the latter film within this subgenre of science fiction, this section investigates what critics meant when they deployed the concept of cyberpunk in reviews of *Akira* and *Ghost in the Shell*.

Potentially, there was a lot at stake in using this term. Calling them cyberpunk effectively placed *Akira* and *Ghost in the Shell* into an already transnational and multimedia subgenre of science fiction. Mike Featherstone and Roger Burrows explain that:

> The term cyberpunk refers to the body of fiction built around the work of William Gibson and other writers, who have constructed visions of the future worlds of cyberspaces, with all their vast range of technological developments and power struggles. It sketches out the dark side of the technological-fix visions of the future, with a wide range of post-human forms which have both theoretical and practical implications. (1995, 3)

Cyberpunk was an unusually reflexive genre from its beginning, deeply concerned with discussions of digital and computing technologies and their impact on culture. As John Markoff suggests, these tropes had an impact on how quickly cyberpunk spread across formats. In an article in the *New York Times* in which he discusses *Akira* at some length, Markoff claims that:

> Now cyberpunk's vision is influencing a much broader group of artists and writers and slowly filtering in the mainstream.... Filmmakers, writers, painters, poets and musicians, influenced by a fascination with the implications of cyberpunk, have so far had the most impact on popular culture. (1990)

As these accounts suggest, the cyberpunk subgenre of science fiction spread quickly from literature into other forms of visual culture and media.

Cyberpunk was also a transnational subgenre. David Morley and Kevin Robins argue that cyberpunk was heavily invested in a Techno-Orientalist image of Japanese culture from Gibson's *Neuromancer* (1984) onwards (1995, 169). Cyberpunk's Techno-Orientalism is explained by Austin Corbett as presenting "Japan as the new home of the cyborg," a stereotype engendered by Japan's technology-related economic boom of the 1980s and 1990s (2009, 45). The emergence of this new subgenre in science fiction thereby coincided with Japan's rise to postwar economic prominence and a concomitant rise in the amounts of Japanese popular culture being translated and adapted across transnational media markets. This goes some way toward explaining why reviewers from Australia to the UK were so keen to assign *Akira* and *Ghost in the Shell* to the cyberpunk genre, as already seen in the quotations from Evenson and O'Connell. However, the circumstances in which critics made these connections reveal additional instability around early attempts to understand anime's genres.

Sometimes, the wider genre of cyberpunk was used to explain *Akira*'s content, as when Markoff claims that Ōtomo "took his inspiration from 'Neuromancer'" (1990). Similarly, the *Sydney Morning Herald*'s Lynden Barber writes that "The influence of the recent brand of science fiction known as cyberpunk, in turn heavily influenced by the work of Phillip K. Dick, is manifest in *Akira*, particularly in its fascination with drug culture" (1990). These assertions are particularly interesting given manga specialist Paul Gravett's claim that "In fact, when Otomo began serializing *Akira* in *Young Magazine* in 1984, he was unaware of Gibson's book, which was not translated into Japanese until 1985" (2004, 155). Consequently, these declarations of genre lineage and influence may be based more in critical assumptions about the cyberpunk subgenre than in Ōtomo's knowledge of the category. These assumptions tell us about how dominant cyberpunk was as a subgenre in this period, with the power to shape texts even in parts of the world where the genre's foundational texts had yet to be translated.

However, the reviews for both *Ghost in the Shell* and *Akira* highlight a form of cyberpunk that *would* have been readily available and widely known in Japan: Ridley Scott's *Blade Runner* (1982). Writing in Australia's *Sun Herald* Rob Lowing explains that "International critics compared the look of [*Akira*] to modern science fiction movie hits like Blade Runner" when it first came out (1990). As evidence of the pattern Lowing identifies, the *Baltimore Sun*'s Stephen Hunter proclaims that we should "Think Ralph Bakshi's 'Wizards,' think 'Blade-Runner' [sic.] as animated by Peter Max (1990)" when watching *Akira*. This example provides an attempt to provide a "high concept" reading of *Akira* that views the film as a mixture of challenging animation styles and cyberpunk genre film.

Ghost in Shell's reviews also reference Scott's *Blade Runner*, as when O'Connell's review ends by stating that "Between the mean-street setting and self-doubting androids, the video suggests an updated Blade Runner— high-quality, futuristic entertainment for a mature audience" (1996). Referencing Martin Scorsese's New York diegesis ("mean-streets") and Scott's film as precursors, O'Connell usefully clarifies the meanings he associates with *Blade Runner* as genre-shorthand. Compare this with Carrie Rickey's cyberpunk associations:

> With its nods to the novels of William Gibson and films such as Blade Runner and Total Recall, the movie trades in familiar virtual realities. Yet as realized by the gifted director Mamoru Oshii, who imagines cityscapes melting into circuit boards, Ghost in the Shell is where virtual reality meets superrealism. (1996)

Unlike O'Connell and Lowing, Rickey, writing for the *Philadelphia Inquirer* stays entirely focused on the cyberpunk genre's highest profile members and texts. The image of cities as circuit boards also usefully explains the cyber aspects of *Ghost in the Shell*'s imagery. In these references to possible points of comparison, the meanings of cyberpunk become reified through its highest profile exemplars. In this way, both *Akira* and *Ghost in the Shell* are brought into a discourse that works to transnationalize and localize at the same time: using a transnationally distributed set of films and books to account for and make sense of a "foreign" set of films.

Ghost in the Shell's reviews were particularly notable for their hybridization of "cyber" ideas. *Daily Variety* labels the film a "cyber-tech thriller" (Street 1995), as does Richard Harrington in the *Washington Post*: "Mamoru Oshii's 'Ghost in the Shell' is masterly Japanimation, a cyber-tech thriller that's miles ahead of such recent live-action cyber-splatter films as 'Johnny Mnemonic'" (1996). Harrington and Street's hybrid suggests an emerging emphasis on the digital media side of the cyberpunk subgenre, and Harrington compounds this impression by creating another new subgenre of "cyber-splatter" films, which helps to differentiate *Ghost in the Shell* from its transnational cyberpunk brethren. The idea that technology was becoming increasingly important is also echoed in Sheila Johnston's proclamation that *Ghost in the Shell* has a "tech noir story" (1995) and in Joe Leydon's complaint that "In the world of 'Ghost in the Shell,' everyone speaks so rapidly in such an obscure high-tech patois, it's often hard to tell just what is going on" (1996). Critical impressions of technology's increasing centrality to the subgenre here begin to shift the discourse around cyberpunk, inflecting it with new anime hybrid offshoots and associations from film noir to the splatter subgenre of horror filmmaking.

Cyberpunk shaped transnational discourse on these two anime films at much the same time that they became evidence for its evolution. *Akira* and *Ghost in the Shell* were by no means solely seen as cyberpunk, and nor were the points of comparison always stable. The unpredictability of genre terms and associations belies the ease with which academics would later assert the centrality of postmodern filmmaking and cyborg narratives in explaining the meanings of these complex anime films. Negative reviews like Eleanor Ringel's perhaps demonstrate these issues best. She writes that "Japanimation is just a ghost of its crazed over-the-top self in 'Ghost in the Shell,' a philosophical animated feature that strives to combine Sartre and 'Speed Racer'" (1996). Though Ringel is likely exaggerating her comparison for effect, this quote is useful for showing the diversity of generic and classificatory associations constructed around *Ghost in the Shell* and *Akira*. As Japanimation, a philosophical animated feature and an attempted juxtapositioning of Sartre and anime television show *Speed Racer* (*Mahha Go Go Go*, 1967–1968), even *Ghost in the Shell*'s perceived failure provides evidence for the challenges involved in making sense of science fiction anime.

From cyberpunk to steampunk anime

Roughly a decade later, when both Ōtomo and Oshii would once again release new science fiction films within years of one another, there were considerable discursive sea changes. *Steamboy* and *The Sky Crawlers* therefore present a good point of comparison for their forebears. Perhaps the most obvious of the changes in anime criticism is the standardization of the critical term "anime." Only three of the reviews examined for this last part of this chapter called these films anything other than anime or Japanese anime. In these moments, "Japanimation" lingered at the edges of anime discourse, and Ōtomo's status as a perceived founder of transnational anime culture is part of the reason for this. J. Hoberman at the *Village Voice* claims that *Akira* "established an American audience for Japanimation" (2005), while Michael O'Sullivan calls Ōtomo "Japanimation icon Katsuhiro ('Akira') Otomo" (2005) and *Variety*'s Leslie Felperin terms him "Leading manga and Japanimation writer-helmer Katsuhiro Otomo" (2004). These titles tantalizingly suggest that it is not Japanimation as a genre that lingers, but rather a critical respect for Ōtomo as a founder of the genre in the USA that shapes this discourse.

It is also the case that Ōtomo and Oshii's previous hit films linger in languorous fashion, legitimating newer anime films. "In 1988, with his debut feature *Akira*, Katsuhiro Ōtomo introduced the world to the post-apocalyptic future, Japanese-style—and spurred a global boom for Japanese animation that has yet to subside" (Schilling 2004). This proclamation in *Screen International* prefaces a largely positive review of *Steamboy*. On its appearance at the Toronto International Film Festival, *The Sky Crawlers* was also given similar treatment. Peter Howell in the *Toronto Star* writes that "Celebrated anime storyteller Mamoru Oshii (Ghost in the Shell) presents The Sky Crawlers, a sci-fi fantasy about a future where endless aerial battles are fought for a TV audience" (2008). Authorial reputation and genre predecessors have become a consistent theme in critical discourse around anime, and the significance of these two directors as stars comes to form an important basis from which to judge the films that they produce. As *The Sky Crawler*'s inclusion at a major film festival also indicates, the producers of these anime films were courting positive critical attention, seeking alternative cinematic entry routes into Western film markets. By placing *The Sky Crawlers* in multiple festivals (see Goodridge 2008 for more information about *The Sky Crawlers'* appearance at the Venice Film Festival), it became possible to build associations between its content and art house cinema circuits, generating journalist- and not fan-derived commentary. This helps to build critical commentary about "quality," as seen when *The Sky Crawlers* won the Future Film Festival Digital Award at Venice (Lyman 2008).

The slippage in Howell's term—sci-fi fantasy—may also imply a shift in the way anime is discussed. For *The Sky Crawlers* in particular, there was a diffuse sense of genre beyond its overriding status as an anime film. For example, Lee Marshall calls the film "Mamoru Oshii's most meditative feature-length animation to date" (2008) in *Screen International* and Nick James of the UK's *Observer* newspaper struggles to place the film. After describing its plot at length he simply gives up that task pronouncing "Weird it is" (2008). In these vagaries linger the traces of *The Sky Crawlers'* refusal of genre tropes, but at another level the slippages in terms also imply, once more, that anime comes in such wide varieties of science fiction as to confound critical vocabulary.

While some critics struggled to place *The Sky Crawlers*, others were more assured in their analyses. Derek Elley calls it a "Retro-futuristic tale, about a bunch of teen pilots whose sole reason to exist is to engage in endless aerial dogfights against a perpetual enemy" (2008) and in doing so picks up a number of recurring themes from the critical discourse around *The Sky Crawlers*. Oshii's sequence of aerial battles were continually commented upon. These comments were often folded into more legitimizing discourse about *The Sky Crawlers'* status as an adaptation. For example, Jason Gray writes, "Based on Hiroshi Mori's eight million-copy selling five-part novel series of the same name, the story focuses on boy and girl teenaged pilots who are raised to engage in aerial battles over Europe for the entertainment of adults" (2008, see also *Screen International*, 2007). Similarly, Schilling writes that rather than science fiction, *The Sky Crawlers* is an "air combat pic … that sent viewers into ecstacy over its gorgeously realistic flight sequences" (2008). Rather than genre, therefore, it was an allusion to the war film and one particular kind of sequence from the film that was most often used to categorize *The Sky Crawlers*.

The adaptation process was also assessed as an attempt to extend Oshii's genre filmmaking to include more women and young people. In an early production report, Brett Bull writes in *Variety* that

> Production I.G's "The Sky Crawlers," which is set to unspool in Japan next year, will contain a romantic theme. For the pic, in which a society of children lives in eternal adolescence, helmer Mamoru Oshii ("Ghost in the Shell") decided to work with young scriptwriter Chihiro Itou so that his message could reach his intended audience. (2007)

So, it may be that the reason *The Sky Crawlers* is so hard to pin down is because of the range of voices apparent in the end product of its adaptation process. The gendered genre issues here, it is worth noting, are quite distinct from those raised around Oshii's earlier cyborg film. Romance rather than the female body dominates the discourse, with one review commentary noting that *The Sky Crawlers* had been "Billed as the Greatest Love Story Ever" (Tartaglione-Vialatte 2008), over and above its status as a science fiction film.

This is not to suggest that science fiction was unimportant to *The Sky Crawlers* and *Steamboy*. Rather, it was an altered, or differently hybridized, form of science fiction genre that critics saw in these films. The idea of *The Sky Crawlers* as a "retro-futurist tale," for example, was part of a wider cluster of genre commentary centering on the concept of steampunk. As Brigid Cherry and Maria Mellins describe it, steampunk was something of an accidental subgenre:

> It was simply a borrowing from the popular use of the suffix in other subgenres of science fiction: where cyberpunk looked to the future for its narrative inspiration, steampunk looked to the past. However, the subgenre is a particularly visual form of fiction organized around advanced science and technology anachronistically retrofitted onto a Victorian-themed—and thus often steam-powered—world. (2011, 6)

Cherry and Mellins specifically name anime as one of the places where steampunk texts have thrived (5). There are hints of this subgenre's presence even in the supposedly "futuristic" world of *The Sky Crawlers*. Marshall, for example, claims that "The only town we see has something retro Eastern European about it, nodding at the steampunk anime tradition most closely associated with Katsuhiro Otomo" (2008) bringing us neatly to Ōtomo's film, *Steamboy*, and noting another science fiction anime shift led by Ōtomo.

Given Marshall's assertion, and the use of the word "steam" in the film's title, it might be reasonable to expect steampunk to dominate *Steamboy*'s reception. There are, indeed, moments of this kind, as when Jeff Shannon explores the film's relationship to steampunk:

> Otomo trades the dystopian sci-fi of his breakthrough 1988 feature "Akira" (the first international anime hit) for a clever overhaul of industrial-age London. He draws inspiration from "The Difference Engine," the 1991 novel by cyberpunk pioneers William Gibson and Bruce Sterling that offered a similar speculation on advanced nineteenth-century technology. (2005)

As before, it is the subgenre's literary past, closely aligned with the earlier cyberpunk tradition, which shapes the understanding of *Steamboy*'s genre. The subgenre is not mentioned by name, however, which is a pattern which would repeat elsewhere. For example, Hoberman's review notes that "Otomo has credited novelist William Gibson as an influence on Akira; with Steamboy, Otomo executes the same switch pulled by Gibson when he went steampunk with the alt-Victorian 19th century of his 1991 collaboration with Bruce Sterling, *The Difference Engine*" (2005). The repetition of details about Gibson and Sterling's novel and the need to explain the periodization normal in steampunk both suggest that the steampunk subgenre was not expected to be widely known or understood. Moreover, the idea that Ōtomo was performing a genre "switch" from one subgenre of science fiction to another is significant. This is a transnational exchange in subgenre concepts and ideas, with US science fiction informing the production of Japanese science fiction anime.

Nor were these the only English-speaking authors from whom Ōtomo was seen to borrow. For example, Roger Ebert opens his review of Ōtomo's film by stating that "'Steamboy' is a noisy, eventful and unsuccessful venture into Victorian-era science fiction, animated by a modern Japanese master. It's like H.G. Wells and Jules Verne meet 'Akira'" (2005). Invoking Ōtomo's 1988 hit film and mashing it together with classic science fiction, Ebert reads a variation on steampunk into his disavowal of *Steamboy*'s genre legitimacy. Schilling, similarly, claims that "huge swathes of cityscape get trashed, in ways that Verne could barely imagine—but will be familiar to fans of Godzilla" (2004) in an attempt to redomesticate this steampunk text within Japanese science fiction (see Figure 2.1). The references to classics of both types—classic Japanese science fiction film and classic English genre fiction—work to differently authenticate Ōtomo's detailed rendition of an alternative version of London in *Steamboy*.

FIGURE 2.1 *Ray Steam uses steampowered jet pack to soar above a sepia-toned London in* Steamboy.

This assessment of *Steamboy* through genre proxies was common. Without overtly calling *Steamboy* a "steampunk" film, many of the reviewers had fun creating puns on the idea of steam-power. Arwa Haider claims that the film "has run out of puff" (2005), Ian Johns asserts that "The film's riveted Escher universe ends up blowing several gaskets" (2005) and Felperin states that Ōtomo "charcoal-filters his ambivalent attitude toward technology through a complex sci-fi plot set in Victorian England" (2004). As these examples demonstrate, the steampunk genre was regularly invoked even when it was not openly named.

These puns provide a way for journalists to signal the film's attention to steampunk-related iconography and themes, and it is in its excesses that its close relationship to the subgenre becomes most obvious. For example, Hoberman claims that "mainly *Steamboy* is about technology. The imaginary steam-powered hardware includes one-man bombers, bathyscapes, and enough elaborately clanking contraptions to keep the world's plumbers in business for the rest of the century" (2005). O'Sullivan similarly contends that "Touted as the most expensive Japanese animated film ever made, 'Steamboy' is right to brag about the lushness of its reimagined late-19th-century world, a metal-spined and wood-ribbed world in which the power of steam has been harnessed like nuclear energy" (2005). In the former example, it is the sheer number of steampunk machines that becomes excessive, in the latter, however, the film began in excess as Japan's most expensive anime and continued this in rethinking steam as a nuclear-scale power source. Positive or negative, therefore, the idea of steampunk runs through the appreciations of

Steamboy's visuals, rendering the film into the subgenre through sly sidelong, and often humorous, glances.

Conclusion

What becomes evident in the shift between the mid-1990s to the mid-2000s is a broadening out of science fiction's place in relation to anime and a greater spectrum of possible genres and subgenres into which anime films can be fitted. Despite the fact that *Steamboy* and *The Sky Crawlers* were viewed as both anime and science fiction by many reviewers, this did not preclude others from placing the films into alternative registers. That *The Sky Crawler*s was positioned in its marketing as a romance film and the fact that reviewers became preoccupied by *Steamboy's* historical setting both speak to the far wider understanding of what anime *can be* than was present in the era of *Akira* and *Ghost in the Shell'*s initial releases.

However, this generic openness is also especially evident around the releases of the earlier films, when competing terms were being used to name and rename this kind of Japanese animated filmmaking. As anime emerged out of the swirling waters of these debates, it allowed the discourse to open out and shift toward ever new subgenres housed within the cultural category of "anime." In this respect, the fact that anime can absorb new forms of science fiction and affix new hybrid concepts to that genre should not be all that surprising.

More importantly, the development of science fiction anime over this period suggests that anime is now increasingly a transnational category of media production, thanks in part to the early film experiments that borrowed from already-transnational film genres. *Ghost in the Shell* was noted as an international co-production, and Oshii's later film, *The Sky Crawlers*, takes in foreign locations and characters. Consequently, if anything, this examination points not to a shift toward transnationalism in anime, but to the idea that anime has always been transnational. It is merely our understanding of it as such that is intensifying over time and sliding along new valances. Not every encounter of this kind is well received. One particularly outraged critic of *Steamboy* asserts that "the filmmaker is tone-deaf: He can't recognize the difference between a true vision of Western hubris and something that feels arbitrary, clichéd, entirely predictable" (Hunter 2005). *Steamboy* discomfits this US critic by stepping into a culturally proximate transnational space, with the director's non-Western worldview challenging the reviewer's sense of his own culture.

Sci fi anime is at the forefront of issues like these because of the ability of these narratives to explore everything from alternative histories to alternative subjectivities. As these reviewers show, science fiction anime has thrived in these liminal spaces of "otherness." Science fiction provided the starting point from which our understanding of "anime" as a category could be tested out and, in return, anime have provided useful spaces in which subgenres can be explored and expanded. In these ways, science fiction has not just been critical to the success of anime; anime has been just as important to the continuing development of a transnational, transmedia genre of science fiction.

3

Anime's Bodies

If any aspect of anime has drawn attention for its mutability, it is anime's depictions of human and humanoid bodies. Body debates in anime range across its genres, and from the industrial remediation of anime characters as toys to the ways female anime bodies are admired and even performed by fans. In all of these ways, discourses about anime have long centered on concepts of the body, which is all the more surprising in a type of media production that contains very few "real" bodies. Christian McCrea suggests that the appeal of anime bodies lies in their "discursive, disruptive and incredibly excessive" natures. He claims that the anime body "is resolutely physical, but never truly available for us to interpret in the way... action films can be interpreted" (2008, 19). The fascination with bodies in anime is at least in part, therefore, a result of anime's ability to depict constantly mutating, metamorphosing and transforming bodies that exceed the possibilities of the real world, even going beyond live-action cinema. These transformations create impossible bodies that cross between genres from romance to horror, sometimes in the same text. Anime's bodies are therefore the subject of this chapter, in which I argue that discussions of anime's bodies play crucial roles in making sense of the genres in which they appear.

Gender studies-inflected debates are crucial here, with discussions of gendered power and dominance in anime frequently compared to Japanese culture's more rigid gender ideologies. Therefore, I begin with an overview of the analyses produced by academics and popular commentators about bodies within anime's varied genres, before focusing on a single example, canonized for its extreme representations of such gender and body issues.

Anime's powerful women have long fascinated commentators on anime (see Chapter 5), often framing debates about anime's cultural and aesthetic difference to other kinds of animation. These discussions of anime's bodies have, for this reason, normally focused on women's representations across the spectrum of anime's genres. While, as I intend to show, these debates about women range from the *shōjo* (adolescent girls) to horror, one particular industrial category has been key to these debates: pornography. While other genres play important roles in discussions of the anime body, pornography's place within anime culture has been perhaps the most emphatically contested beyond academic discussions, becoming a crucial part of anime's difference from other kinds of animation. During critical attempts to account for anime pornography, certain texts have come to define the discourse more than others. In this chapter, therefore, I examine the range of anime bodies discussed by academics before analyzing how one particular medium, the original video anime (OVA), and one film series of that type, *Urotsukidōji* (Hideki Takayama, 1987–1994), have shaped our understanding of anime's bodies, and with them, anime's body genres.

Anime bodies in Japan: From Disneyfication to toyetics

Before examining how anime's bodies have been understood transculturally, however, it is important to note that the anime body is also important in Japan. Not all of the body discussions in Japan are focused on the kinds of extreme anime bodies that have come to dominate English criticism, however. Manga and anime pioneer Osamu Tezuka has himself discussed the importance of transnational influences on the look of his characters. In his autobiography *My Life in Manga* (*Boku no Manga Jinsei*), for example, Tezuka talks at length about how he modeled Astro Boy after Mickey Mouse, mimicking Mickey Mouse's shape and Disney's method of keeping both of a character's ears on screen (1997, 111–113, see Chapter 4). Tezuka also reportedly borrowed his large character eyes from those of the Fleischer brothers' character Betty Boop (Ladd and Deneroff 2009). This transnational influence is significant for the way it commingles genres and styles, making even early anime part of global animation body debates.

The design and depiction of characters in anime are also frequently the subject of books on manga authors and animators in Japan. Usually titled *irasuto*, from the English "illustrations," these image archives focus primarily on anime and manga characters (for a representative example, see Harada 2008). Images of anime characters also routinely grace the front covers of specialist magazines like *Animage* (*Animēju*), *Animedia* and *Newtype* in Japan in the manner of the film stars and idols of other Japanese media industries. This kind of character representation is a product of anime's reliance on popular characters that can be exploited across a wide range of media formats. In Japan, this reliance on character has been recognized in the growth of a *kyara bijinesu*, or character business, in which characters are used as concepts around which entire franchises can be created. Such was famously the case, for example, when Takashi Okazaki had a figurine made of his *dōjinshi* character, Afro Samurai, which later became the central protagonist for a transnational anime co-production involving US star Samuel L. Jackson (Condry 2013, 80–82).

In many cases, the character business in Japan reimagines anime's heroes and heroines (and villains) to a wide range of new ends in order to extend the reach or fandom for a set of characters. Often, this involves more exploitative scenarios than those usually seen in their anime narratives. For example, Kyoto Animation's *nichijōkei* (everyday, or slice of life, see Chapter 6) anime *K'On!* (2009 and 2010) heroines are frequently depicted in more sexualized and provocative poses on the covers of popular anime magazines in Japan than those featured in the show's *moe*-style content, which is designed to produce protective feelings in fans (for example, see http://animage.jp/back_number/am_201403.html). For my purposes, the interest generated in this kind of character exploitation, a form of "fan service" (LaMarre 2006b), comes from the way it can create dramatic shifts in genre between an anime text and its promotional surround in Japanese magazine culture. As a result, these kinds of images acknowledge the importance of particular adult (usually male) fans while also indicating how central characters and their bodies are within anime's domestic culture.

As this suggests, there is a highly pornographic end of the Japanese anime market, but it remains the case that not all of the bodies of anime characters are understood or discussed in terms of exploitation. Japanese psychologist Tamaji Saitō, for example, has discussed the birth of a new kind of character in anime, the "phallic girl" or beautiful fighting girl of whom he claims that:

> The icon of the beautiful fighting girl is an extraordinary invention capable of encapsulating polymorphous perversity in a stable form. She radiates the potential for an omnidirectional sexuality latent with pedophilia, homosexuality, fetishism, sadism, masochism, and other perversions, yet she behaves as if she were completely unaware of it all. (trans. J Keith Vincent and Dawn Lawson, [2000] 2011, loc.2189)

In Saitō's reading of anime's women, therefore, ambiguity rules. His most important intervention is in reading this "thoroughly fictional construct" as one which "nonethess attains a paradoxical reality in the process of being desired and consumed" by otaku fans (loc. 287). Saitō's observation about the "paradoxical reality" of Japanese anime women is thus bound up in their real-world consumption and in the ways fans interpret them psychologically.

Other Japanese scholars are more tentative in their claims, noting not the "polymorphous perversity" of anime's characters, but their connections to indexical realism. For example, Misao Minamida argues for a reading of anime characters' closeness to real people in an analysis of Isao Takahata's anime adaptation of *Anne of Green Gables* (*Akage no An* literally, *Red-haired Anne*, 1979) and within a popular anime series with a racoon protagonist, titled *Rascal* (Hiroshi et al., 1977). Minamida wishes to evaluate this relationship "because I think it [*Rascal*] is a work that masters the potential of anime on the point of drawing characters as 'real people'" (2000, 34). This link to the "real" is one Minamida goes on to trace through the faithful adaptation work undertaken by Takahata for his contribution to Tōei Dōga's *Masterpiece Theater* series, but also through the ways these anime depict the everyday activities of their characters (34–36). In this variety of anime bodies, it is not the extremity or instability or exploitation of the body that shapes discourse, but the closeness of even anthropomorphized animal characters to lived human experiences and everyday events that gains significance.

Marc Steinberg's *Anime's Media Mix* offers a third, this time more industrial, interpretation of the anime body's significance (2012). In his detailed historical account, Steinberg quotes from a wide range of Japanese sources detailing the importance of characters to anime's economic success. He argues that as toys and other merchandise, anime's bodies are literalized and extended into new worlds. With the business of anime built around characters, Steinberg argues that "The character is a particular combination of name and visual design that is in some sense independent from any particular medium" (2012, 83). In this respect, at least, Steinberg's industrial observations accord with Saitō's psychological understanding of anime characters' meanings for Japanese fans. Crucially, it is the ability of characters to appeal to audiences as affective bodies within and beyond film and television that acts as a marker of their potential for success.

From big eyes to big breasts: Anime's bodies in critical commentary outside Japan

As this range of appreciations shows, there is no single approach to anime bodies, nor a single genre or issue around which anime body debates coalesce. However, there are noticeable groupings of discourse that attend to anime's genres. Early in English-language commentary on anime, divisions between *shōjo* and *shōnen* manga and anime were grounded in aesthetic analyses of the body. For example, in one of the earlier books on anime in English, Antonia Levi compares the two categories, arguing that:

Girls' and women's *manga* (*shōjo* manga) were precisely the opposite [of *shōnen*]. They focused on emotions and personal relationships. Plots were weak. Eyes, however, were enormous. Almost nothing happened, but you knew exactly how everyone felt about whatever it was that wasn't happening. (1996, 9)

The link between affect and physicality is presented as a core theme in *shōjo* texts. The focus here on eyes in female character bodies in anime also helps to differentiate these texts from other, more masculine-oriented ones (though, as Chapter 5 shows, these divisions are hard to maintain).

The idea that anime contained characters with "enormous" eyes became something of a theme within English-language criticism. This seems to have begun with Frederik L. Schodt's *Manga! Manga! The World of Japanese Comics*, in which he asserts manga's role as an aesthetic origin point for *shōjo* styles, especially the aesthetics of the eye. Schodt writes that

by far the most striking visual aspect of girls' comics is the orblike eyes of the characters…. In contrast to men's and boys' comics, where the male characters have thick, arched Kabuki-style eyebrows and glaring eyes, heroines in girls' comics are generally drawn with pencil-thin eyebrows, long, full eyelashes, and eyes the size of window panes that emote gentleness and femininity. Over the years artists have also come to draw a star next to the pupil that perhaps represents dreams, yearning, and romance—and beneath the star to then place one or more highlights. (1983, 91)

Romantic, gentle and overtly feminine in these interpretations, the large eyes of anime and manga have gone on to influence many aspects of the wider subcultures around Japanese media.

For example, fans have long emulated these *shōjo* eyes in everyday and "cosplay" situations (Winge 2006). As early as 1995, Rick Marin et al. were interviewing anime fans in New York who were wearing contact lenses to "simulate little 'toon twinkles in the corners of his eyes." Moreover, this aesthetic has become part of critical understandings of anime, even used in reviews of live-action films based on anime. For example, one reviewer of the Wachowski's failed blockbuster version of anime *Speed Racer* (Andy and Lana Wachowski, 2008) said, "This frenetic adaptation of the beloved 1960s Japanese cartoon bears little resemblance to that anime classic of yore, unless you count Christina Ricci's saucerlike brown eyes" (Hornaday 2008, for more, see Denison 2014). Satirical though this reading may be, it confirms the status of big eyes as one of anime's core aesthetic tropes.

However, to think that the *shōjo* and their bodies can be defined solely through these "window pane" eyes would belittle the varied modes through which anime's female characters have been understood. Annalee Newitz began a conversation in the mid-1990s about the magical abilities of *shōjo* characters, particularly their powers of transformation. In what Newitz terms the "romantic comedy genre" of anime, presumably a translation of the Japanese *rabu kome* or "love comedy" genre, she names the "chief subgenre: 'magical girls.'" Among these magical girls, Newitz notes a penchant for traditional gender roles and "slapstick-style encounters which are sexy but innocent" (1995, 4). Into these encounters, Newitz reads a regressive set of patriarchal pleasures available to Japanese and US fans alike.

Susan J. Napier, by contrast, reads the magical girls of anime in slightly different ways. Her analysis reveals a range of *shōjo* characters who "all possess some form of psychic or occult power" while "at the same time as they can be seen as intimately related with a young girl's normal femininity" (1998, 93). Napier argues that these versions of the *shōjo* were especially important for appearing during a period of significant change for Japanese women, dubbing them "*shōjo* fantasies" (105) that allow women's power to be explored through the liminal status of the teenaged girl protagonist.

In one particularly notable (and commented upon) example of the *shōjo* category, Rumiko Takahashi's *Ranma ½* (anime TV series were produced in 1989 and 1989–1992 engendering a multimedia franchise), Newitz examines gender trouble at the heart of the anime's narrative about bodily transformations. When the protagonist, Ranma, is splashed with water of varying temperatures he shifts back and forth between being a *shōnen* and a *shōjo* character, the latter signaled as his enchanted form through the use of red hair and an ample bosom. For audiences, Newitz argues that "Quite simply, *Ranma ½* demonstrates to the young man who enjoys romantic comedy *anime* that he is constantly in danger of becoming a girl." (6) Transformations from male into female bodies are figured here as a site of disquieting Otherness, with Ranma's female form equating to "male fears at the heart of the comedy romance genre" (Ibid.). Napier's considerations of transformation and magic build on this early work and lead her to conclude that "although references to genitalia are conspicuous by their virtual absence in *Ranma ½*, the sexual signifier of breasts is constantly evoked throughout the series to denote that something is 'wrong'" (2005, 54). She goes on to link Ranma's gender swapping with Japanese transsexual *bishōnen* (beautiful boy) narratives as another potential subgenre with which it might be possible to associate *Ranma ½*. (60) Within these discussions, Ranma's female form becomes a problem for both gender and genre, shifting between the *shōnen* and *shōjo* in ways that these authors argue gives greater credence to the former category over the latter, thereby suggesting a bias against women in anime.

Transformations of other kinds are picked up on by Anne Allison and Frenchy Lunning. Lunning argues that the *shōjo* body is abject, that there is nothing "under the ruffles":

> To the extent that gender becomes a fictive notion in favor of a magical state of shape-shifting, they swivel and switch dangerously, as if announcing the absence of an original gender state. For the creators of manga and anime, the shōjo body offers a substrate upon which is inscribed the tension between a desire to do away with gender and the inability to express gender conflict without gender. As a representation of the abject, the shōjo character becomes a thing of phantasm (7)

To argue that these often active, powerful and complicated protagonists lack a "core" denies the subjectivity of women in anime (for counter-commentaries to this view, see Saitō [2000] 2011 or Sugawa Shimada 2011). Allison, by contrast, links transformative powers of anime's women to an altogether more materialist requisite: the need to create merchandising-led anime shows.

Allison argues that in many series, but especially those aimed at children:

> The fascination with bodies and their reconstruction into fusions of insect/ machine, human/tool, nature/technology proceeds along two axes.... The first is transformation (*henshin*), and the second is union (*gattai*): assembling the individual bodies, robots and weapons... into superconglomerates. (2006, 106–107)

Even though Allison is primarily writing about live-action series like *Power Rangers* (1975—in Japan; 1993—in the USA) in this analysis, her observations hold for many team-oriented anime television series. Allison's analysis also suggests good reason for the appearance of "super-deformed" or *chibi* characters in anime—cute, truncated versions of characters that can be easily transformed into merchandising objects.

Allison, like Steinberg, thereby asserts that commodification is a crucial part of anime culture. She describes *Sailor Moon* (*Bishōjo Senshi Sērā Mūn*, 1992–1997) in these terms:

> The star of the show is a 14-year-old girl, Usagi Tsukino (Serena in English), who, guided by her talking cat, Luna, transforms into the superhero Sailor Moon by activating various sources of moon power, such as a penlike device called "moon prism" and the tiara she wears when "morphed." (2000, 269)

Allison explains how important the shift from *shōjo* to an adult female body becomes within *Sailor Moon*, stating that "her body becomes first naked and then reclothed, starting with a sailor bodysuit and followed by a miniskirted sailor outfit with a plunging neckline that shows off her newly developed breasts." (272) *Sailor Moon*'s transformation sequences thereby invert the logic of *Ranma ½*'s comedy with the adult female body, and specifically breasts, used to imply capability, power and self-confidence (for more on *Sailor Moon*, see Chapter 6). It is also, however, a commodified body, reliant on objects of power (that were turned into merchandising in Japan) for the ability to transform from child to adult. It is here that her work accords with Lunning's claims about the "fantasy of endless diversion" (2011, 8) at work at the heart of *shōjo* texts. In this way, Lunning and Allison both position anime's representations of women as liminal: as occupying an uncertain space that relies on replicability (through merchandise) while revolving around an empty center.

If the *shōjo* category of anime is invested in the liminal status of women's bodies, held in tension between male and female or young girl and adulthood, the women represented in other genres of anime cleave closer to the kinds of debates usually limned for "body genres" in US cinema, particularly horror and science fiction's cyborg narratives. In the previous chapter, the idea of the cyborg was introduced as a post-human anime body, but it is worth noting that these debates about anime's cyborgs extend far beyond the discussions of *Ghost in the Shell*. For example, the *mecha* genre, discussed more fulsomely in Chapter 6, is a key part of these debates. It is usually defined in the following terms: "*Mecha* films and shows place an emphasis on mechanical elements, especially robots and giant mechanical suits" (Ruh 2005, 73). Borrowing heavily from live-action *tokusatsu* (special effects) genre predecessors like the *Ultraman* (*Urotoraman*) and *Masked Rider* (*Kamen Raidā*) franchises (Allison 2006; Onoue et al. 2012), these anime present different sorts of transformation from what Allison calls *gattai*, offering more physical interminglings of the body and technology.

Nor is this discourse about intermingling restricted to discussions of women's bodies in anime. Brian Ruh reads the robots that grow from protagonist, Naota's, forehead in *FLCL* (OVAs 2000–2001) as symbolic of his sexual awakening process, and Naota's merger with robot, Canti, at times of strife as a sign of the protagonist's maturation process (2005). In Ruh's estimation, therefore, the male cyborg is relatively normative and combines with robots in ways that enable a discussion of the *shōnen*'s liminal cultural status. By contrast, the transformations of Tetsuo at the end of *Akira* are understood by Napier as an example of the "monstrous adolescent" whose "frenzy of metamorphosis" allows the audience to be overwhelmed by the on-screen catastrophe (2005, 46). Napier extends this frenzy to cyborg characters like Sho, who merges with "bio-booster armour" in the *Guyver* franchise (OVAs 1989–1991) to become "a recognizable version of the universal fantasy of a weakling's transformation into a superhero" (2005, 92). However, this transformation is anything but pleasant for Sho, leading Napier to conclude that men's bodies are not as accepting of metamorphosis as women's in anime narratives.

This may help to explain the preponderance for investigating cyborg women in academic accounts of anime. For example, in an unusual discussion of a romantically framed cyborg, Thomas LaMarre's analysis of Chi from *Chobits* (2002) takes Silvio's argument about form and content further, arguing that the series formulates its cyborg woman as "a metaphysical problem." LaMarre contends that "The woman-ness of Chi is an effect or symptom of something else, something beyond Chi as a physical being (a computer)" (2006b, 54). In *Chobits*, the resolution to the problem of the cyborg woman is a platonic, yet sexualized, relationship. LaMarre calls this platonic love, which:

> implies a love of ideal forms over and above the crass material intercourse of bodies, even while soft-porn images of bodies remain desirable and even necessary. For *Chobits* is not simply about love over lust, or about ideal forms over matter. *Chobits* also includes a great deal of sex, or something like it. (57–58)

LaMarre's distinction between sexed and sexless relationships in science fiction anime is particularly significant for the way it can be mapped onto the romantic comedies and "sexless" *shōjo* texts discussed earlier to explain fan service and many of the other generically incongruous moments instantiated by anime's magical girls.

Original Video Animation (OVA): Bringing anime's bodies into disrepute?

From discussions of cyborgs' metamorphoses and platonic sex, it is a short step to the discourses about anime's darker fringes and more explicit and extreme bodies. One category of industrial production has been continually invoked as a source for the disreputable anime body: Original Video Animation (OVA). Jonathan Clements, rehearsing a long-standing debate about whether the correct term for anime on VHS is OVA or OAV, quotes Yoshiharu Tokugi. Tokugi argues that OVA is as an industrial term used to denote "straight to video" releases whereas Original Animation Video (OAV) is a marketing term created to denote a new VHS text and not "a repurposed work" (1999, 307, quoted in Clements 2013a, 167). Clements' frustration about this lingering debate emerges when he declares that "such quibbles seem pointless—the acronyms have persisted interchangeably in English, one suspects, because monoglot pundits wish to brag that they can understand one element on a page of Japanese text" (Ibid.). While Clements' assessment is devastatingly dismissive of the debate, he raises an important issue by quoting Tokugi. While the name of the category may not matter, there seems to be lingering confusion about what it contains and when to deploy it.

Something as simple as the production of "straight to video" anime would seem straightforward enough. However, as Tokugi asserts, these home video releases comprise virtually every kind of anime text: from feature-length anime films, through to single television-length-episodes of serialized anime, to collections of repurposed anime epsiodes or shorts. As this variety suggests, anime producers have been canny about the ways home video can be made to support new kinds of productions. Famously, director Mamoru Oshii was one of the founding members of Headgear, a company set up specifically so that the creators of the *Patlabor* (1988–1989) OVA series would remain beneficiaries of any subsequent remakes and extensions of their work (Ruh 2004, 75). This kind of OVA series acts like a "calling card" to industry, and if they "acquired enough of a following to justify their upgrade into TV serials and movies" (Clements 2013a, 168), then they could become the origin points for an entire franchise of anime texts.

However, this does not mean the relationship between "traditional" media and OVAs has been straightforward. High-profile OVA series will often receive short theatrical releases, as in the case of *Garden of Sinners* (*Kara no Kyōkai*, Ufotable, 2007–), a long-running OVA series of films, usually about an hour in length, that have enjoyed theatrical releases in Tokyo before being more widely released on VHS, DVD and Blu-ray (Joo et al. 2013). Advertising also plays an important role in the repackaging of anime texts on OVA. Take, for example, Katsuhiro Ōtomo's *Freedom* (2006), a series of anime advertisements for Cup Noodles that were later collected and repackaged across several Blu-ray and DVD releases.

Or, alternatively, there are oddities like Studio Ghibli's *Short Short* (2005, for more, see Chapter 7), which collated the studio's advertising and music video works. In a bundling of perhaps even more obscure works, the *Fullmetal Alchemist Premium OVA Collection* (released by Aniplex in Japan in 2006 and by Funimation in the USA in 2009, see Figure 3.1) offered up animation created for a special theme park ride at Universal Studios Japan along with short promotional videos for the film *Conqueror of Shamballa*

FIGURE 3.1 *Chibi wrap party from the* Fullmetal Alchemist Premium OVA Collection.

(Seiji Mizushima, 2005), including one done as live action in which a statue of one of the main characters, Alphonse, takes a journey to *Fullmetal Alchemist*'s production studio, Bones. This in addition to the reproduction of television shows and films on sell-through video and digital formats, as well as the kinds of "midquels" described by Clements (2013a, 168) and sequels described by Tsugata. The contradictory, highly commercialized content of home video anime releases in Japan might go some way to explaining why there has been such contestation about what to call it. In addition, though, this new set of home viewing technologies fostered a new set of markets.

In *Anime Gaku* (*Anime Studies*), Nobuyuki Tsugata argues that the first OVA was *Dallos* (Mamoru Oshii), released in 1983 (2011b). Clements notes that in fact, "Dallos was not initially intended as the first 'original video anime.' To many of its makers, it was regarded instead as a 'failed' television project" (2013a, 167–68). Tsugata claims that by the height of the boom in home video in 1989, there were over 400 OVA releases per year (2011b, 32) and elsewhere, he explains this popularity by arguing that the success of OVAs was in part down to the appearance of young adult and adult anime (using the imported English term "adult anime" to describe these films, 2011, 32, and 2005, 160). About the latter, Tsugata writes that the serialization of these adult-oriented OVA anime led to some enormously popular series including *Cream Lemon* (1984–) with nearly 40 OVAs, while science fiction fantasy *Legend of the Galactic Heroes* (*Ginga Eiyū Densetsu*, 1988–1997) achieved an extraordinary 110 OVA volumes (Tsugata 2005, 160).

Cream Lemon is an overtly pornographic work that shifts story worlds and protagonists across the series. McCarthy and Clements accord it importance, arguing that the:

> erotic OAV opened up the possibility of showing erotica without such artifices [as seen in television anime]; the intended audience would know what they were getting. On video, with no possibility of offending the uninterested, erotica could thrive, and in this new market audiences got their first taste of *Cream Lemon* from Fairy Dust. (1998, 42)

In this, *Cream Lemon* and other erotic anime arose alongside a broader market for violence and pornographic live-action works, known as V-Cinema. Alexander Zahlten has done groundbreaking work on Tōei's V-Cinema in his PhD thesis and explains that Tōei's V-Cinema market seems to have grown up independent of its earlier work in OVAs, which began in 1986 (2007, 340). But the markets are parallel, with adult-oriented pornographic and violent films generally feeding a niche for adult-viewing materials without the need to pander to younger viewers.

These adult home cinema texts have been translated from industrial categories like OVAs and V-Cinema into new generic categories as they have moved abroad. However, McCarthy and Clements argue erotic anime take many forms, and that despite the notoriety of some of them, there "is no indication that they 'took over the market' in any sense" (1998, 43). These *ero* (from "erotic") texts, as they term them, were also differently generic inside and outside Japan. For example, McCarthy and Clements argue that the long-running *Cream Lemon* series was popular enough in Japan to create a new subgenre of texts with "lemon" references in their titles (47). Outside Japan, this new industrial category of OVAs became just another set of anime texts being distributed on video, which was fast becoming the dominant means for consuming anime.

As a consequence, when violent pornographic anime like *Urotsukidōji*, *Dirty Pair* (1985–1990) or *Vampire Hunter Yōko* (*Mamono Hantā Yōko*, 1990–1995) arrived in the USA and UK, they were recontextualized by their distributors to form a very different understanding of "anime" or "Japanimation" to that perceived in Japan. Abroad, where the terms *ero* and "adult anime" were less used, numerous Japanese terms came to be deployed to describe the subgenres of pornography making their ways to the USA and UK, in particular *hentai*. Susan J. Napier explains that the term means "pornography" (2005, x), but elsewhere, Philip Brophy proclaims that it means "perverse" (2005, 130) whereas, Mark McLelland explains that the use of the term *hentai* to refer to erotic or sexual manga and anime in general is not a Japanese but an English innovation. In Japanese *hentai* can reference sexual material but only of an extreme, "abnormal" or "perverse" kind; it is not a general category. (2006, 3)

Susan Pointon's early article on Japanese animated pornography has been influential in painting all of anime pornography as *hentai*. However, Pointon was referring specifically to a single anime OVA series: *Urotsukidōji*.

She notes *Urotsukidōji*'s generic hybridity, arguing that "When viewed in isolation, this sex/magic/horror/romance synthesis may seem as alien to a western audience as the exaggerated genital dimensions" of one of the main demonic characters, but that "it follows the conventions of fantasy horror texts which were laid down in the late Edo period" (1997, 50). Nevertheless, Pointon also declares that "these examples of *hentai*, a sub-genre of Japanese animation that literally translates as perverted, have managed through word of mouth to achieve a cult status among young adolescent males" (43) outside Japan. This recognition of *hentai* as a subgenre is important, and McCarthy and Clements attempted to address the slippage around anime pornography in their book on *ero* anime. In that book, McCarthy and Clements present an holistic view of sex in anime showing just how diverse anime's engagements with this body genre have been. However, to do this regenrification work, they named a subgenre that now often replaces the idea of *hentai* in English: what they term "tits and tentacle" pornographic anime, many of which, they argue, are the product of the new OVA culture in Japan (1998).

Urotsukidōji: Legend of a controversy

Worst of all, because most lovingly crafted, were the Japanese cartoons known as anime... [that] often feature scenes of women being gang-raped by lascivious, leering monsters, aliens with tentacles that entwine and bind the victims before multiply penetrating them through various orifices. Heavily cut by the Board was a scene in which a monster with a huge metal phallus rapes a victim orally, exploding in her mouth into spikes which penetrate the cheeks.... In many of these cartoons, there seems to be an underlying hatred (or is it fear?) of women, which can only be slaked by the destruction of the female principle... It is frightening to view the exorcising of such violent fantasies in cartoon of such technical brilliance. (British Board of Film Classification Report 1994–1995, 20, quoted in McCarthy and Clements 1998, 92)

This is a truncated quotation from a report by the British Board of Film Classification, the UK's official film censor, which recounts in detail the offense given by a variety of scenes in the *Urotsukidōji* OVA series. The language used in the report is as explicit as the cut scenes from the series, and the report tars all of anime with the *Overfiend*'s phallic brush: anime "hate" women, they delight in killing them and these "violent fantasies" are all the worse for being technically accomplished (see Figure 3.2). Anime's problem, this report suggests, is its treatment of the female body and its representation of that body in extremis.

McCarthy and Clements quote this BBFC report in greater detail than I have done, by way of explaining the furore that arose around the (censored) releases of the *Urotsukidōji* OVA series. They argue that:

> The two titles that did the most to create the modern-day anime business in the West have also arguably damaged it, by encouraging false expectations from the foreign audience. "Everyone" has seen *Akira*. "Everyone" has heard of the *Overfiend*.... within the journalistic community, it is the *Overfiend* that is most likely to get column-inches, and all anime, not just the erotic subgenres, are damned by association. (1998, 82)

Both authors were working in the UK's anime industries, reporting on and translating texts for distribution. Their assessment arises from a privileged position of knowledge and reflects the real fears of a fanbase that worried that *hentai*, or violent "perverse" anime pornography, would become all that anime was ever known for abroad.

FIGURE 3.2 *Demonic imagery from* Urotsukidōji: Legend of the Overfiend.

However, returning to this debate now, and examining wider review and newspaper coverage of anime texts from the period of the mid-1990s when the *Urotsukidōji* OVA series was released, reveals some slightly different patterns of discourse than might be expected. I have focused on UK news coverage as this is where the most overt debates were recorded (between the BBFC and fans, and by critics like McCarthy and Clements). However, as a useful point of comparison, I begin by examining the US coverage of Central Park Media's release of this series.

In *Video Week*, the kinds of promotion undertaken for the *Urotsukidōji* series start to be made clear. On the release of the *Urotsukidoji Perfect Collection* (Central Park Media, 1993), for example, press notes are quoted that court controversy: "Company touts Collection as entire story with 40 min. of outtakes deemed 'so sexually violent that it could not be included in the theatrical features'" (*Video Week*, 1993). Far from shying away from possible conflicts, the distributors were seeking even greater controversy for the films as the series went on. It is interesting to note, therefore, that US reviewers did not always respond to these shock tactics. Richard Harrington's 1993 review of the first in the series, *Urotsukidoji: Legend of the Overfiend* in the *Washington Post*, commented that it "could just as well have been subtitled 'Legend of the Oversexedfiends.' This Japanese animation feature is so relentlessly drenched in graphic scenes of perverse sex and ultra-violence that no one's likely to challenge its 'NC-17' rating. Iron-cast stomachs only!" His take on the film is humorous and his response to its content is to critique, not damn, its insistence on "perverse sex and ultra-violence." He finishes his review by commenting that "The 108-minute film has been dubbed 'erotic grotesque,' but only the second term seems deserved." This is a direct reference to the Japanese genre of erotic-grotesque-nonsense media production, implying either a press kit for the film that tried to situate it beyond pornography for US audiences or a deep knowledge on Harrington's part about Japanese media culture. The fact that the term recurs in the same newspaper when Desson Howe offers a shorter review of the same film is perhaps suggestive of the former (1993).

So if the US distributors attempted to place the *Urotsukidōji* series in relation to both existing Japanese genres of media and notions of extremis, how did the UK respond to the Overfiend? McCarthy and Clements quote an article by David Lister of the *Independent* as an example of the kinds of histrionic responses *Urotsukidōji* engendered (1998, 91). Lister writes with concern about the "rape and abuse scenes" whose victims are "usually under-age and often doe-eyed schoolgirls—a popular theme in Japanese films" (1993). However, despite all of the concerns he ends his response by quoting Kanjee Bates, a fanzine editor, who blames the UK's positioning of anime alongside Disney texts in shops for the controversy, and not the films themselves. Bates says, just before worrying about the ease with which children can buy adult VHS tapes in the UK, that "it is regrettable that the only Manga films shown over here were the sex and violence ones, as there were many art films in the genre." By giving Bates the last word, Lister confirms that there are problems with anime sex and violence in the UK, but the fanzine editor deflects the controversy onto UK retail chains and away from the content of the anime itself.

This kind of worried but not histrionic critique can be found in many other reviews and commentaries on the *Urotsukidōji* series. For example, when the first in the series was shown at a special screening at the London ICA, Derek Malcolm related that "there are special late-night performances of Hideki Takayama's controversial Urotsukidoji: Legend of the Overfiend, praised for its brilliant technique, but accused of sexism, sadism and amorality" (1992). In this, Malcom could be quoting from the BBFC's later report on the series despite pre-dating it, so close is the language used. Once more, it is a pre-existing sense of controversy that shapes the response, but the tone of the review is balanced nevertheless.

Jonathan Romney's review of this same film for a National Film Theatre (NFT) anime festival in 1995 accords it a "cult" status two years later, describing the film as an appeal to the Lolita complex which "seems to go way overboard." Romney states that "It starts off as a raunchy college-kids romp, then turns into a horrendous feast of entrail-spurting and nightmare sexuality" (1995). The genre mixing is where Romney seems to have problems with *Urotsukidōji*, and its shift in gears between sex comedy and body horror is his central point of contention.

Rather than wholeheartedly condemning the *Urotsukidōji* series, therefore, critical responses show an acknowledgment of its extreme content working in concert with understandings of its genre film status and even its technical accomplishment. However, it is also worth noting that by 1995, mainstream UK newspapers were making New Year Resolution lists that included items like: "Watch some manga films, read a graphic novel and be generally more aware of the cartoon renaissance" (*Observer*, 1995) So, while McCarthy and Clements are right in arguing that *Urotsukidōji* and its ilk shaped discourses about the sexualized violence inherent in many of the anime being brought to the UK by major distributors like Manga Entertainment, not all of the responses were straightforward dismissals of the potential of anime as popular culture or art. While many journalists found the content of the *Urotsukidōji* series bemusing and at times grotesque, they were able nonetheless to see value, too.

Conclusions

As an extreme form of pornography, the "tits and tentacle" or *hentai* genre of anime pornography was neither the main form of anime being produced in Japan in the 1980s, nor even necessarily representative of the wider *ero* genres of pornography that would have been available to distributors at the time. Moreover, in Japan, the genre itself is usually named as either *ero* or adult anime, without the histrionic labels invented outside Japan. The regenrification of these pornographic anime thereby reveals more about the media markets for animation outside Japan, and about distributor attempts to broaden the scope of those markets, than they do about animated Japanese pornography.

Titles like the *Urotsukidōji* series allowed Western distributors to create a new and controversial kind of anime that could augment the success of *Akira* by emphasizing that film's violence and metamorphic passages as key pleasures for the newly emerging foreign adult audiences for anime. This attempt to create a new market was met by gatekeeper fans with trepidation if not outright concern, as shown by Bates' comments about the laxness of the UK's VHS retailers that comes hot on the heels of the UK firestorm over video nasties (Egan 2007, for more, see Saitō [2000] 2011, loc. 2142). In these respects, opinions about anime were as reliant on the technology of video in the UK as they were back in Japan, though the debates shifted considerably.

In more general terms, it was the way the *Urotsukidōji* series treated bodies that seems to have generated disquiet. It became, therefore, one of the key texts around which popular and academic debates over anime and the body began to be formulated, as seen in Pointon's early article. These debates have been formulated around the aesthetics as well as the content of anime. It is not just the fact that bodies are transformed, exploded or mutated that concerned commentators, it was the fact that they did so *differently* to other kinds of animation. The newness of anime's bodies, from the big eyes of the *shōjo* to the *mecha*-clad *shōnen*, to the adults and children victimized in pornographic anime, was perhaps unsurprisingly challenging to critics and censors. It has been a difference that academics have leapt upon, producing wide-ranging assessments of anime bodies, often in conjunction with important zeitgeist-inflected theories of gender and genre. Such is certainly visible in the shifting discussions of the *shōjo*, who moves through discourse from active heroine to an abject, soulless, but well-dressed, character type.

The absence of a real referent for anime's bodies conjoins the two in discourse. The discussions of cyborg women in this chapter and the previous one attest as much, envisioning the adaptive body of the cyborg woman as both object of investigation within narratives and a subject position that shifts across them. As Sharalyn Orbaugh argues in an article about cyborg affect and the limits of the human, "Given the nature of the medium, film requires a *visible* protagonist" (155). This, she argues, is why the narrative of the *Ghost in the Shell* sequel, *Innocence* (Mamoru Oshii,

2004), shifts to Major Motoko Kusanagi's second-in-command, Batō, once the Major becomes incorporeal. As Orbaugh's argument suggests, one of the most compelling reasons for the scholarly and popular commentary on anime's bodies is this: anime bodies challenge our conceptualizations of what it means to be human. Anime contains so many anthropomorphized, mutating, transforming, displaced and exploding bodies because these bodies defamiliarize our concepts not just of animation's cultural purposes and potential, but of humanity itself.

4

Early Anime Histories: Japan and America

Japanese animation has not always been anime (see Introduction and Chapter 2). Taking a step back from the earliest moments of transnational history investigated in the opening chapters, the second section of this book maps anime's history in relation to a range of genres that have developed concurrent with new periods, technologies and transnational exchanges in Japanese animation texts. The aim is to introduce the history of some of the bigger generic threads running through three specific periods of anime: first, to chart the rise of "children's animation" in Japan and to see how Japanese animation was reproduced for a children's market when Japanese television animation first traveled to the USA.

In Chapter 5, I examine a second technological shift, from "film" and cel animation to its remediation on home video formats. Specifically, I investigate the rise of fan discourses during the "VHS" era, considering which anime genres fans discussed in early fan/professional specialist magazines. Finally, in Chapter 6, I examine how digital distribution has reshaped the markets for anime, allowing new kinds of anime fan creativity, and with that creativity, new kinds of anime genres to be popularized through their dispersal to global fan communities. Each of the chapters deals with at least one broad industrial category: film and television in this chapter, then home video in Chapter 5 and digital formats in Chapter 6. I do not mean to suggest that new technologies determine anime's meanings; rather, I show how new technologies present new opportunities for anime to travel and spread, both inside and outside Japan. This section therefore broadly examines the expansion of anime's genres concurrent with expansions in anime distribution—from the earliest attempts to position anime in relation to children and education, through to an expansion of genres in the early years of television and home cinema, through to an explosion of anime genres in the post-digital landscape. But, I argue that even within this expanding generic landscape, there are still moments of hidden, obscured or misunderstood anime genrification taking place.

This chapter, by contrast to the approach taken in others, begins with the pre-history of anime, looking at how academics and critics in Japanese and English scholarship have made sense of the earliest periods of Japanese animation. I then move on to a consideration of anime's early life as a television format in Japan and the USA. In this way, I hope to show how child audiences shaped the early existence of Japanese animation and how debates about child audiences recurred and framed anime as it moved into television and across national contexts.

Japanese animation before anime

One of the first things to note is that there is little agreement about the origins of Japanese animation. Daisuke Miyao (2002), Nobuyuki Tsugata (2005) and Jonathan Clements (2013a) all cite the *utsushi-e* ("reflected or projected pictures," a relative of magic lantern technologies) as a possible precursor to Japanese animation. As Tsugata explains it, these were color pictures painted on glass that were then projected onto screens in a darkened room. Lenses, moving the glass slides, or replacing them, created the illusion of movement (2005, 30). Miyao, however, cautions that

> the two systems [animation and *utsushi-e*] are entirely different: the movement of pictures in *utsushi-e* or "projected pictures" involved direct manipulation of the apparatus, while movement in animation is generated in the course of film production. Nevertheless, particularly for audiences of the early period, there was probably no firm distinction between *utsushi-e* and animation. (2002, 193)

The lack of division between *utsushi-e* and animation was largely a product, Clements argues, of a lack of language with which to describe early animation. By his reckoning, animation became just one among the many *misemono* "see-world-things" that formed just one part of hybridized theatrical or side-show events (2013a, 23, see also Gerow 2010, 99–100).

A later form of Japanese street theater, *kamishibai* (paper theater), has also been proffered as the origin point for television anime and is argued to have grown out of these same traditions:

> *Kamishibai* may be best known today as one of the direct precursors of postwar manga and anime, but over its forty-year heyday [1920s–1960s] it

enjoyed enormous popularity, at times eclipsing rival entertainment media for children such as movies or radio (in the 1930s and 1940s) and manga (in the 1950s). (Orbaugh 2012, 79)

Clements links this street theater to Japan's *benshi* tradition, live narrators of the silent cinema in Japan, as *kamishibai* narrators would "set up their stands in street and parks, and tell a story by slotting card pictures in an out of frame like a proscenium arch, sometimes mounted on the back of a bicycle" (2013a, 21; see also LaMarre 2009, 192–193 for a discussion of *kamishibai*'s links to anime). The connection between the two media comes from the inter- and postwar work of artists who would go on to become popular manga artists including Sanpei Shirato and Shigeru Mizuki (Orbaugh 2012, nb3, 98; Foster 2009a, 165). These two *kamishibai* artists would later come to dominate important postwar manga genres like the *gekiga* ("dramatic pictures") and *yōkai* manga ("ghosts/demons/spirits"), respectively. Notably, *kamishibai* performances were commercialized through sales of sweets and aimed explicitly at child audiences, making the comparison between *kamishibai* and manga, and the commodification of early television anime, all the stronger.

However, Clements (2013a) and Tsugata (2005) both argue for an historical view of Japanese animation as an outgrowth of a multitude of theatrical and media traditions in Japan that included early trick films, theatrical "events" and a wide range of magic lantern and other *misemono* attractions. In these earliest moments of cinema and media events, between the late 1890s and the mid-1910s, there seems to have been little restriction on the participants at these sideshows. Given the concerns that would begin to emerge later, it is highly likely that large number of families and children would have been among those watching these early films, magic lantern shows and animated shorts.

There is much debate about which animated film was the first to be screened in Japan, but early "animations" included imports of Georges Méliès' trick films (*majutsu eiga* or "magic films" in Japanese), which were hybrid live-action and animation films that made use of many of the "special effects" techniques that would later become associated with stop motion and pixilation (Furniss 1998). Other early animation distributed in Japan includes works by James Stuart Blackton and Émile Cohl. Of particular note were the short animated films released under the *Kid Deko* title, or *Dekobō Shingajō* (*Kid Deko's New Picture Book*), which Yamaguchi (2004) claims played to sold-out theaters, but about which Frederick S. Litten shows there is much to debate (2014). Litten argues that the term *Dekobō Shingajō* became a generic description for a variety of imported short animated films, masking who the individual foreign animators were and where their animation was coming from. Regardless of which foreign animation came first, these animated and trick films have been proposed as early influences on Japan's first generation of animators (Yamaguchi 2004, 44).

Nobuyuki Tsugata argues that three animators began the Japanese animation industry:

> The established theory for the beginning of domestic animation says that in 1917 three people, cartoonists Ōten Shimokawa and Junichi Kōuchi and a skilled western-style artist, Seitarō Kitayama, variously and independently produced short animations. The one who produced the most works from among these three people was Kitayama, but Taishō period [1912-26] animation was mostly things drawn from nonsense cartoons ["*manga*"] and folk tales like *Kachi-Kachi Mountain* and *Momotarō*. (2011b, 24)

Yamaguchi concurs with these dates and points out that it is difficult to separate out the true beginning of Japanese animation because these three animators even began their preparations in the same year as one another, in 1916 (2004, 44). Technically, though, Simon Richmond is among those to claim that Shimokawa's *Mukuzo Imokawa the Doorman* (*Imokawa Mukuzo Genkanban no Maki*) was the first of the three to be released, screened in Tokyo in January of 1917 (2009, 2; see also Clements 2013a, 25–26 for the debates about which film came first).

These were not Japanese animation as we know them today. Shimokawa's film was made by taking images of chalk drawings on a blackboard that were erased and redrawn. Kitayama's productions were for a new division of Nikkatsu Mukōjima Studio, and he produced what Yamaguchi calls "paper anime," (2004, 48) which Tsugata describes as "drawing whole images on one sheet of paper, one by one", though he explains that Kitayama later "moved over to paper-cut animation" (2005, 58). Kōuchi, similar to Shimokawa's later work, seems to have favored ink on paper drawings for his animation technique (see images in Yamaguchi 2004, 47–48). There was, as this suggests, a lot of experimental animation being undertaken in the first years of Japanese animation.

Tsugata's observation about the content of these early animated short films is important for what it tells us about their potential audiences. Borrowing from local myths and legends meant that these early animated works would have been familiar to Japanese audiences, but perhaps especially to younger audiences and families. The humorous nonsense cartoons, likewise, had been appearing in a wide range of publication types from newspapers to journals (Silverberg 2006). Though the latter may have been favored by adults, there is a clear cross-generational set of appeals in the earliest animation produced in Japan.

Another reason that folktales and comedy "gag" animation found favor with animators was because they were working, from the very beginning, under an increasingly strict censorship regime. Between 1917 and 1939, a series of regulations and laws were put in place by the Japanese authorities that drastically shaped the content and styles of early Japanese animation. The first regulations, from the police, were put in place in July 1917 and came in response to the phenomenal popularity of films called *Zigomar* (three French films were released under this title in Japan in 1912) as that series became connected in public discourse with criminal behavior in Japan's youth (Gerow 2010, 52–53, 176 and 181–191). In 1914, for example, one survey of educators reported that films "harmed the health of children due to impure air and the lack of light," and a further Bureau of Education note sent home to parents warned that films also "easily teach evil and wicked methods and naturally infect children with the vices of obscenity and cruelty" (quoted in Gerow 2010, 180).

It is against the backdrop of this kind of anti-film hysteria that age restrictions on films were put in place in 1917, including the first age-related restriction that forbade children under the age of 15 from seeing "Category A" films. The first animated Japanese film to be restricted was only one of a few then in existence, Kōuchi's *Young Chame's Airgun* (*Chame no Kūkijū*) which was made in 1917. As Tsugata points out, in this early phase of its history, there was no sense of division between animation and other kinds of filmmaking in Japan, which meant that Kōuchi's animated film about a child playing with an airgun incited concerns around child morality just as any other live-action film might have done (2011b, 36).

These early regulations also had the unexpected result of creating the first genres of Japanese animation. In 1921, the Japanese government began to recognize animation as a category of filmmaking, and in 1922 "the Ministry of Education established a sort of subsidy system for the use of film in elementary education and supported the production of films for pedagogical purposes" (Miyao 2002, 203). Animators, particularly Kitayama and a later animator named Sanae Yamamoto, made animated educational films on diverse topics from banking to agriculture (Clements 2013a, 31–32; Miyao 2002, 204). Though the topics suggest that these films were educational, they do not suggest that they were necessarily aimed at children, particularly with films made on topics like Yamamoto's 1926 film *The Spread of Syphilis* (*Baidoku no Denpa*). It is, however, difficult to know much about the expansion of educational animation, simply because, like so many other kinds of filmmaking, huge amounts of these films were destroyed by the Great Kantō Earthquake and the fires that raged through Tokyo in its aftermath. However, these educational animated films, along with Kitayama's work animating live-action film titles and doing special-effects work, are credited with keeping the industry afloat during this period of natural disaster and fast-changing censorship (Clements 2013a).

Other types of early Japanese animation were more clearly aimed at a general or young audience, however. In response to the 1939 Film Law (*Eiga Hō*), and with the introduction of cel animation in the mid-1920s in Japan, the industry shifted its focus. Some of the most memorable, and obviously paternalistic if not overtly child-oriented, animation of this period was produced during Japan's Fifteen Years War (1931–1945). As Miyao argues, the war brought money into Japanese animation, thanks to military sponsorship of propaganda animation. This produced some very well-known franchises including the *Norakuro* franchise and two famous films based on the legend of *Momotarō*. Thomas LaMarre explains the former:

> Norakuro began his adventures as an accident-prone soldier in a dog regiment under the command of Buru the Bulldog. The Stray Black dog [a translation of Norakuro] enjoyed such popularity that the manga were soon adapted in animation, with some episodes adapted repeatedly. (2008, 88)

The *Momotarō* films likewise made use of animal characters to mask the nationalism and racism at work in these war-time propaganda films. Director Mitsuyo Seo was a key figure in this period directing a version of *Norakuro, Private Second Class* (*Norakuro Nitōhei*, see Figure 4.1) in

FIGURE 4.1 Norakuro, Private Second Class *and war-time propaganda.*

1935 before going on to make both *Momotarō* films, noted as Japan's first feature-length animation, even though the first, *Momotarō's Sea Eagles* (*Momotarō no Umiwashi*, 1943), was still relatively short at 37 minutes (Tsugata 2005, 139). The second, *Momotarō's Divine Sea Warriors* (*Momotarō no Umi no Shinpei*, 1945), was another first in length, at 74 minutes. Clements explains how the success of the former made it a recruitment tool for young boys in Japan, but that by the sequel, the privations of war had begun to bite in Japan and the more accomplished second film had far less impact than the first (2013a, 63–65).

The anthropomorphism displayed within all of these films, which pitch "good" Japanese folktale and animal figures against "bad" animals representing the Allied forces, has been critiqued by LaMarre as "speciesism": "the displacement of race and racism (relations between humans as imagined in racial terms) onto relations between humans and animals" (2008, 76). LaMarre and Clements' analyses reveal the child-audience, or at least the young adult, audience sought by these propaganda filmmakers. Moreover, as propaganda, their nationalist messages demonstrate how animation, particularly cel animation by the period of the Fifteen Years War, was being addressed to a mass, general audience. In this respect, the war united the production of animation in Japan into a single mainstream genre of production, aimed at all and solely intended for Japanese consumption. It was during the War that cel animation became the highest profile form of animation in Japan, and it was this legacy of production that led into television animation in the postwar period.

Television and the birth of "anime" in Japan

Three factors were key to the growth of postwar, post-Occupation (1945–1952), Japanese animation. First, the recovery of the Japanese economy in the postwar period and the rise of commercial culture; second, the expansion of Japan's animation industry during and after the Occupation period; and, finally, the rise of television. These three factors go hand-in-hand, and all three were necessary to the birth of what we now think of as "anime."

Though it is a radical simplification, the postwar period was a turbulent one for the Japanese economy, and with it, for the nascent animation industry. For Japan, it brought cultural upheavals as the USA occupied and reconceptualized Japanese society through a new constitution and new institutions, including those supporting children. In 1947, the newly established Education Bureau published *The Fundamental Law of Education*, the purpose of which was to remove nationalists and politics from classrooms and to ensure that all children, including girls and the children of the *burakumin* (untouchables), would receive education alongside boys (General Headquarters, SCAP, 1948, and Takamae 2002, 182–183). Modern family life also began to change with the rapid postwar urban reconstruction and expansion, and the move of families into city suburbs and away from traditional hometowns (Robertson 1988). With modernization also came new machines, not least of which were televisions, which entered into Japanese homes from 1953 onwards. Children's entertainment began to shift and change in response, for example, with manga rental shops becoming popular before giving way to the cheap weekly "phone book" anthologies that are still being sold today (Ito 2008), and with *kamishibai* and cinema gradually losing status in relation to television. The fast-developing animation industry, consequently, began to invest in entertainment specifically made for children and for the new medium of television.

At the film studios, particularly Tōhō, the Occupation period saw the rise of unions, and with them, strikes—one of which Hayao Miyazaki and Isao Takahata were famously involved with at Tōei (McCarthy 1999, 30). The US Occupation also brought with it large numbers of imported US animated films and shorts, perhaps most obviously the works of the Disney and Fleischer studios (see Clements 2013a, 83, for a full list). The same was also to be true within the burgeoning television market in Japan, which began in 1953 but really blossomed with the coverage of the marriage of Japan's crown prince Akihito in 1959 and the Tokyo Olympics in 1964 (Chun 2007). But, even before those pivotal events, Clements and Tamamuro (2003, xv) state that "The first American series to be shown on Japanese television was the Fleischer brothers' animated *Superman* in 1955" (originally produced in the USA in 1941–1943). Broadcasts like these had a notable impact on early children's genres in Japan, with stories of superheroes and their ilk popular from the earliest moments of children's postwar media culture in Japan.

The recovery, however, enabled the expansion and proliferation of animation studios in Japan in the postwar years. In 1945, Kenzō Masaoka, who had earlier founded the Nihon Manga Eiga-sha (Japan Manga Films Company), established a new company called Nihon Dōga-sha (Japanese Animation Company, Nichidō for short) with fellow animators Sanae Yamamoto and Yasuji Murata. This company was to become Japan's biggest and most powerful early animation company when it was "rebranded as a subsidiary of Tōei in 1956" becoming Tōei Dōga (later renamed Tōei Animation, see Clements 2013a, 75–94). The company was important because it provided a training program for the animators who would go on to form many of Japan's current animation studios, because it trained the first real star-directors of Japanese animation industry and because Tōei Dōga produced the highest quality feature length animation available in Japan at that time (Yamaguchi 2004, 64–68).

Tōei Dōga also, significantly, focused on the production of films suitable for general audiences, including its famous postwar "first": the first feature-length color film *Hakujaden* in 1958 (variously translated, but known in the USA as *Panda and the Magic Serpent*). Borrowing from Asian folklore, *Hakujaden* is one of a series of films made by Tōei Dōga in this period that borrowed from myths and folktales from across Asia, from India to China (see Figure 4.2). In this way, department chief Hiroshi Ōkawa "doggedly pursued both finance and audiences in Asia" that would allow these films to be seen transnationally (Clements 2013a, 98).

Perhaps the most famous of the animators to pass through Tōei Dōga was Osamu Tezuka. Tezuka, already well known as a manga artist in the 1950s, was hired to adapt one of his manga, *My Sun Wukong* (or *My Son Goku, Boku no Songokū)* retitled as *Journey to the West* (*Saiyūki*, Daisaku Shirakawa and Taiji Yabushita, 1960),[1] another story concept borrowed from Asian folklore (Schodt 2007, 62), and also to work on two further Tōei Dōga films, *Arabian Nights: Sinbad the Sailor* (*Arabian Naito: Shinobaddo no Bōken*, Sanae Yamamoto, 1962) and *Doggie March* (*Wanwan Chūshingura*, Daisaku Shirakawa, 1963) (Clements 2013a, 113).

However, Tezuka's time working at Tōei Dōga has been presented in very mixed ways. On the one hand, Clements notes that Tezuka worked on the

FIGURE 4.2 Hakujaden, *Japan's first color feature film.*

storyboards for *Journey to the West*, and that Tezuka lured away Tōei Dōga's animation staff when he set up his own company (2013a, 114). On the other hand, Fred Patten's unsigned column in *NewtypeUSA* magazine in 2003 reports that Tezuka was dismissive of Tōei Dōga's importance when appearing at a fan convention in the USA:

> When fans asked him to tell about his career as a director for Toei, he just laughed. He explained that Toei licensed the right to base the movie upon his popular *My Son Goku* manga, and gave him a "co-director" credit with Yabushita just for the publicity value. The only time he was even close to the production was when Toei brought him into the studio to take publicity photos of him standing amidst the animators at their drawing tables. But it was true that these visits to the Toei studio did help inspire him to start his own studio in 1961. (*NewtypeUSA* 2003)

Wherever the truth of Tezuka's involvement at Tōei Dōga might lie, it remains that Tōei Dōga has been essential to the industrial history of Japanese animation. Moreover, the fact that Tōei Dōga might be willing to capitalize on the star power of Tezuka's name relatively early in the post-Occupation period also suggests a shift in the animation industry in Japan toward what would come to be known as "media mix" practices, wherein anime borrows heavily from other media like manga for its appeals, and is in turn used to sell a wide range of merchandising and licensed goods.

It was, however, Tezuka's formation of Tezuka Osamu Productions in 1961 (which later became Mushi Productions) that changed Japanese animation, bringing children's animation to Japanese television. Although Tezuka's already famous manga *Astro Boy* has been credited as the first television animation series in Japanese history (*Mighty Atom, Tetsuwan Atomu* 1963–1966), anime historians have long known that a previous series of short three-minute animations, *Otogi Manga Calendar* (1961–1964), by Otogi Pro began in 1962 and ran to over 300 episodes (Clements 2013a, 90). With that caveat, it is fair to say that *Astro Boy* was the first animated series on Japanese television that had the basic format of what we think of as television anime today, but it is not quite right to call it the first television anime. Perhaps more significant is that *Astro Boy*, a science fiction series centering on the adventures of a robot made to look like a boy, has many of the science fiction themes that would come to dominate anime in later years (see Chapter 2). But perhaps the most important facet of Tezuka's long-running *Astro Boy* series was the way it came to shape the industry for television animation in Japan.

One way in which *Astro Boy* shaped the industry is something now referred to as "Tezuka's Curse." Marc Steinberg recounts,

Tezuka had made the problematic decision to undersell his Atomu series to the TV station. Aiming to quell the TV station's anxiety about the cost of animation production and undersell the competition in advance, Tezuka sold each episode for far less than it cost Mushi Production to make it. (There is some debate about the actual amount Tezuka asked for, but the most commonly cited sum is 550,000 yen, when it is said to have cost 2.5 million yen to produce each episode.) This fateful move—known to the animation industry today as Tezuka's curse—guaranteed that anime would develop as a transmedia system. (2012, 39–40)

As the next section shows, part of this transmedia necessity would come through distribution of *Astro Boy* to the USA, but within Japan, Steinberg notes that it was early sponsorship from Meiji Chocolates and early merchandising that began the prominence of the *kyara*, or character, business in Japan, where anime relies on licensing, sponsorship and merchandising for the majority of its profits (2012). Clements questions the conception of Tezuka's industrial strategy as a "curse," seeing it rather as a gamble within an unstable industry that caused Tezuka to use risky production strategies (2013b). Curse or simply industrial necessity (after all, it was the Japanese television companies that initially balked at the high relative cost of animation production), Tezuka's impact on Japanese animation was significant for the foresight he showed in aligning animation texts with a wider commercial set of child-oriented commodities from chocolate to toys. In this way, *Astro Boy* inaugurated the "largely character-based media-commodity system that persists to this day" (Steinberg 2012, 43) in anime.

Stylistically, too, Tezuka and Mushi Production's pragmatic, cost-saving decisions about how to produce *Astro Boy* would radically shape the industry and its aesthetics for good. Figure 4.3 is the list of techniques implemented for *Astro Boy* that are recounted by many anime historians (Schodt 2007, 71–72; Steinberg 2012, 15–16; Yamaguchi 2004, 80). Many of these cost-saving techniques had been used by animators before, particularly by US television animators like the Hanna-Barbera and Filmation companies (Wells 2003). Moreover, some techniques, like the reuse of footage, were being used throughout children's television in Japan throughout the 1960s and 1970s, for example, when live-action *tokusatsu* (special effects) shows reused expensive special-effects sequences (Denison 2015).

While not unique, Tezuka's version of "limited" or "reduced" animation is important for the way it has been adopted as a style of animation in Japan, long after being a necessary pragmatic choice. For example, when Major Motoko Kusanagi philosophically narrates over the top of an unmoving image in *Ghost in the Shell*, or when we view Gainax's notorious still sequence in

Neon Genesis Evangelion, in which there is no movement for whole minutes of on-screen time, we can see the lingering traces of the *tome-e*, or still shots, used by Tezuka. There are also similar reuses of footage in contemporary anime transformation sequences (notably *Sailor Moon*, see Chapter 3) and it is still possible to see, in the framing of characters and their sometimes disjointed movements onscreen, the limited numbers of frames being produced for many anime shows. In this regard, Tezuka's limited animation style has become an industry aesthetic of choice, and one that continues to dominate anime aesthetics, particularly at the lower-budget end of children's anime.

Tezuka's Animation Aesthetic

1 Shooting three frames of film for every drawing instead of one or two to create the illusion of fluid movement

2 Using only one drawing in a *tome*, or "still" shot, when shooting close-ups of character's faces

3 Zooming in or out on face shots or physically sliding a single drawing under the camera to create the illusion of movement with a single drawing

4 Shooting a single short sequence of animated drawings and then repeating it again and again while sliding the background image ....

5 When a character moved an arm or leg, animating only that portion ....

6 Animation of the mouth alone ...

7 Creating a "bank system" of images to save on the total number of drawings, allowing reuse of the same drawings in different situations

8 Using more short takes in place of single long take that usually required more movement

Quoted from Schodt (2007, 71–72).

FIGURE 4.3: *Tezuka's limited animation.*

Early television anime in America

Tezuka's was not the only company to emerge as an important part of Japanese animation in the postwar period. In fact, had *Astro Boy* not beaten other animation companies to distribution, being broadcast as a New Year's program in 1963, then several of Tezuka's rival companies would have happily filled that "first" television anime slot. In the year or so that followed *Astro Boy*'s appearance, new animated television shows started to emerge from a wide range of companies. Some—like Otogi Pro and TCJ, the makers of *Tetsujin 28* (1964), an early giant robot animation series—made the majority of their revenues from television advertising in this period. Others—like Tatsunoko Productions, the makers of *Speed Racer* (*Mahha Go Go Go*, 1967) and *Kagaku Ninjatai Gatchman* (*Battle of the Planets*, and later, *G Force*, 1972)—were formed specifically to produce animated television shows. Although Otogi Pro and TCJ pre-dated Tōei Dōga's successes, and although Tatsunoko Pro was founded by a manga artist, Tatsuo Yoshida, and his siblings to exploit his manga designs, Tōei Dōga remained an important feeder for new animation studios in the years that followed. Most notably, Tōei Dōga trained Hayao Miyazaki and Isao Takahata, who would go on to found Studio Ghibli in 1985; moreover, it was Tōei Dōga that gave rise to some of the more innovative studios of today, including Sunrise and Madhouse.

This burgeoning new animated production culture did not stay local for long. Anime's international distribution goes back further than television. Japanese animation went to film festivals fairly early on, for example, when "art animation" (Tsugata 2005, 71) director Noburō Ōfuji's color cellophane remake of his own film, *The Whale* (*Kujira*, 1952), won an award at the Cannes film festival in 1952 (Yamaguchi 2004, 53). In addition, Fred Patten has noted that there is a lost history anime in the USA—that of 16mm film rental libraries, which began in the 1950s and were still running up to the advent of home video in the 1980s. Patten contends that some of the video rental libraries included localized, translated versions of Japanese animated films, especially those of Tōei Dōga and Tezuka's Mushi Productions. For example, *Treasure Island Revisited* (*Shin Takarajima*, a 1965 TV special by Mushi Pro that was colorized for the US market by Fred Ladd), *The Little Norse Prince* (*Taiyō no Ōji: Horusu no Daibōken*, Isao Takahata, 1968), *Panda and the Magic Serpent* and *Arabian Nights: Sinbad the Sailor* were all released in the 16mm format, and others were also shown as matinees on US cable television (2004a and 2004b). If nothing else, this early form of hidden film export from Japan attests to the child-friendly nature of many of the films being produced by Tōei Dōga and Mushi Productions. It also suggests that television's dominant market position was not simply a product of animated films lacking distribution to the USA, but rather more a product of the greater presence that television afforded to animation.

What is perhaps most notable about the discourse around Japanese animated television's early export to the USA was its importance as child-friendly programming. Fred Ladd, one of the major importer-translator-redubbing impresarios of early Japanese animation in the USA, famously had to "save" three of six *Astro Boy* cartoons rejected by "Standards and Practices" at NBC by cutting sequences and hiding the deaths of characters through dialogue changes (2009). This was to become the hallmark of Japanese animation in the USA before the advent of home video cultures—a constant push from pressure government and pressure groups like ACT (Action for Children's Television) and therefore from US re-producers—for Japanese animation to be produced in ways that did not challenge US conceptions of morality and child-friendly content.

However, as animation production matured in Japan, so too did its themes, and, as Ladd explains about *Speed Racer*, which he redubbed and edited for its US release:

> True, the series was not without violence (after all, the year was 1967 and violence seemed to have become the order of the day for all anime; Tokyo broadcasters had no reservations about airing such content for Japanese boys and girls). But in *Astro Boy* and *Gigantor*, we learned how to turn apparent violence into comic violence. (2009, 78)

Already, therefore, by 1967, there was a palpable sense that the Japanese animation market did not align with its US counterpart, and that content permissible in Japan was simply unacceptable to US broadcasters.

Conclusion

As a children's entertainment form, therefore, early Japanese animation was continually being curtailed. The US re-producers and distributors came to form an important pressure group in this regard, pressuring Japanese animators not just toward more child-friendly content, but also toward more transnational productions. The former can be seen in the negotiations over the content of Tezuka's *Kimba the White Lion* (*Janguru Taitei*, 1965) even before it went into production in Japan. NBC required Tezuka to re-plan his narrative, making the series episodic rather than serial in format, they also refused to let "Leo" or "Kimba" age or die during the series and they curtailed Tezuka's original plan for 78 episodes down to 52 to suit the US broadcasting schedules (Ladd and Deneroff 2009, 52). In this way, even the earliest Japanese animated television became a product of transnational pressures and exchanges.

Like *Astro Boy*, too, there was a constant discourse about the perceived violence of Japanese television animation. These shows became caught up in the wider US movements to "protect" children from violent cartoon conflicts and deaths (see Mittell 2004 for a detailed account). Writing in Japan about the little-discussed *Marine Boy* (an amalgam of three series from the *Marine*

Boy franchise, 1965–1969), Satoshi Kusanagi explains that the show was sold to Seven Arts in the USA by K. Fujita Associates, and that "three of the 78 episodes were deleted" on the show's American broadcast, due to levels of violence that, even though they were comic violence, went beyond what was permissible at the time (2003, 70). These associations of violence would re-emerge in the VHS-era as anime's content matured along with its original audiences and the expansion of the manga market in Japan, causing a continually re-emerging debate about animation violence with each newly emerging technology of distribution.

While Japanese television animation came to be a major prime-time (in Japan "golden hour") presence, in the USA it is important to remember that even Astro Boy and Kimba were relegated to the syndication market. These shows, up to and including the "remake" hybrid anime of *Robotech* (1985) and *G-Force* in the late 1970s and early 1980s, may have laid the foundations for anime fandom in the USA that is explored in the next chapter, but they were never themselves a major cultural force at the time. Even *Speed Racer*, which Ladd asserts was the most popular of the anime released before the video era, was shown by regional stations rather than on major US network television channels. This meant that all of these anime tended to have patchy, partial distribution. Even *Astro Boy* began to be broadcast in the USA on a single local New York syndicate station.

Moreover, these were all highly "Americanized" versions of anime, with entirely new soundtracks and, in some cases, amalgamations of unrelated anime shows, perhaps especially in the case of *Robotech* (Ruh 2010). As Brian Ruh argues, by the 1970s, "American television producers not only adapted anime for U.S. broadcast but began changing the shows around to generate programs that were almost entirely American creations" (2010, 31). Just at the moment when anime became a recognizable category of animation in Japan, therefore, it was mutating into a new form of animation elsewhere. From the earliest moments of its history, Japanese animation has been a constantly changing commodity, shifting from art to commercial forms, from short to long to serialized production and from a tenuous craft industry to a major cultural industry. That children have been important throughout the early history of Japanese animation is perhaps clear from the continual attempts by authorities to control the content of animation. As a cultural form, if not as a culture of production, therefore, the children's category of Japanese animation has played an integral role in its development.

5

Anime, Video and the *Shōjo* and *Shōnen* Genres

Anime was first discovered by the American public in March 1976.

(PATTEN 2004C)

In Fred Patten's estimation, March 20, 1976, was the date on which US audiences first saw anime as anime in a broadcast of *Brave Raideen* (*Yusha Raideen*) on Japanese-American community television channels, complete with English subtitles. In this moment, Patten claims, US audiences were first able to see Japanese animation unadulterated by the localization processes common among previous imports including *Astro Boy* and *Speed Racer*. However, this is just one of the important shifts that took place between *Astro Boy*'s appearance on Japanese and US television and the advent of home video technologies that affected how anime came to be a transnationally recognized category of cinema and television. This chapter considers the way genres of anime began to bifurcate along gender lines in Japan, and how these divisions between anime texts aided the growth of an international fanbase, questioning which of those gendered genres held sway in the UK in the earliest moments of international anime fandom.

In the previous chapter, I introduced some of the hidden ways that anime films circulated in US culture before the advent of anime television's transnational re-creation and flow. In the epigraph here, Fred Patten points to another influential, but relatively invisible, form of anime flow: the broadcast of anime on local stations serving the Japan's diasporic population in the USA. Patten argues that through this distribution network, "American awareness of anime was no longer limited to the few who went to the trouble of tuning in to a Japanese-community TV channel because fans with VCRs were dubbing copies and showing them at sci-fi and comic book clubs" (2004c). From a local diasporic broadcast event, Patten charts the beginnings of an underground, grassroots fan culture in the USA, one that was taking the dissemination of anime into its own hands.

It was from the moment that home video technologies entered the Japanese and US markets that anime started to really capture the global imagination. This was only possible, however, because of the growth and diversification of genres that had already developed in Japan. I argue in this chapter that it was the early divisions between *shōnen* (boys') and *shōjo* (girls') anime genres that came to define this period, particularly within Japan and within the emerging UK and US fan cultures. To explain this process, I turn first to the Japanese market and the expansion of anime's genres in the 1970s and early 1980s, before turning to an examination of *Anime UK*, which was the UK's foremost fanzine before it became a professional subculture magazine in the early 1990s.

Through an examination of the discourses about anime's genres in this fan-led publication, I reveal how important the idea of genre was to the emerging fan cultures for anime. Having examined the prehistory of anime in the USA, I want to focus on the UK to give a sense of how anime's genres were coming to be understood as fully transnational phenomena in this period, and not just as an exclusive set of exchanges between Japan and the USA. Additionally, the UK's anime fans have not received the same level of attention as has been devoted to their counterparts in the USA. This is a significant oversight, not least because UK fans have always been incredibly active in their attempts to evangelize on behalf of the texts they love and were in a very different position as regards the distribution of anime during the early period of international VHS exchanges. As *Anime UK* notes in only its second issue, it was already being distributed back to the USA as a leading fan magazine, and in the same issue, the editors note that the UK had more early fan conventions than the USA, demonstrating the rapid growth of the UK anime fanbase and the value that US fans were placing on the opinions of their fellow-fans in this seemingly tertiary market for anime distribution (1991). For these reasons, the UK offers an important point of comparison to US discourses about anime's VHS-era history.

It is worth noting, however, that there is debate about when the transnational VHS-era of anime began. Video tape technologies were available from the mid-1950s onwards, and there was an international race to exploit the medium. However, the popular adoption of video as home viewing technology came from the battle between Sony's Betamax tapes and JVC's

VHS in the mid-1970s. In 1988, Betamax was dropped by Sony in the face of the growing popularity of VHS, which would come to define the home video market (Wasser 2001, 49–50). In terms of anime fandom, VHS quickly became a crucial fan technology. It was, for example, video's potential as a home recording technology that began the debates about fan recordings of programming that later exploded between industry and fans in the digital era (see Chapter 6).

Within US anime fandom, Sean Leonard argues that:

Fans used the introduction of the video cassette recorder (VCR) to share raw untranslated anime with others, as a slew of fantastic imagery and incomprehensible language bombarded audiences at the back of science fiction conventions. The birth of fan distribution followed, releasing anime shows upon a vast underground network of fans throughout the country. By 1990, fans started to "fansub," or to translate and subtitle anime videos. Many fans started anime companies, becoming the industry leaders of today. (2005, 282)

What Leonard says is borne out by the way Fred Patten, John Ledford and other fan culture leaders later went "professional," for example, with Ledford co-founding the influential AD Vision anime licensing and distribution company in the USA.

However, Patten has reported that this mixed fan-professional history of anime in the USA has created confusion around which anime video was released "first" in America. This is simply because there are so many possible contenders, dependent upon *to whom* the videos were being sold. Patten claims that a range of titles could all lay claim to the title, from the *Akira Production Report* (1990) to *Astro Boy* (released in 1989) to *Voltron*, and the Americanized version of Hayao Miyazaki's *Nausicaa of the Valley of the Wind* (*Kaze no Tani no Naushika*, Hayao Miyazaki, 1984) released on VHS as the significantly cut *Warriors of the Wind* in the 1980s. However, he comes down on the side of "U.S. Rendition's first two videos"—which were "*Dangaioh* Volume 1 and *GunBuster* Volume 1, both subtitled—unmistakably anime"—as the first, fan-approved anime VHS releases in the USA (2003). These debates reveal confusion and consternation about who anime was "for" in the USA. Compared to Leonard's comments, there are also omens of a forthcoming collision between industry and fans, as both appear to have taken to video releases at roughly the same time, and in many cases disagreed about who the US audiences for anime were.

As the market continued to expand, these tensions and potential collisions between industrial and fan interests would become more apparent. But what kinds of texts would become "anime" and lay the groundwork for what we think of as anime today? Certainly, some were the kinds of pornographic and "extreme" OVAs discussed in Chapter 2, but these were not, by any means, the defining texts or genres of the 1970s to the mid-1990s.

Japanese anime diversifies: New markets, new genres

Jonathan Clements (2013a) contends that soon after *Astro Boy* was broadcast, the market for anime changed in Japan. Most commentators note that as television expanded, so too did the time given over to animation on Japanese television, leading to the first "boom" in anime in Japan that started from the late 1970s (Tsugata 2005, 81). Therefore, this section briefly charts some of the major changes involved in the expansion of television anime in Japan, before moving on to a consideration of the way UK fandom grew concurrently in the VHS-era of anime. Clements sees the beginnings of this boom when "*Little Witch Sally* [*Mahō Tsukai Sarī*, 1966] opened a new discourse in Japanese animation, with the first steps in bifurcating what had previously been regarded as a '*children's*' market into separate thematic strands for boys and girls" (2013a, 137 emphasis in original). Masami Toku reflects upon the similar division occurring in manga: that they had "split into boys' (*shōnen*) and girls' (*shōjo*) comics" in the postwar period (2007, 19). This bifurcation is important to understanding the anime genres that would develop inside and beyond Japan.

Yasuo Yamaguchi summarizes the rise of the *shōjo* genre in the following terms:

> Anime for girls came to be recognised as a genre in the second half of the 1960s, going into a golden era in the 1970s. After that, it became a little stagnant in the 1980s, but *Pretty Soldier Sailor Moon* [*Bishōjo Senshi Sērā Mūn*] (Tōei Dōga), which was broadcast on Asahi Television in 1992, bucked this trend, resurrecting it. It was also very popular in Europe. (2004, 105)

Yamaguchi's account, though brief, is indicative of an apparent boom and bust cycle of *shōjo* anime production that emerged in Japan from *Sally the Witch* (an alternative translation of *Mahō Tsukai Sarī*) through to *Sailor Moon*.

Yamaguchi charts the rise of both the boys' and girls' genres of anime (see Figure 5.1) and in doing so reveals that although girls' anime was maturing as a separate genre across the 1970s, its hits were not as numerous, nor as seemingly likely to spawn cycles of production by comparison to *shōnen*

	Shōnen Anime		Shōjo Anime
Year	Text	Year	Text
1970	Adventures of Hutch the Honeybee (Konchū Monogatari: Minashigo Hatchi, Fuji TV)	1970	Magical Mako (Mahō no Mako-chan, Tōri Dōga, NET)
1972	Science Ninja Team Gatchaman (Kagaku Ninjatai Gatchaman, Fuji TV)		·
1973	Neo-Human Casshern (Shinzō Ningen Kyashān, Fuji TV)	1973	Fables of the Green Forest (Yama Nezumi Rokkī chakku, Zuiyō Enterprises, Mainichi Broadcasting)
1974	Hurricane Polymar (Hariken Porimā, NET)		
1975	Space Battleship Yamato (Uchū Senkan Yamato, NET)		
1975	Time Bokan (Taimu Bokan, Fuji TV)	1976	Candy Candy (Tōei Dōga, NET; started on Asahi TV)
1977	Time Bokan New Series: Yatterman (Taimu Bokan Shinshirīzu Yattāman, Fuji TV)		
1979	Time Bokan New Series: Zenderman (Taimu Bokan Shinshirīzu: Zendaman, Fuji TV)	1979	Rose of Versailles (Bersaiyu no Bara, Tokyo Movie Shinsha, Nippon TV)

FIGURE 5.1 *Comparison of Japanese boys' and girls' genres through texts. Data amalgamated from Yasuo Yamaguchi 2004, 104–106.*

cycles like the *Time Bokan* series. Furthermore, Yamaguchi's analysis of the *shōjo* texts indicates that the *shōjo* genre's heroines also matured over the period from the 1960s to the end of the 1970s (see also Sugawa Shimada 2011). The early heroines, like Akko from Tōei Dōga's *The Secret of Akko-chan* (*Himitsu no Akko-chan*, 1969), were considerably stylized younger looking girls, but by the end of the 1970s and early 1980s, older-seeming heroines like the long-limbed heroines of *Sailor Moon*, at 14 years old, and the cross-dressing young adult "Lady Oscar" from *Rose of Versailles* were a regular feature of the genre (see Saitō [2000] 2011 for a full history of anime's fighting women). These aging heroines may suggest attempts to continue seeking anime audiences from among an aging generation of female viewers in Japan, but it may also suggest that the *shōjo* genre was becoming hybridized with its *shōnen* counterparts.

Other anime genres were using texts aimed at both genders of Japanese audiences, perhaps most notably seen in the sports genre. Yamaguchi cites *Attack No.1* (*Atakku No.1*, 1969) as a response to the success of *shōnen* text *Star of the Giants* (*Kyōjin no Hoshi*, 1968). *Star of the Giants* is a baseball-themed series that, Clements argues, is "a landmark show for a number of other reasons, not least the attempt it represents to expand anime beyond the children's ghetto" (2013a, 139). Misao Minamida, similarly, sees in *Aim for the Ace!* (*Ēsu o Nerau!*, 1973–1974), a tennis-themed sports anime, a scent of "feminine sensibility" that helps it to stand up to analysis in comparison to other anime of its kind (2000, 12). Sports anime, therefore, from the late 1960s onwards were not just aimed at boys, but had a habit of seeking out, and crossing between, the *shōnen* and *shōjo* genre archetypes and audiences.

Attack No. 1 is a particularly interesting example in this respect, because its appearance in Japanese culture in the late 1960s seems to have been a specific appeal to two kinds of audiences. First, the show centered on the exploits of an all-female volleyball team, making it an early example of the team-oriented *shōjo* anime that would be popularized with *Sailor Moon*; but, additionally, *Attack No. 1*'s production by Tokyo Movie fell between the real-life successes of the Japanese women's volleyball teams at the Tokyo Olympics in 1964, where they won gold, and the Mexico Olympics, where they achieved silver (for more, see Yamaguchi 2004, 105). Broadcast shortly after those successes, *Attack No. 1* offers an example of anime capitalizing on real-world success stories in order to heighten ratings and expand a genre's meanings.

The development of both of these gendered audiences, *shōnen* and *shōjo*, of anime is at least in part a product of the expanding worlds of manga. The 1960s saw the first "generation" of female manga artists, known as "The Magnificent 24s," which refers to Shōwa 24 or 1949 (they are also known as the *24nen gumi* in Japanese, sometimes also as the 49ers). Deborah Shamoon argues that these women manga artists changed the remit and meanings of the *shōjo*: "This groups of artists, of whom Ikeda Ryoko is one, dealt openly with politics, sexuality, and with the psychological development and interiority of characters" (2007, 5). Ryoko Ikeda was the creator of *Rose of Versailles* (*Berusaiyu no Bara*, 1979–1980) (Gravett 2004, 78–79), one of the first breakout hit manga of the *shōjo* genre to be written by a woman (for more on Ikeda's politics and the male-dominated manga industry before The Magnificent 24s, see McKnight 2010). *Rose of Versailles* has become one of the best-known examples of a thread of same-sex love (*dōseiai*) stories running through *shōjo* anime, from Osamu Tezuka's *Princess Knight* (*Ribon no Kishi*, 1967–1968) to more recent texts like the French Revolution-set *Chevallier*

D'Eon (2006–2007). Deborah Shamoon says of *Rose of Versailles* that it "helped transform shojo manga into a genre that could encompass vast epics, complex psychological portraits, political commentary, and adult romance" (2007, 14).

The expansion of the *shōjo* subgenres in this boom period substantiated several archetypes of anime heroine, not least anime's magical girls and beautiful fighting girls. Though found across genres, Akiko Sugawa-Shimada defines "Magical Girl anime as TV anime made for girls which feature a prepubescent girl or girls with magical powers … primarily designed for girl audiences" (2011, 126). Like Clements, Sugawa-Shimada traces this trend back to *Sally the Witch*, but sees these magical girls transforming in the 1970s and 1980s in response to "emerging gender equality" that allowed for new kinds of "femininity, sexuality, self-assertion and self-expression" on the part of Japanese women and female characters in anime, citing *Magical Angel Creamy Mami* (*Mahō no Tenshi Kurīmī Mami*, 1983–1984) as a popular early example (165).

Tamaki Saitō ([2000] 2011) goes further than this, listing thirteen different lineages of anime heroine in his work on the beautiful fighting women of anime. Among these traditions in anime production, he notes a wide variety of female character types including the magical girl, transforming girl, "idol works" in which female characters act as popular culture idols, "splash of crimson" stories about militaristic women that Saitō traces back to the work of manga artist Shotarō Ishinomori (creator of *Kamen Rider* and *Power Rangers*), a "Takarazuka" or "sartorial perversion" lineage of cross-dressing female characters in male drag, a "Pygmalian" lineage, a "grit and determination" type linked to sports anime and a range of multiply "othered" female character types that includes alien girls, mediums (*miko*) and "hunters." As the sheer range of character types suggests, the *shōjo* genre quickly divided internally, with a multitude of subgenres presenting a wide range of female characters to audiences that would become part of the global discourses on anime's representational strategies and genres.

Similarly, Noboyuki Tsugata attests to the influence of *shōnen* science fiction texts in producing anime "booms" within Japanese culture. He argues that *Astro Boy* was at the crest of anime's initial wave of popularity, before *Space Battleship Yamato* inculcated the second "boom," with Gainax's *Neon Genesis Evangelion* at the forefront of a third "boom" in the 1990s (2011b, 30). Tsugata muses that:

> If you think about why this was, there was little sense of the "young adult generation's existence" in things from this period—television anime continually produced shows that were based on *Shōnen Jump's* serial manga originals, including *Dragonball* [1986–1989], *Saint Seiya* [*Seitōshi Seiya*, 1986–1989] and *City Hunter* [1987–1988]; and, things

like brave youth stories, which began with *Brave Exkaiser* [*Yusha Ekusukaizā*, 1990–1991] were being broadcast, and family-based works including things like *Chibi Mariko-chan* [1990–1992], ie family and young boy-oriented anime became the mainstream. (2011b, 31)

He argues that the young adult boom came with the advent of video, when Japanese anime audiences could be made niche, rather than mainstream, allowing greater generic and content freedom to industry (see discussion of OVA in Chapter 3). Tsugata's collection of texts and his understanding of a further shift in the 1980s toward two specific categories of anime on television—*shōnen* anime and family anime—is indicative of the lessening importance of *shōjo* anime in this period and the rise to mainstream dominance of science fiction *shōnen* anime.

The dominant position of *shōnen* within the 1970s and 1980s anime markets is evident in the creation of anime's first massive multimedia franchises, particularly the *Space Battleship Yamato* and the longer-lived, ongoing, *Gundam* franchises. Minamida argues that:

If summed up, the flow of the 20th century, up to the present, would be classified as: the dawn starts from *Astro Boy*, and from *Space Battleship Yamato* there was a period of expansion, then from *Mobile Suit Gundam* there was a period of maturity, until with *Neon Genesis Evangelion* it reached an apex. (Minamida 2000, 7)

As with Tsugata, Minamida's list of texts is intended to show the nexus points around which the anime industry and its genres changed in Japan. The overlap between these lists—from booms to phases of anime production—simply demonstrates how important certain texts are within the discourses around anime in Japan. What is notable is how many more shifts take place after the advent of home video than before it, with the roughly fifteen-year period between *Space Battleship Yamato* and *Neon Genesis Evangelion* marked by three phases, almost mapping across the whole of VHS's life span as the dominant home video viewing technology. Notably, all of these texts fall under the broad rubric of science fiction when discussed within and outside Japan (Napier 2005; Yamaguchi 2004). Even more notably, they encapsulate discourses around the *mecha* genre of *shōnen* anime production.

In one of the more obvious signs of *Mobile Suit Gundam*'s transnational franchise popularity, *Animerica* magazine released a special issue on *Gundam* that offers a near-encyclopedic analysis of its production and franchise of texts, including the vast merchandising network that had emerged around it.

Within a republication of that special issue in 2002, Benjamin Wright cites lucky timing for the success of the *mecha* anime genre in the late 1970s and early 1980s:

Two years after *Star Wars*, 1979 was the year when anime mecha came of age. It also marked the birth of what would become Japan's biggest mecha anime franchise. It was the year that a TV series called *Mobile Suit Gundam* premiered. (5)

By contrast, both Patten (2003) and Yamaguchi trace the *mecha* genre back to a 1972 Sunrise production called *Mazinger Z* (created by Gō Nagai), which Yamaguchi claims began a "giant robot boom" in the 1970s in Japan that culminated with the *Gundam* franchise (2004, 116). These parallel histories, one transnational the other local, are both important contexts for the success of the *Gundam* franchise.

Yamaguchi notes that the series was not initially successful (117), and that it was in syndication (Wright 2002, 6) and through its toy lines that *Gundam* became a fully fledged hit. Mark Simmons declares that "One of the major reasons for the *Gundam* saga's stunning longevity is its sheer adaptability. Each new series introduces new creators, new worlds, new narrative ideas, and new visual aesthetics" (2002). This kind of franchising was not common within anime production at the time, and the continual reinvention of *Gundam* under new directors and animation staff might make this less of a franchise and more of a brand entity, or a branded-subgenre of *mecha* anime in its own right.

Wright even notes the idea of franchise stages within *Gundam*:

The first age of *Gundam* began in 1979 and gave birth to the idea of Real Robots. The second age of *Gundam* was 1985 to 1988, when [Yoshiyuki] Tomino's vision was told through the continuing stories of *Zeta*, *ZZ*, and *Char's Counterattack*. The third age of *Gundam*—1989 to 1993—saw continuity pockmarked by reverse-engineered sidestories and saw the first attempt at revitalization. The franchise's third age came to an end with *Victory Gundam*, a series which also stands as the transition to the fourth age … the age of parallel worlds. (2002, 9)

The "ages" of *Gundam* are significant benchmarks in ways of conceptualizing a Japanese anime franchise. Here, Wright does so in accordance with both changes to creative personnel and shifts within the genre, moving away from "Real Robots" toward "parallel worlds" over time.

Ian Condry argues that "*Gundam* also helped to solidify the idea that 'real' anime was that which appealed to adults." For Condry,

The term "real" in "real robots" primarily indicated an emotional seriousness, but more broadly indicated a dividing line in terms of the age of the audience, the kinds of toys produced, and in the style of the anime, particularly in terms of more brutal representations of war and fighting. (2013, 126)

Like their *shōjo* contemporaries, then, the robots of *mecha* anime started to subdivide into two genres, one of super robots, who were the protagonists of shows aimed at younger audiences, and the subgenre of real robots, who populated a young adult subgenre (Tsugata 2011b, 30–33). Within these generations and subgenres of *shōnen* anime, therefore, we start to see the kinds of genre and franchise productions that would become the norm for the Japanese "mainstream" of anime in the decades to come.

The *shōnen* genre's many points of fracture indicate its mutability, which may help to explain its longevity. However, the popularity of *Shōnen Jump* manga-derived anime, often appealing across gender demographics, does offer at least one point of commonality within the genre. As Tsugata explained earlier, since at least the 1980s, *Shōnen Jump* manga have acted as origin points for highly popular *shōnen* franchises that now include long-running multimedia franchises like those based on *Bleach* (2004–2012) and *Naruto* (original anime from 2002 to 2007, with a second series 2007–). As these fractures within the categories of *shōnen* and *shōjo* indicate, they might, like anime, be now considered as meta-genres that have produced a wide range of genres, or at least subgenres, which have themselves been changing over time. The genre mixing inherent in these works, be it with sports, *mecha* or heroes and heroines from the other meta-category, can be seen as a necessary set of industrial attempts to extend and expand the reach of texts. The question remains, how did audiences see those texts once they shifted out of their Japanese context? And additionally, how did the meanings of these shifting genres solidify within the transnational consumption context?

UK fans and anime's transnational genres

The UK's anime fans were in a very different position to their US counterparts in the pre-internet, video-era of anime. Before the rise of Manga Entertainment, there was little specialist distribution of anime in the UK. Helen McCarthy outlines the early 1990s situation for fans in the first issue of *Anime UK*:

How can you actually buy anime in the UK? Well, for the most part, you can't. Since this country's video trade firmly believes that no-one over the age of seven watches "cartoons," the few anime features that have made it over from Japan go onto obscure kidvid labels which all seem to share the unfortunate characteristic of folding within a year and dumping their stock onto market stalls and car boot sales. (1991–1992, 16)

UK anime fandom, as a consequence of this dearth of distribution, relied upon an inherently transnational network of exchanges. By necessity, the UK's anime fans sought out tapes through fan conventions, from Europe and from the USA, and *Anime UK*, in recognition of that fact, provided lists of contacts when they announced new US releases, and had information about how to send payments and whom to trust within the transnational anime distribution networks.

When *Anime UK* began to be published in the early 1990s, the VHS-era was well underway. Indeed, just a few years later in the decade DVD would begin to encroach on VHS's markets, changing the landscape of home viewing and the market for anime (see Chapter 7). In addition, when *Anime UK* started to be published, the shift toward *shōnen* anime as the dominant genre of Japanese anime had also already taken place. Perhaps as a consequence of these industrial shifts, the discussions of *shōjo* characters are more usual than discussions of *shōjo* as a genre within its pages. Will Overton's "Nadia Notes," for example, relates the genres of Hideaki Anno and Hayao Miyazaki's *Nadia: The Secret of Blue Water* (*Fushigi no Umi no Nadia*, 1990–1991) as "a combination of high adventure, exotic settings, fantastic machines … and appealing characters" but warns that the female characters "spend a lot of time sans clothing" suggesting a male implied audience for the text (1992–1993, 24). Similarly, Helen McCarthy names *Project A-Ko* (1986) as a "girls school story for the 21st century!" (1992a, 6) but stops short of naming it *shōjo*, while Paul Munson Siter's feature on *RG Veda* (*Seiden: Rigu Vēda*, 1991–1992), designed by the CLAMP group of all-female manga artists, notes that "Those of you who can't stand the rather slender, androgynous body shapes, long flowing hair and elongated limbs that is a hallmark of the so-called 'shojo style' will probably hate the art" (1993, 26). These prevarications imply assumptions about the gender of UK fans on the part of the writers, with coverage of masculine genres reinforcing this impression.

Peter J. Evans, however, does deal with anime's heroines head-on in an article titled "The Beautiful and the Terrible." He writes,

I find it a constant joy that anime continues to give us a plethora of strong, competent, sensible heroines who do not exist purely as a prize or objective for the male "hero." There is really no other genre that treats women in the same way, and yet this positive view of the female is so often tempered by a streak of needless exploitation, sexism and generalised hatred of the female that most of the good that can and has been done by anime in this field is forgotten. (1993, 27–28)

For Evans this paradox runs through anime's representations of women, making the *shōjo* a character that is alternately heroine and victim, with anime sitting at a generic level above the characters contained in texts and the audiences those texts are aimed at.

However, as Evans' analysis shows, *shōjo* images litter the pages of *Anime UK*, and the magazine routinely reviewed and provided features on *mecha* anime that featured *shōjo* heroines—for example, Dafydd Neal Dyar's reflections on a decade of *Dirty Pair* works (1985–1990), from manga to OVA and television anime. Dyar's assessment of the show is concerned, in the main, with two recurring issues: the uses of psychic powers and the protagonists' changing character designs and costumes. For example, Dyar notes that the protagonists became younger as they shifted from manga into anime:

> The girls (they hardly looked like grown women any more) were much more chan-like [a diminutive suffix used to refer to girls in Japan] in both face and figure, at times almost terminally cute, and their behaviour more adolescent. Kei's bangs puffed out in front like Woody Woodpecker's topknot, somewhat concealed by her now-trademark headband. Yuri's hair turned indigo blue and the "spears" of hair in front of her ears extended to a length worthy of Urusei Yatsura's Lum. (1992, 10)

The descriptions of these "terminally cute" girl protagonists and references to a previously successful manga and anime from Rumiko Takahashi, a well-known comedy manga artist whose characters often shifted between registers (especially in *Ranma ½*, see Napier 2005), push the coverage of *The Dirty Pair* into a hybrid position somewhere between the *shōnen* and *shōjo* categories.

The inclusion of female protagonists in otherwise *shōnen* genre anime actually became the focus of much of the coverage contained within early issues of *Anime UK*. Despite the fact that the Dirty Pair carry guns and were the protagonists of their show, their spectacularly small bikini-style costumes and seeming haplessness were used to place them as *shōjo* protagonists within the *shōnen* genre that relied upon their central, but highly objectified positions within the narrative. Even within the same issue of *Anime UK*, similar refrains about *shōjo* characters in *shōnen* texts abound. For example, *Bubblegum Crisis* (1987–1991), initially an OVA series, is described as follows:

> The concept came from Toshimutsu Suzuki, but the show was stolen, in the view of most fans, by character designer Ken-Ichi Sonoda. His creations,

in particular the four-girl techno-commando team the Knight Sabers, had enormous appeal, both for their looks—Sonoda is the arch-exponent of the Cute Female Fighter—and for the mix of characteristics, ideas and attitudes that make them believable people. (1992, 25)

Cute Female Fighters are given archetypal status in this coverage, raised up from a borrowed *shōjo* aesthetic into a *shōnen* genre type. Moreover, it is the concept of the *kawaisa*, or cuteness, which traverses the categories (Kinsella 1995).

This is not to say that the coverage of anime's genres in *Anime UK* was dominated by Cute Female Fighters. *Mobile Suit Gundam* (*Kidō Senshi Gandamu*, 1979–1980) is perhaps the single text, or franchise of texts, to which most space is given over in *Anime UK*. Covered across three issues in a three-part analysis, again by Dyar (1992–1993, 1993a and 1993b), the articles on the *Gundam* franchise focus on the science, chronology and society of the *Gundam* universe, ending with a production history. Perhaps surprisingly, within this extended discussion of the franchise, very few mentions of genre occur, except where the *Gundam* saga's inventive approach to science and space becomes essential to recounting the physics and narrative of the show. While genre may not drive the narrative of Dyar's coverage, images of *Gundam*'s "Mobile SUITS," as he terms them, grace two of the three issues and are described and compared in detail (1992–1993 and 1993b). In contextualizing this franchise, then, it is not the *shōnen* hero, Amuro Rei, of the early part of the franchise who takes center stage, but the *mecha* designs that give their name to a whole subgenre of anime.

Similarly, the *shōnen* genre has become so pervasive at this point in anime history that its texts become the focus for localization. *Anime UK*'s first issue coverage of Mamoru Oshii and Headgear's *Mobile Police Patlabor* (*Kidō Keisatsu Patoreibā*, see Figure 5.2) OVA and anime television series, for example, is explained through some perhaps surprising references:

Most importantly, it has plenty of humour, from the inherent wry laughter familiar to aficionados of the copshow genre to the sheer slapstick—there's a wonderful episode of the tv series in which an albino alligator is prowling the sewers of Tokyo, giving rise to a couple of chase sequences which are pure Keystone Kops [*sic*]. (1992, 6)

Patlabor, which follows the exploits of a *mecha*-team of Tokyo police officers as they battle crime in a world that has been enriched by *mecha*-labor suits, is carefully aligned here with an international genre—the cop

FIGURE 5.2 *A girl and her* mecha, *Noa Izumi in* Mobile Police Patlabor.

show—and with a local, early British cinema example of comedy police film, the *Keystone Cops*, or *Kops*, that began under Mack Sennett's company in the 1910s in England. This example is an interesting one simply for its long reach back into the history of UK filmmaking in order to find a local point of comparison for *Patlabor's* sometimes outlandish comedy style. Through this example, the author is able to give a sense of local anchorage for the *mecha* genre, despite its alien point of origin for British viewers (for whom, however, the *Keystone Cops* were also likely to be a relatively distant cultural memory).

Similarly, to suggest that only Japan's most transnational anime were given space in *Anime UK* would be to drastically underestimate the knowledge of Japanese culture and anime's domestic production history routinely displayed in this magazine. Throughout its early issues, *Anime UK*'s editors made sure to include articles on anime that were less likely to be freely available, and which were distinct from the "dominant" *shōnen* genres being debated. McCarthy's coverage of Hayao Miyazaki's *Porco Rosso* (*Kurenai no Buta*, 1992) is a good example (1992b), as is the review of *Night on the Galactic Railroad* (*Ginga Tetsudō no Yoru*, Gisaburō Sugii, 1985) in Issue 2 (*Anime UK*, 1992, 30). These analyses gave *Anime UK* an educative edge and worked in the proselytizing mode of much early anime fandom. What they also did, however, was begin to build fan knowledge around genres and directors who would come to define anime in more recent times.

Conclusion

By the time the end of the video-era was approaching, anime's genres had expanded far beyond the children's market analyzed in Chapter 4, taking in a wide spread of gender-related genres and topics. Across the period of video's primacy, anime continued to shift and be replayed, with new generations of fans brought into contact with anime that was not originally made for them. This was as true in Japan, where syndication made a hit of *Gundam*, and OVAs spawned new kinds of anime genres and fandom including the rise of the otaku (Tsugata 2011b), as it was in the USA, where VHS and then DVDs allowed whole new national fanbases to build (Cubbison 2005; Leonard 2005). In the UK, as VHS gave way to DVD, anime fandom developed into a committed subculture that reached into the grassroots of the UK's already burgeoning fanbases for fantasy and science fiction.

Within this fan-oriented milieu, two texts came that changed transnational and local fandom. One was *Sailor Moon* (1992–1997), whose female protagonists reclaimed the *shōjo* heroines of texts like *The Dirty Pair* and *Patlabor* and created a new inflection on the "magical girl" subgenre that continues to be popular today in hits like *Puella Magi Madoka Magica* (*Mahō Shōjo Madoka Magika*, 2011), whose cute title belies the genre-deconstruction at the heart of the text. Also deconstructing its genre, *Neon Genesis Evangelion* has been claimed to have revitalized the *mecha* and *shōnen* genres of anime in the mid-1990s (Azuma 2009), and Susan J. Napier argues that it "defamiliarizes" its "rather hackneyed story line." She continues, "This is particularly true in the second half of the series, in which the tortured psychology of the main characters and a variety of enigmatic apocalyptic elements begin to intrude into the conventional action-packed plot" (2002, 424). From a single genre into gendered genres through to texts that rework and begin to deconstruct the premises of those categories, anime's maturation during the video-era demonstrates how important it is to contextualize the cycles of production running from *Astro Boy* through to *Neon Genesis Evangelion*, and how attention to those contexts of production and reception is all the more necessary as the circumstances of production and reception become more diffuse.

6

Post-Video Anime: Digital Media and the Revelation of Anime's Hidden Genres

Anime has exploded into the digital era. Anime has become globally visible as never before, and its transnational life has become problematic for industry as never before. In previous decades, when the spread of anime was contained by high reproduction costs and the degrading quality of fan-subtitled videos (fansubs), Jorge Diaz Cintas and Pablo Muñoz Sánchez claim that it was "implicitly acknowledged by fansubbers as well as by Japanese copyright holders that the free distribution of fansubs can have a very positive impact in the promotion of a given anime series in other countries" (2006, 44). However, this changed with the "digital turn" of the 1990s (Hesmondhalgh 2007), as Lance Heiskell of US anime distributor, FUNimation, explains:

> At this stage, fansubbing has gone from something that requires a significant time investment and a level of technical expertise on the part of the potential viewer to mass penetration, with video quality that is sometimes beyond what anime companies themselves are able to provide on their legit releases. (Quoted in Koulikov 2008)

Fans have thereby become a newly potent force in anime culture, and one whose activities in the post-digital media world are not always welcome. For this reason, the first section of this chapter details the major shifts within the post-digital landscape of transnational anime (re)production and distribution.

This analysis is motivated by the fact that anime's genres have continued to proliferate as fans search for new anime experiences online, often utilizing emerging new media technologies as an aid in this process. This new relationship between industry, fans and anime genres is the focus of this chapter. Problems in identifying and standardizing our understanding of those anime genres persist as much because of, as despite of, these changes. In this chapter, and in Chapter 9, I argue that better distribution does not equate to universal genres or meanings for anime, nor to agreement about how to recognize anime's categories. Rather than anime universally being "what we collectively believe it to be" (Tudor 1974, 139), anime's genres remain contingent on context; what is an anime genre in one place may not be a genre elsewhere (Condry 2013). In Chapter 9, I discuss how time lags in official distribution and a transnational understanding of the horror genre have shaped responses to "horror" anime both within and outside Japan. In this chapter, by contrast, I look at how new genres can form in Japan that can be differently recognized outside of anime's home market.

To give this analysis shape, I focus on a genre that has only recently emerged in Japan out of a very specific tradition in anime production, but which has had a longer and more diverse existence in its English equivalent. The Japanese version of this genre is called *nichijōkei* (literally, "everyday-style"), whereas to English fans, the small set of texts usually described in this way fit into a larger and older category known as "slice of life" anime. I focus in the main on the assertion of this newly emerging genre, led by recent research from Japan's Kinema Jumpo Research Office, that provides a detailed history and definition of *nichijōkei* anime, with contemporary news and specialist Japanese media accounts of the genre. By considering how genres of anime are differently constituted through such discourses, I intend to show how contextually and culturally dependent genrification is, and how thinking cross-culturally can produce distinct genre understandings and meanings even when the texts in question are contiguous. The inherent multiplicity of anime's possible categorizations leads into the new areas of analysis investigated in the final section of this book, where I argue that brands, physical spaces and delays in distribution all have the potential to radically effect how we think about anime's categorization in culture.

Digital anime and fans: From online discussion to online distribution

Before discussing one genre's different international labels and history, however, it is first worth considering how shifts towards digital and computer-based distribution technologies have changed the relationship between fans and industry. Multiple histories of digital technology vie for attention in relation to anime. On the one hand, there is a history of digital anime production in

Japan, which has been expertly charted by Japanese (Masuda 2007; Mikami 2011) and non-Japanese scholars alike (Clements 2013a; Steinberg 2012). On the other hand, there is a transnational history of anime that has received only piecemeal attention. It is to this transnational history of digital anime distribution that I now turn.

Ramon Lobato's bifurcation of film distribution into formal and informal circuits is useful here (2012). In treating the two as equally important, rather than contesting the legitimacy of one over the illegality of the other, Lobato presents a useful lens through which a consideration of anime's parallel legitimate and shadow economies of distribution might be undertaken. The informal distribution work of fans has become one of anime's driving transnational forces, and so their work is considered alongside the work of industry here (for more debate on how to position this fan-work, see Condry 2010 and 2013; Jenkins 2006b; Leonard 2005). In this section, I aim to chart just a few of the interactions between fans and industry in a period of technological upheaval that produced heightened tensions in order to reflect on the creative practices of both groups in relation to anime's genres. Throughout, I focus on creativity and the mechanisms through which anime has been digitally distributed in order to question how these emerging distribution practices have broadened access to anime's lesser-distributed genres for international anime fans.

It is worth noting that the shift to digital distribution took place in the wake of Japan's rising international "soft power" profile (McGray 2002): a wave of transnational exports and Japanese media "hits" overseas that briefly gave the impression of Japan as a new cultural superpower. Anime was at the vanguard of this new cultural wave, most notably the *Pokémon* franchise and the films of Hayao Miyazaki. However, discussion of these "hits" masked the uncertain industrial production conditions behind these successful crossovers:

> The comic book, the television show, and the trading cards were not part of Pokémon's original marketing strategy. It is only in such third-wave markets as Italy and Israel that the rollouts of the various products were fully coordinated and integrated…. the greatest strength of Pokémon is that it is a multidimensional, inter-related set of products and activities, but the multidimensionality was emergent, rather than planned. (Tobin 2004, 10)

Joseph Tobin proclaims that *Pokémon* was lucky and it was flexible, with a wide range of products from its Japanese media mix (Steinberg 2012) ready for deployment in new global locales. Similarly, I have argued elsewhere that Studio Ghibli's deal with Miramax and Disney in the USA opened up new distribution routes for the company, but that its products were nowhere near as successful abroad as they were at home (Denison 2007). Rather than seeing Japanese anime's rise as a product of "national cool," (McGray 2002) therefore, I view anime's rising global profile as a product of long-term growth in the transnational fandom for anime, and as related to technological developments, shifting distribution patterns, industrial diversification (media mix) and increased co-operation between Japan's media industries and international distribution partners. Perhaps most significant in this period was the changing distribution of anime, first from VHS on to DVD and then on into internet distribution.

The picture of distribution becomes increasingly muddled as anime moves into the realms of digital distribution, with significant overlaps between new and older forms of home media. DVD is an important medium here. Like Blu-ray since, DVD's technical capacity to store far more high quality data than VHS (though perhaps not so impressive by comparison to LaserDisc) engendered real shifts in formal distribution practices. Although many Japanese DVD producers continue to serialize anime shows with just one or two episodes per disc (DVD in Japan also enabled different versions of texts to be distributed and a proliferation of accompanying special extras to be included, see Clements 2013a, 203), in the USA "volumes" of anime shows containing three or four episodes have been more common. By the late 1990s, US anime distributors had embraced the new technology of DVD and by the turn of the millennium DVD had reportedly become a "$65-million" a year business (Cubbison 2005, 50).

DVD quickly became the normative home viewing technology, and fans in the mid-2000s were already nostalgically discussing the way certain high-profile anime texts, most notably *Ghost in the Shell*, had received DVD releases packed with special features (Harrison 2004). More significantly for fans, however, DVD effectively ended the subtitling versus dubbing debate. Laurie Cubbison notes that "The impact of DVD on anime is really based on its ability to do two things: turn subtitles on and off and switch between multiple audio tracks"; but, she goes on to discuss the importance of Americanized special features like interviews with US voice actors as a way of providing non-Japanese fans with "a more fully developed" viewing experience (2005, 50 and 51).

Despite the increasing dominance of online distribution, this "fully developed," mode of DVD distribution continues to play important roles for the industry. For example, companies like Right Stuf! in the USA have shifted toward producing beautiful "premium" editions of anime shows in elaborate box-sets and with exclusive extras. For example, their DVD/Blu-ray version of the *Blossoms of Tomorrow* anime show (*Hanasaku Iroha*, 2011) contains an English language art book, translated interviews with the Japanese production team and reproduced illustrations. As the title *Blossoms of Tomorrow* intimates, Right Stuf! has become the key US distributor of more marginalized *shōjo* and other female-audience-oriented anime in the USA, expanding into a tranche of neglected genres and giving them a transnational push. In addition, Right Stuf!'s website has diversified into a community hub, with news updates and fan forums, as well as being an online retailer of a wide range of anime-related goods (Right Stuf!.com, n.d.). In this way, Right Stuf! has shifted from retailer into community nexus, embedding online consumption into wider fan practices. I mention Right Stuf! merely as an example of a wider transnational industry trend away from traditional promotion toward a form of distribution that integrates community-formation and maintenance as part of anime distribution practice.

Other retailers, too, have radically shifted away from the Japanese model of serialization, and now it is far more common to see FUNimation, Manga Entertainment, MVM and others producing half-season and full-season or series collections on DVD. In the UK, Manga Entertainment has diversified its web presence similar to Right Stuf!, with its website acting as a news and retail venue, in addition to providing fans with a regular blog, Facebook site and Twitter feed. Manga Entertainment has also expanded its range of anime genre distribution far beyond its initial interests in adult-oriented horror, action and science fiction, and now includes DVD box-sets of *shōnen* titles like *Naruto* and *One Piece*, while also bringing across a wide range of high-profile films and niche genres as diverse as horror and slice of life shows to the UK (*Anime News Network*, n.d.). These changes come as a consequence of anime distributors having to compete with formal and informal online distributors, forcing them to go online themselves through a range of social media outlets. Traditional retailers are also bringing a wider range of genres to the USA and UK as a result of shifts in the fan markets over the last two to three decades.

Fans' online activities are therefore necessary, desired and yet challenging to distributors attempting to attract anime consumers. Moreover, the most "participatory" members of the online anime community have expanded on the VHS-era's fan distribution practices to create a separate, informal shadow market of exchanges in anime texts. The disagreements about fans' roles in the digital anime explosion are easily boiled down to two positions: first, that fans are important grassroots pro-sumers (a portmanteau of producer and consumer), active in their efforts to promote and spread anime through a participatory fan culture (Jenkins 2006b). On the other side of the debate are those who frame fan activities as interloping on industry:

a sector within anime fandom retaliates with an addled notion of hyper-ownership, superseding that of the rights holders and sometimes even that of the original creators. In the rhetoric of the most fanatical fansubbers and video pirates, access should be mandatory…and irrespective of the adverse effect this might have on revenue. (Clements 2013a, 209)

Both positions have merit. Fans' informal distribution circuits began with relatively closed communities sharing files through IRC (Internet Relay Chat) channels, copying VHS and later DVDs and physically sending them to people within their fan networks. However, this changed with the introduction of online distribution and reproduction technologies and access to high-speed internet connections (Cintas and Sánchez 2006).

As a result of a fast-changing distribution landscape, fans of anime now occupy a spectrum of positions rather than the two outlined earlier. Many anime fans simply consume their anime online, legally or otherwise, while others, like fan subtitlers, use expertise in Japanese language to translate anime, or technical skills with computer software to encode, time or proofread subtitles, creating "fansubs." Even within the fan subtitling community, however, there are ethics debates. The differing ideologies at work can be read even at the level of how fans distribute the works they subtitle (Lee 2009). Elsewhere, I have posited a generational shift in fan subtitling practices, with earlier generations framing their activities as promotional and as filling gaps in distribution, while more recent generations of fansubbers are openly entering into (and even seeking) conflict with industry (Denison 2011).

A particularly visceral debate has opened up around "speed subbing" practices. Those partaking in "speed subbing" are seen as a problem both within and outside the formal channels of anime distribution. Tofusensei, an anime fan subtitler, claims in an interview that:

> Bittorent leveled the playing field, so you had a whole influx of new people coming in doing speed subs, because if you were the first person to release a file, you were going to get that notoriety, that attention. People would recognize you and be interested in you. It really is a competition; there are people who are friends and people who are enemies. (Bertschy 2008a)

The distribution mechanism Tofusensei mentions, BitTorrent, is a peer-to-peer file-sharing program preferred by many fan subtitling groups and feared by industry (as seen in the earlier quote from Heiskell) for its ability to enable digital fan distribution of high quality audiovisual texts, and, moreover, permanent distribution in the form of downloadable anime. Tofusensei's comments show how this new technology has affected the fan community around anime, generating competitive practices rather than communal ones and creating intra-community friction.

In terms of genres, some older fan-distributor practices were emulated, with certain fansubbing groups focusing on anime texts like *Rose of Versailles* that had never received formal distribution. On the flip side, speed subbing groups tend to focus on already-formally distributed and popular texts, undermining the work of overseas distribution companies. One of the most frequently speed subbed texts, for example, was *shōnen* anime *Naruto*, which was already a popular transnational hit (Denison 2011). By reinforcing the most popular transnational hits in an attempt to gain prestige within the online fanbase, speed subbing has become one of the most obvious points of tension as anime's formal distributors have raced to keep pace with their informal competition.

Other aspects of anime's participatory fandom have now started to develop into substantial categories of anime in their own rights. Anime fans are more creative than the debates about fansubbing allow. Anime Music Videos (AMVs) have, for example, become a new field of anime fan production in recent years. Lev Manovich (2009) notes that these fan pro-sumers see themselves more as editors than filmmakers, using digital software to re-edit anime texts against a new sonic backdrop, usually rock or popular songs. The combination of these two genres—music videos and anime—presents a distinctively different tradition of fan production to fans' translation and subtitling activities. In AMVs, fan pro-sumers interpret moods, restage battle and action sequences or parody anime content by refracting anime texts through new, usually non-Japanese music. This new genre has been building in popularity with Condry noting the rising inclusion of AMV competitions at fan conventions (2013, see also http://www.anime-expo.org/schedule/amv-contest/), and with AMVs now warranting their own fan community websites.

Fans' creativity is dispersing across multiple digital media formats and is likely to continue to bring new genres and new interpretations of anime texts as they are reversioned by fan pro-sumers. A particularly notable example of live-action fan adaptation has emerged with the Thousand Pounds Action Company, an independent company of stunt people and martial artists in California who make live-action short films based on fan favorites like *Naruto* (Green 2012). Their work may not extend the genres of anime, nor do they pay attention to the rights of original copyright holders, but this company's attempts to engage anime fans is an indication of how powerful a gatekeeping force anime fans have become within wider US fan cultures.

In another version of creative adaptation, OtaKing77077 has posted a two-minute short anime version of *Star Wars* (George Lucas, 1977), featuring an impressive space battle akin to the best of early television anime (http://www.youtube.com/user/OtaKing77077). These kinds of creativity have become more available to fans in the digital age, with everything from cameras to computer editing software enabling the emergence of new kinds of creative voices. Many anime scholars are pointing to the home production of anime, especially that of Makoto Shinkai, as a new wave of anime fan-turned-producer (LaMarre 2009), following in the wake of the earlier Gainax company, itself begun as a product of fan production and creative work (Clements 2013a). In these examples of fans-turned-producers, we can see a breaking down of the barriers between production and reception, and the emergence of more fluid anime cultures, thanks to digital technologies.

This is clear from the way the transnational anime industry has been developing online. Simulcasting, or near-simultaneous broadcasting, of anime in Japan and the USA has been the most common response to speed subbing activities by fans. While in Japan the broadcasts remain part of television schedules, in the USA these simulcasts happen online. FUNimation, for example, one of the most influential US anime distributors, launched its own online television channel in 2005 (Anime News Network 2005), adding mobile phone access in 2008 and high-definition anime streaming in 2010 as a means to keep pace with rapidly shifting new media distribution technologies (Anime News Network 2008a, 2010). FUNimation also has deals with online streaming websites like Hulu, archiving box-sets of anime for US fans. However, it also streamed some of its most popular anime direct through its own website, with mixed results.

One Piece, a huge franchise in Japan, was a particularly ironic problem for FUNimation as this anime about pirates was itself pirated:

> As anime fans know, *FUNimation Entertainment* and *Toei Animation* had planned for the first ever online *simulcast* of the series "*One Piece*" tonight at 9:00 pm CDT., just one hour after its premiere on Japan's *Fuji Television*. Unfortunately, in the last 24 hours we have determined that the *FUNimation* servers were compromised, even though we employ strict security standards. An unknown individual accessed and posted episode 403 online and as a direct result of this illegal act, all U.S. and Canadian fans will be deprived of access to this great anime series for the immediate future. We will make every effort to locate and prosecute the perpetrator(s) to the fullest extent of the law and will provide updates regarding this most serious matter. (Quoted in Anime News Network 2009)

To be clear, the hacking of FUNimation's servers goes well beyond the capabilities, interests and practices of most fan subtitlers. The language used by FUNimation is significant, though, for the paternalistic way it positions the company. Its withdrawal of services to legitimate consumers is, on the surface, used as a means of disciplining the fan community for the actions of a rogue few. However, the underlying reason for FUNimation's paternalistic response and language more likely lies in something they do not comment upon—the downloads of the illegally obtained episode 403 by large numbers of "ordinary" fans online.

Nevertheless, the anime distribution market has shifted with the introduction of simulcasting, moving away from digital downloads and toward the more ephemeral markets of "streaming" distribution. Streaming websites use client software to deliver videos to computers in compressed packets, enabling a continual "stream" of sound and images to be unpacked on users' screens. These video streams are not automatically archived on users' computers, making them reliant on the centrally held anime archives on the streaming providers' websites. Within the realms of anime, the most significant such website to emerge has been Crunchyroll.

Officially formed in 2006, Crunchyroll was initially a shadow market fansub-linking website that did not contain formally distributed texts. Its founders sought, and got, venture capital from the Venrock group, gaining an initial investment of around $4 million, before being bought out by the Chernin group for nearly $100 million in 2013 (Spangler 2013). This investment has allowed Crunchyroll to become one of only a few success stories in digital anime distribution, gaining the support of most of Japan's top animation studios and dominating the online market for simulcasting and box-set-style streaming distribution of contemporary anime texts. Crunchyroll's success has come through a mixed economy of subscriptions, now in excess of 200,000 members (Anime News Network 2013), and ad-supported streaming of anime television shows, thereby managing to monetize even those unwilling to pay for their services. In an interview, one of Crunchyroll's co-founders, Vu Nguyen, states that "Bringing content that's not easily accessible in the US using traditional media sources" was their main aim, placing the expansion of anime's genres at the heart of Crunchyroll's purpose (Bertschy 2008b).

Their system for organizing genres is perhaps surprising, but also representative of the kinds of permissive generic landscape developing online. Within the fifteen categories of anime listed, only five are given Japanese labels, among them *ecchi* ("H," or *hentai*, see Chapter 3) and *seinen* (which is translated as "mature" by the website) alongside the more established *mecha*, *shōnen* and *shōjo* groupings. Many of these texts are cross-listed in multiple categories, for example the *ecchi* show *Dragon Crisis* (*Doragun Kuraishisu!* 2011) can also be found under *shōnen*, action, romance and fantasy. While this cross-listing makes sense in terms of attracting audiences, the variance in the listings for *Dragon Crisis!*, a show that follows protagonist Ryūji Kisaragi's adventures with a magical girl and his second cousin Eriko, also demonstrates the genre mixing found at the heart of most anime texts. This show may be *ecchi* and have romance elements, but it is nonetheless classified on the masculine side of the adventure and fantasy genres by its inclusion within the *shōnen* category.

Perhaps more important for this chapter are the inclusions of genres that have emerged, largely thanks to online distribution. For example, Crunchyroll now lists nearly twenty "sports" anime that include *Prince of Tennis* (*Tenisu no Ōjisama*, 2001–2005), as well as Kyoto Animation's popular swimming drama, *Free!—Iwatobi Swim Club* (*Furī*, 2013, second season 2014) which Crunchyroll simulcast with Japan. In popularizing this long-popular local Japanese genre of anime sports dramas, Crunchyroll has expanded upon the scant distribution that this genre previously received on VHS and DVD.

Likewise, Crunchyroll has adopted the label "slice of life" to describe over fifty of the titles it carries. Although these titles cross between genres, they are a far cry from the kinds of genres discussed in this book up to now. For example, at one end they include the vignette show *Kaasan—Mom's Life* (*Mainichi Kaasan*, 2009–2012) and Madhouse Animation's short five-minute episode series of kitten drama *Chi's Sweet Home* (2008 and 2009). At perhaps the other end, there is *Peeping Life* (2009–), a series of rotoscoped 3D CG anime shorts that cover humorous aspects of everyday Japanese life. In between these aesthetic extremes are anime that cover a wide range of topics, from brothers who want to go into space (*Space Brothers, Uchū Kyōdai*, 2012–2014), to fantasies like *Natsume's Book of Friends* (*Natsume Yūjinchō*, 2008, 2009, 2011, 2012) through to a variety of anime about young girls working everywhere from hot springs (*Hanasaku Iroha*) through to cafes (*Wagnaria!, Working!!*, 2010, 2011) to myriad stories about school girls including popular titles like *Hayate the Combat Butler* (*Hayate no Gotoku!*, 2008–). The range of these texts indicates the porousness of the slice of life genre, and also the way it is used to model any number of anime that relate stories about everything from cute animals to high concept fantasies that happen to feature aspects of everyday Japanese life. As a catch-all for new kinds of anime, and particularly offshoots of the *shōjo* meta-genre, the slice of life genre presents a puzzle for uniform processes of genrification.

Slice of the everyday: The reformulation of "slice of life" as "*nichijōkei*" anime in Japan

It is for this reason that I turn now to a particular slippage between the idea of "slice of life" and a roughly approximate Japanese genre term, *nichijōkei* anime. In the UK, the release of a hit from Japan called *K'On!* (*Keion!* 2009, 2010 with a film in 2011 and several OVAs) was met with consensus about this text belonging to the slice of life genre. For example, *Neo* magazine proclaimed that its range of school girl protagonists shows "the durability of these character types, especially in a slice of life show such as this" (2011, 62). Within Japan, however, these school girl musicians were the focus of a massive hit franchise based on a newly emergent genre critically recognized as *nichijōkei* anime.

The reason for this slippage can be located in Japanese critical attempts to recapture this genre as a new form of local anime production. Motoko Tanaka, for example, has been among those reading the *nichijōkei* genre as an offshoot of recent literary trends in Japan that have shifted focus from outward-looking perspectives (positive and nihilistic) toward a focus on inner, everyday aspects of Japanese life (2014), from the *mukokuseki* (stateless) and *sekaikei* (though not a direct translation, the meaning aligns with the concept of world-in-peril stories) to the *nichijōkei*. This section charts some of these categories in relation to debates about anime's recent history before moving on to examine how technologies and digital distribution have aligned with the emergence of *nichijōkei* texts, taking *K'On!* as a case study.

As a representational medium, with no necessary links to indexical realism, most authors writing about anime have tended to focus on its penchant for outlandish, even otherworldly, imagery. Susan J. Napier, quoting animator Mamoru Oshii, opens her first book analyzing anime with a discussion of anime's global or *mukokuseki* potential, its potential to cross borders becoming essentially stateless (Napier, 26). Napier takes this to mean that anime provides "a realm that exists in counterpoint to modern Japan" that creates in anime "a site of resistance to the conformity of Japanese society" (26). Koichi Iwabuchi takes this a stage further than Napier and asks about the *mukokuseki*,

> If it is indeed the case that the Japaneseness of Japanese animation derives…from its erasure of physical signs of Japaneseness, is not the Japan that Western audiences are at long last coming to appreciate, and even yearn for, an animated, race-less and culture-less, virtual version of Japan? (33)

Anime, in these accounts, thereby becomes a site for the denial of Japaneseness, presumably then also of the everyday structures underpinning Japanese cultural practices and society. What to think, then, when anime commentators in Japan start to declare the existence of a new genre about the everyday aspects of Japanese life?

Nichijōkei are, by contrast to the *mukokuseki*, texts about life that are more ordinary than ordinary (Kinema Junpō 2011). The researchers of the "*Nichijōkei Anime*": *The Theory of Hits* ("*Nichijōkei Anime*": *Hitto no Hōsoku)* book explain the emergence of *nichijōkei* texts using past precursors like the long-running *Sazae-san* (1969–), *Crayon Shin-chan* (1992–) and *Chibi Maruko-chan* (1990–1992, 1995–). This genealogical approach to the *nichijōkei* genre's history in anime enables a set of propositions that set out how the local and everyday have come to manifest in this genre. The ordinariness of *nichijōkei* texts is often alluded to elsewhere as part of a "healing" (*iyashikei*) trend in Japan, for example, seen in the inward looking, gentle progression of time in *nichijōkei* anime. "In the *nichijōkei* manga, time passes slowly and that fact makes the audience feel the link with their real lives" (Kinema Junpō 2011, 105). Aging characters in *nichijōkei* are thereby seen as a sign of the shift in genres between precursors like the ageless Sazae-san, Maruko-chan and Shin-chan, and the *nichijōkei*'s new group of school girl heroines.

However, recognition of *nichijōkei* anime as a genre is still developing in Japan. In an interview, Murakami, an employee of the Animate anime retail company, Japan's largest manga and anime chain, claims that,

I became aware of it when I knew about *Lucky Star*. But looking back on it, there was already *Azumanga Daioh* [anime TV series 2002] and *Strawberry Marshmallow* [2003–2005]. Because it wasn't a genre yet, I only considered *Strawberry Marshmallow* as *Strawberry Marshmallow*. However, *K-ON!* followed *Lucky Star* [2007] and similar manga have become popular, then I thought there might be a genre of these manga. The word *nichijōkei* appeared only a couple years ago. If I think back, the first work was *Azumanga Daioh*. (*Screen Plus*, 20–21, trans. Hiroko Furukawa)

Here, the professed lack of clarity from this employee-fan clearly signals that these "everyday" anime have yet to become entirely commonplace, and that their categorization as *nichijōkei* remains fraught.

The heroines of anime like *Lucky Star* and *K'On!* are important for other reasons, though. Several authors proclaim a link between these *nichijōkei* anime and the concept of *moe*. The Kinema Junpō research group argues that "*Nichijōkei* can be defined as a category for works which describe everyday events of pretty girls who makes the audience feel '*moe*'" (2011, 31, trans. Hiroko Furukawa). This chimes with claims in a special issue of *Screen Plus* magazine that focused on the *K'On!* film (Naoko Yamada, 2011), wherein a book store employee from Akihabara says in interview that

Nichijōkei manga are for young readers and it is certain that they have an aspect of *moe*. There are pretty girls and although there isn't a deep story, like something interesting happening,... Almost all of the main characters are girls. (Takashi Matsumaru quoted in *Screen Plus* 2011, 18, trans. Hiroko Furukawa)

The concept of *moe* is here located in *bishōjo* or pretty girl characters. Patrick Galbraith suggests that *moe* is relatively recent: "In the 1990s, the word appeared on the bulletin board website 2channel in discussion of young, cute and innocent anime girls, and a burning passion for them" (2009). Tanaka argues that these *nichijōkei* shows reject the male teen protagonists of the *sekaikei* genre of nihilistic science fiction in favor of female-centered shows to engender affect on the part of male *otaku* consumers. She claims that this "is because they [male characters] would be a distraction for male *otaku* consumers who have *moe* feelings for the beautiful girls and wish purely to 'possess' them rather than to fall in love with them" (2014). In this regard, therefore, *nichijōkei*'s generic content is closely linked to its original context of consumption.

Moe, however, is an expansive term. In Japan, it is used to describe everything from *ero*-video game productions, where the female characters are intended to be sexually desired by *otaku* consumers (Galbraith 2009), to Koto Toguchi's review of *nichijōkei* for *Screen Plus* magazine, where it is claimed that *moe* is "like a relationship between a pet and its owner. The feeling is like that of the owner who sees the pet playing happily" (2011, 25, trans. Hiroko Furukawa). This latter definition accords with recent English-language work on *moe* by Michael R. Bowman, wherein he links *moe* to *kawaisa* or cute cultures and sees it as an audience response to the "concentrated appeal" (2011, 18) of characters. By linking the fetishization of these school girl characters with the everyday cultures of Japanese schoolgirls, these *nichijōkei* texts are seen as making their content "safe" for consumption by cross-gender, multigenerational audiences. More importantly, however, these accounts suggest that the *moe* attributes of these characters are included specifically to ensure the adoption of texts by gatekeeper fans in Japan.

The extreme fetishization of the ordinary within the girls' relationships with one another thereby becomes a way to offset the transgressive potential of these *nichijōkei* texts: by making these representations feed into a mythos about pets and ownership, the discourse frames the older male audience for these texts as less problematic. Jonathan Clements declares that this explains the perfecting of reality featured in *nichijōkei* texts:

> "Mundane" anime drama has none of the overcast skies or compromised shooting schedules of live-action television. Its sunsets are always beautiful; its scenery always quintessentially seasonal; its framing always perfect. Even in its quest for realism, it renders the everyday hyperreal. (2013a, 201)

In the fetishizing of the everyday, from relationships to environments, the everyday itself becomes unnaturally perfect in these accounts. The local success of *nichijōkei* texts is thereby attributed to everything from *moe* character facets to the beauty of backdrops that used to define the new genre through a sense of the everyday that is more ordinary than ordinary.

Additionally, the recognition of this genre by local commentators in Japan comes from industry, because *nichijōkei* anime are big business in Japan and not just niche-oriented texts. *Nichijōkei* anime texts form part of a wider multimedia network of production. When they are successful, as in the case of *K'On!*, they become the central intellectual property at the heart of a widespread cultural phenomenon. A *Nikkei Entertainment* article struggles to "solve" the question of *K'On!*'s success, proclaiming that "it developed into a 'social phenomenon' with crazy sales of products from Blu-ray and CDs, to merchandising, and of things used by the characters in the show" (Kanai 2011, 23). Viewed through an industrial lens, then, the *nichijōkei* genre is not, as other commentators have claimed, simply a progression from generic precursors like *Crayon Shin-chan*. It is also borne out of industrial precursor hits like *The Melancholy of Haruhi Suzumiya* (*Suzumiya Haruhi no Yūutsu*, 2006–2009), which was Kyoto Animation's first big hit series from 2006 before it began producing *nichijōkei* titles including *Lucky Star* and *K'On!*

Conclusion

Japanese commentators were careful to link the new *nichijōkei* genre of anime to new media technologies. The *Kinema Junpō* group, for example, argue that *Lucky Star*'s success in anime was due to its informal distribution on video sharing websites (2011, 90). Further, they claim that

> Originally, anime fans and PC users had closely layered practices and from this kind of exchange anime fan sites were established and that timing, out of which a movement arose, was consistent with the period around 2002 and 2004 when blogs themselves became popular. This also overlaps with the period in which the *Azumanga Daioh* television anime broadcasts began. (85)

Suggestive overlaps and assertions of the impact of new technologies thereby closely associate the rising *nichijōkei* genre of anime with a new media-savvy group of fans who had the power to spread digital versions of *Lucky Star* and other *nichijōkei* across their globalizing informal distribution networks.

The rise of this new genre in Japan is reported as being a product of the "new" genre's reliance on anime history and domestic anime production contexts. It is the multitude of attendant goods, special events, musical tie-ups and franchised production that allowed texts like *K'On!* to cross between media empires and what *Nikkei Entertainment* proclaims are genuine "social phenomena" (2011, 23). Without that context, and with the wider context of recent genre developments in fields like Japanese literature, the *nichijōkei* genre's apparent newness recedes until it becomes merely another kind of slice of life anime within the transnational markets for anime online. Paying attention to cross-cultural contexts is therefore important if we want to understand the fast-moving worlds of genre in anime's digital era.

7

Ghibli Genre: Toshio Suzuki and Studio Ghibli's Brand Identity

Studio Ghibli has become one of the world's most recognizable animation brands. In Japan, its films are routinely the biggest of box-office hits, and any film by its most famous filmmaker, Hayao Miyazaki, is likely to garner record-breaking audiences and box-office takings that exceed $100 million. Studio Ghibli's films have also been among anime's most successful exports, thanks to a deal that has seen the Disney conglomerate releasing Miyazaki's films on America's cinema screens. But "Studio Ghibli" means different things depending on the context in which its works are being consumed. Most notably, the extent of Studio Ghibli's brand is observably different within and outside of Japan. This chapter questions how Studio Ghibli's meanings are carried through its brand identity and who communicates that brand.

In doing so, the relationship between genres and brands within animation is interrogated, and the shifting meanings of Studio Ghibli are considered in relation to the tensions between facets of proprietary branding and generic elements of production. This investigation is carried out by analyzing the discourses circulating around Studio Ghibli's US and domestic Japanese brand identities (following Grainge 2008 and Mittell 2004). Paul Grainge argues that:

If contemporary cinema is defined by the migration of texts across media, branding has become central to the analysis of films' extended commercial environment, as well as to the space created through, and in relation to, the cultural lexicon of film. (Grainge 2008, 11)

I argue in this chapter that the Studio Ghibli brand has been created and managed by one of the Studio's three founding partners: Toshio Suzuki. Though Suzuki has been rather eclipsed by his more famous partners, film directors Hayao Miyazaki and Isao Takahata, I want to argue that he has been instrumental in deciding the content of Ghibli's films, and in the creation of Studio Ghibli as Japan's most successful animation studio. Consequently, I attempt to understand Suzuki's creation of Studio Ghibli as a distinctive brand presence within Japan's complex anime marketplace through an analysis of the Studio's extended commercial environment.

US animation and branded genres: The shifting meanings of "Studio Ghibli"

Brands are often held at the opposite end of an industrial spectrum from genres, as when Rick Altman argues that:

> Hollywood's stock-in-trade is the romantic combination of genres, not the classical practice of genre purity. In one sense, this is hardly surprising; by definition, genres are broad *public* categories shared across the entire industry, and Hollywood studios have little interest in anything that must be shared with their competitors. On the contrary, they are primarily concerned to create cycles of films that will be identified with only a single studio. (1999, 59 emphasis in original)

Altman divorces genres (public categories) from brands (in the guise of proprietary film cycles). In doing so, he separates out popular film franchises, with their famous characters, stars and directors, from the wider cultural categories into which those "owned" entities might be placed. It is interesting to note, however, that Altman does not include Hollywood's animated films in his discussion.

Animation is often left out of discussions of Hollywood genres, not least because it has been industrially and ideologically dominated by the productions of only a handful of companies. US animation studios, principally Disney, but, to a lesser extent, studios like Warner Brothers, Pixar and DreamWorks, have come to define US animation. Their proprietary film cycles so dominate the market for feature film animation in the USA that they offer an alternative to the concept of subgenres: proprietary or branded subgenres. Disney offers the most obvious example with films, television channels, theme parks and merchandising, creating a brand network in which films act as a nexus point in promotional and consumption activities (deCordorva 1994; Langer 1992; Wasko 2002). Writing in 1997, animation scholar Philip Kelly Denslow contends that "In Hollywood, marketing or thinking about a film as animation automatically throws it into the sphere of influence of the Walt Disney Company" (2). Writing before the expansion of computer-generated (CG) animation films, Denslow sees Disney animation as coeval with the US animation market. While this may go a step too far (Disney has always had competition), the assertion that a studio brand might operate as a shorthand for the dominant type of animation within the US market lends weight to the idea that studio brands organize the "genrifcation process" (Altman 1999) in US animation.

Kevin S. Sandler's introduction to *Reading the Rabbit: Explorations in Warner Bros. Animation* (1998) also explores the way animation brands compete within the US market. Sandler situates this difference in aesthetic terms, arguing that "While the Fleischer brothers filled the frame with the fantastic and the impossible, and Disney saturated the screen with sentimentality and hyperrealism, Warner Bros.... dealt in a zany universe somewhere between the two extremes" (6). The competition between these house styles of animation, each with its own unique production milieu and aesthetic, has led to conceptualizations of US animation as filled not with subgenres, but with brands competing to dominate a broadly defined "family" animation genre. Consequently, the company brands operating within this market are fiercely protective of their meanings and spaces, often absorbing competitors through partnerships and conglomeration practices (Grainge 2008). As a result, US animation brands come to own swathes of production with shared meanings, in line with the way subgenres have absorbed ever-new proprietary film production cycles.

Studio Ghibli has begun to take on branded subgenre associations as a part of the US animation market. Famously partnered with Disney as its US distributor in 1996, Studio Ghibli's films have been repackaged for the US market through a layered understanding of brand meanings.[1] This layering is revealed in the complex brand associations forged between the Disney conglomerate and Studio Ghibli's films. While Studio Ghibli's highest profile US releases have come to audiences directly through Disney's core brand, Ghibli's more challenging films have been shunted into Disney's peripheral brand spaces. For example, the theatrical release of *Princess Mononoke* (*Mononokehime*, 1996) was orchestrated through Disney art house subsidiary Miramax (for more on Miramax in this period, see Perren 2012). More recently, too, Hayao Miyazaki's *The Wind Rises* (*Kaze tachinu*, 2014) was released through Disney's Touchstone Pictures.

However, when Disney has been directly responsible for releasing Studio Ghibli's films in the USA, reviewers have been quick to examine the relationship between the studios. Claudia Puig, in *USA Today*, for example, compares the studios to Disney's detriment:

> Even though Disney released this film, *Spirited Away* points up just how by-the-numbers the studio's [Disney's] fare can be. But perhaps most striking is the way this fanciful tale creates an alternate reality along the lines of a vivid childhood dream or a detailed rendering of a classic fairy tale. (2002)

Here Puig argues that Studio Ghibli's *Spirited Away* has co-opted the branded animation space traditionally occupied by Disney, and that in doing so Ghibli's film reveals a loss of creativity within the US studio. The juxtaposition of animation brands may not work well for Disney in this instance, but it does reveal a commingling of Studio Ghibli and Disney's brand meanings, and the beginnings of a Studio Ghibli brand of animation in the USA.

Hayao Miyazaki was crucial to this new branded subgenre around Studio Ghibli in the USA, particularly as the Disney conglomerate sought to build up a new brand-genre complex around Studio Ghibli's films. From the first Miramax-produced trailer for *Princess Mononoke*, claims were made about Hayao Miyazaki being a "master animator" and subsequent trailers continued this pattern. For *Howl's Moving Castle* (*Haoru no Ugoku Shiro*, 2004), for example, Miyazaki was labeled a "master filmmaker" and an Academy Award winner. This award has since become an integral part of Miyazaki's brandname status in the USA. When *Spirited Away* won the Academy Award for Best Animated Feature, Disney posted a full-page congratulatory advertisement in US trade journal *Variety* (2003) saying, "The Walt Disney Studios thanks the Academy of Motion Pictures Arts & Sciences and proudly congratulates Academy Award winner Hayao Miyazaki" emphasizing their own connections with Miyazaki's rising directorial star. Disney thereby worked to create a layered set of brand associations with Ghibli's films. *Spirited Away*'s main US poster reads "Walt Disney Studios Presents" above a strap line saying, "A Studio Ghibli Film" included above the title: "Miyazaki's *Spirited Away*" (2003, 5), blending together Disney, Ghibli and Miyazaki to create a layered brand.

The success of Disney's branding campaign can be seen when reviewers conflate Miyazaki's name with particular kinds of animation. For instance, *Time* magazine's Richard Corliss compares animation studio styles in his review of *Spirited Away* saying,

> The animation here doesn't boast the meticulously rendered character expressions of the early Disney features. Nor does it go for the slam-bang effects of Shrek and the other canny computerized cartoons that have

dominated the box office. Instead, Miyazaki goes for—and gets—the big picture, the grand emotion, one spectacular set piece stacked on another in brilliant colors and design. (2002)

Elsewhere, critics connect these spectacular set pieces with the fantasy genre. For example, Joe Morgenstern of the *Wall Street Journal* reviews *Spirited Away* claiming,

> Classic fantasies—and "Spirited Away" is bound to become one—often have themes that grown-ups can point to and say, Look, this stuff is worthy because it teaches a lesson … . But I don't want to dwell on didactics here, even though "Spirited Away" has much to say about many worthy things: the life of the spirit, materialist greed, the importance of words, the power of love. The most important thing about this film is its explosively exuberant invention—startling images and stunning designs. (2002)

In these ways, Miyazaki's brandname comes to take in aspects of genres familiar to US audiences, from fairytales to fantasy, but these claims are usually offered alongside ones about the uniqueness of his animation's spectacle and visual design.

The sense of a branded subgenre of Studio Ghibli animation is usually aligned with Miyazaki, but it does extend beyond his films. For example, reviewers of *Tales from Earthsea* (*Gedo Senki*, 2006), directed by Hayao Miyazaki's son Gorō Miyazaki, found fault with *Earthsea* through internal comparisons of Studio Ghibli's films claiming that "Other scenes are surprisingly empty for a Ghibli film. The animation is a step and a half less fluid than Hayao Miyazaki's most recent film, 'Ponyo'" (Hartlaub, 2010) and, "The layouts have the striking look one associates with Studio Ghibli productions but the character drawings are dull and inexpressive" (Honeycutt, 2010). Likewise, lesser releases, such as that undertaken for *The Cat Returns* (*Neko no Ongaeshi*, Hiroyuki Morita, 2002), bounce branding discourses back and forth between the Studio and its most famous director, as when Lisa Nesselson writes, "Animated by Hiroyuki Morita—a protege of Hayao Miyazaki—story draws more from fairy tales than the eerie transformative productions by Studio Ghibli" (2003). Here, Morita's legitimacy is conferred by Miyazaki, and perceived shortfalls emerge out of comparisons between *The Cat Returns* and the Studio's wider oeuvre, suggesting an extension of the Studio Ghibli brand beyond Miyazaki and into the realms of a wider branded subgenre.

However, the status of the branded subgenre of Studio Ghibli animation is perhaps most clearly outlined in relation to what has been widely reported to be Hayao Miyazaki's final film, *The Wind Rises* (*Kaze Tachinu*, 2014). At that moment, the meanings of Studio Ghibli and Miyazaki were eulogized by reviewers, leading Ann Hornaday to reflect on the brand of animation now represented by Studio Ghibli in the US marketplace:

That 1997 movie [*Princess Mononoke*] was the first time many American filmgoers entered Miyazaki's world of myth, magic and lyrical, finely detailed imagery; happily, there are now generations of children who have grown up cherishing such Miyazaki classics as "My Neighbor Totoro," "Kiki's Delivery Service," "Spirited Away" and "Howl's Moving Castle" the way their parents played and re-played "Snow White," "101 Dalmatians" and "The Aristocats." (2014)

Ghiblis: The Studio Ghibli brand in Japan

The "myth, magic and lyrical, finely detailed imagery" attributed to Miyazaki and Studio Ghibli has become so well known that references to its branded subgenre of animation are appearing within wider media commentary on animation. In one recent example, in a promotional article about Dean DeBlois' *How to Train Your Dragon 2* (2014), Ali Plumb writes that "Unlike Pixar or, say, Studio Ghibli, DreamWorks has no hard-and-fast house style" (2014, 78). Studio Ghibli's house style, its consistent aesthetic, has come, as a consequence of comments like these, to represent a specific kind of branded subgenre in animation criticism. In a further example, discussing the recent release of Paul Grimault's *The King and the Mockingbird* (completed in 1980) the same issue of *Empire* magazine states, "There's beautiful visual and verbal comedy, and the film has the creative spontaneity of a dream, foreshadowing Spirited Away (it influenced Miyazaki)" (Osmond 2014). With uncannily similar phrasing, *Total Film*'s review of *The King and The Mockingbird* also claims that "Hayao Miyazaki cites it as a major influence, and fans of Studio Ghibli will thrill to the tenderly explored themes—class, nature, love, grief—and poetic, witty visuals" (Graham 2014). In these comments, a rich intertextual chain of influence is woven between Japanese and French animation history. But what these comments do not reveal is a more recent *industrial* connection forged between Paul Grimault's film and Studio Ghibli.

Studio Ghibli's Japanese language website made the link between Grimault's film and Studio Ghibli clear when it announced a new line of world animation DVDs for the Japanese market (in conjunction with Walt Disney Studios Home Entertainment). This new sub-brand of Studio Ghibli merchandise would extend the Studio's meanings to take in films:

that have left an impression on Takahata and Miyazaki, including recommended works of the past and a selection of works from around the world. This project was a response to the box office success of Paul Grimault's *The King and the Mockingbird*, which we released last year. (http://www.ghibli.jp/30profile/000152.html)

The influence is thus reciprocal: Miyazaki and his Studio may well have been influenced by Grimault's animated work, but so too has *The King and the Mockingbird* now received a new lease of life, thanks to Japan's most powerful animation studio. In this way, Studio Ghibli's animation brand is beginning to echo the practices of the USA's biggest animation conglomerates, buying up what it sees as similar texts and incorporating them under its umbrella to extend its brand meanings. This sort of practice may be the future of Studio Ghibli, following Toshio Suzuki's recent declaration that Ghibli will cease feature animation production in 2014 (Anime News Network, 2014a).

Studio Ghibli's expansion into distribution indicates the heightened presence of the Studio Ghibli brand in Japan's crowded anime mediascape (see Chapter 8). Unlike the USA, where powerful animation brands stand in the place of subgenres, anime has diversified into a vast multigeneric landscape in its home market (see Chapters 2, 3 and 9). In Japan, therefore, Studio Ghibli's brand needs to be understood in relation to a different discussion of animation and genre. Consequently, the sections that follow focus on the work of Toshio Suzuki at Studio Ghibli, and his attempts to create and expand Studio Ghibli's brand meanings over the course of his near thirty-year tenure at the Studio. Studio Ghibli has been remarkably open about its branding and production practices, publishing books on its advertising, (auto-) biographies of leading company members, and publishing its own history in a range of formats, alongside cinema pamphlets produced for film releases and the statements made to Japan's specialist film press about the growth and activities of the Studio. I mine these sources hereafter to help capture a sense of what Studio Ghibli means in Japan.

Studio Ghibli's official Japanese histories reveal a complex, intertextual and diversified brand presence. It would be more proper, for example, to refer to the *Studios* Ghibli, as its official website reveals the existence of several animation production houses incorporated under the brand, including one announced in 2014 called "Ghibli West" in Toyota, in Aichi Prefecture (Studio Ghibli 2009). Moreover, not all of these studios are housed directly under the "Ghibli" brand:

Separate to Studio Ghibli we have established a brand called "Studio Kajino" in order to do live action; and, up to now, we have done production and distribution for Hideaki Anno's live action film *Shiki-jitsu* (2000), and have helped by participating in the overseas distribution of Katsuyuki Motohiro's work *Satorare* (2001). (Studio Ghibli n.d.)

Studio Kajino, led by animator Yoshiyuki Momose (who directed the experimental short *Ghiblies 2, Giburīsu 2*, 2002,[2] distributed as a double bill with *The Cat Returns* in Japan), has produced live-action films and CG-animated music videos, extending the Studio Ghibli brand in new directions. Studio Ghibli is thus a broader industrial presence in Japan than its "handcrafted" animation discourse in the USA might suggest.

The array of sub-brands operating around the core brand of Studio Ghibli makes an aesthetic identification of the brand even more difficult. Figure 7.1 is an attempt to map the more significant sub-brands operating under the core brand of "Studio Ghibli" in Japan. As it shows, beneath the layer of film production and consumption, Studio Ghibli has developed several ancillary brands, each of which feeds back into the core meanings of the Studio. Studio Ghibli has developed a series of distinctive logos to represent its core and subsidiary brands, perhaps most famously an image of Totoro from *My Neighbour Totoro* (*Tonari no Totoro*, Miyazaki, 1988) drawn on a blue background in a manner reminiscent of Disney's famous

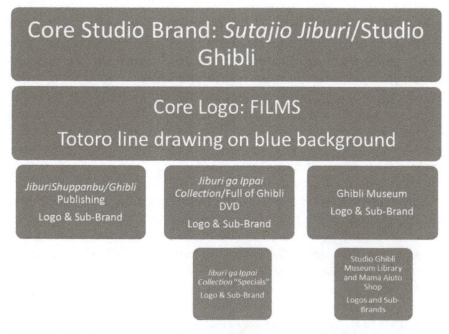

FIGURE 7.1 *Representation of the brand hierarchy at Studio Ghibli in Japan.*

logo. This logo has become a standard part of Studio Ghibli's web presence, its newspaper advertising and it now graces the beginning of each Studio Ghibli film release, helping to expand Totoro's meanings from a character into a brand icon.

However, for home video and DVD, this Totoro logo is framed by another—the *Jiburi ga Ippai Collection* logo. This logo marks the movement of the Studio into the realms of distribution, and by retaining the DVD rights to the Japanese market, Ghibli has been able to retain control over the presentation of their films to the public in Japan. This logo, with its natural, woodland iconography, borrowed again from *My Neighbour Totoro*, draws attention to other core facets of the Studio's brand—its projected interests in environmentalism and its reputation for producing beautiful animation of natural phenomena like rain, wind and forests.

While Studio Ghibli's high-profile animated feature films remain crucial to the company's cultural presence in Japan, its productions are broader than this suggests. For example, Hayao Miyazaki and other animators have made short films shown exclusively at the Studio Ghibli Art Museum in Mitaka, and the DVD label *Full of Ghibli: Specials* (*Jiburi ga Ippai Collection: Supesharu*) acts as another distribution sub-brand of Studio Ghibli's *Jiburi ga Ippai Collection* label, releasing behind-the-scenes informational DVDs and other ancillary Studio Ghibli products (Figure 7.1). This includes a DVD titled *Short Short* (*Shōto Shōto*, 2005). *Short Short* offers insight into Ghibli's branding work for *other* Japanese companies, offering a compilation of the Studio's television advertisements, channel idents and music video productions up to 2005, made for a wide range of Japanese clients. Far from being a studio with a recognizable "house style" in Japan then, Studio Ghibli's aesthetic meanings reach across the history of world animation and across the creative spectrum from CG animation to live-action filmmaking. Through ancillary filmmaking and distribution, Studio Ghibli's Japanese brand extends far beyond anime feature filmmaking too, offering "special" content to local fan-collectors and to those able to experience physical branded spaces like its specialist retail outlets and Art Museum (Denison 2010).

The Studio Ghibli Art Museum, situated within the Inokashira Park in Mitaka, close to Tokyo, acts as a collation of Studio Ghibli's brand meanings and activities. The museum's park location speaks to the Studio's longstanding interest in environmental themes, seen in films like *Princess Mononoke* and *Pom Poko* (*Heisei Tanuki Gassen Pom Poko*, 1994), but also to Ghibli's emphasis on local partnerships. The Art Museum was built by a collective called "The Tokuma Memorial Cultural Foundation for Animation" comprised of Ghibli's then parent company Tokuma Publishing, the NTV network, Miyazaki and Takahata and, perhaps more unusually, Mitaka City. The building project itself became the work of another sub-brand of Studio Ghibli, originally called

"Museo D'Arte Ghibli Co., Ltd." before being renamed for the in-museum shop it runs, "Mamma Auito Co., Ltd."[3] These changes in the Studio's sub-brands and its collaborations show how insistently *local* Studio Ghibli's brand identity can be, making connections to local cities as well as local media cultures. It also suggests a fundamentally complex brand networking and collaboration system at the heart of Japanese popular culture production.

Contrary to the complexities of its creation, the finished product of the Studio Ghibli Art Museum tells a different story, one of emphatically (albeit whimsically) branded space. The Art Museum operates as a collection of Studio Ghibli's brand activities, offering a physical hub through which dominant aspects of the Studio's various sub-brands can be explored. Built from designs by Hayao Miyazaki, the Art Museum was created to the specifications of, and manifesto by, Studio Ghibli's star director. This manifesto was translated into English for a museum guidebook in 2007, in which Miyazaki proclaims:

> The displays will be …
>> Not only for the benefit of people who are already fans of Studio Ghibli
>> Not a procession of artwork from past Ghibli films as if it were "a museum of the past"
>> A place where visitors can enjoy by just looking, can understand the artists' spirits, and can gain new insights into animation
>> Original works and pictures will be made to be exhibited at the museum
>> A projection room and an exhibit room will be made, showing movement and life
>> (Original short films will be produced to be released in the museum!)
>> Ghibli's past films will be probed for understanding at a deeper level
>
> (HAYAO MIYAZAKI, quoted in Tsukue and Tamura 2007, 1–2)

The brand ambition is clear: Miyazaki's desire to make the museum a living space for housing Ghibli's growing cultural meanings can be seen in the bespoke films, in his desire to investigate the Studio's past and to connect his Studio to the wider world of animation. As Figure 7.1 illustrates, the Studio Ghibli Art Museum brand has expanded the Studio's remit, taking in new publishing and retail elements in addition to the branded spaces afforded by the museum itself.

Perhaps more significantly, the Art Museum has incorporated Miyazaki's manifesto through the creation of spaces that nostalgically celebrate and extend Studio Ghibli's history within world animation culture. While not "a museum of the past," the Art Museum's "Beginnings of Movement Room" (*Ugoki Hajime no Heya*) offers a permanent exhibition of early moving image technologies, all of which are presented through the lens of Studio Ghibli's anime characters and films. For example, a zoetrope is constructed using characters from Miyazaki's *My Neighbour Totoro*; panorama boxes are placed around the walls offering layered scenes from feature anime like *Princess Mononoke*; and a short reel of film from *Spirited Away* is used to demonstrate differences in film gauges. By inserting its animation into this historicizing of animation production, the Art Museum projects Studio Ghibli's brand meanings back through the history of animation, forging associations with traditions in animation production and a conceptualization of their product both as traditionally focused craft and as part of an artform with a long history.

In the temporary exhibition spaces too, the Art Museum has sought to balance between celebrating the art of Studio Ghibli (and other producers of world animation) and its commercial brand. Celebratory special exhibitions about new feature films, for example, Hayao Miyazaki's *Spirited Away* and *Ponyo* (*Gake no Ue no Ponyo*, 2008), have attempted to break down the process of animation, providing cases filled with background art, storyboards and explanations of CG-animation. However, these same exhibitions have also sought to demonstrate the Studio's popular success. For example, the *Spirited Away* exhibition (2001–2002) rooms contained the Golden Bear award that Miyazaki won at the Berlin Film Festival, placed atop a stack of original pencil sketches for the film. For *Ponyo* (2009–2010), the special exhibition space suggested a younger audience, providing interactive displays, including one with a little figure of Ponyo trapped in a jelly that children could press their hands into. In aligning these branded experiences of Studio Ghibli's filmmaking with art, the Art Museum disguises its placement of visitors within a branded and highly commercialized space.

Toshio Suzuki: The face of Studio Ghibli

The idea of a disguised commercial aspect to Studio Ghibli would be an apt way for describing the one member of its founding triumvirate who has remained relatively obscure outside Japan: Toshio Suzuki. Suzuki was, ironically, recently named the "face of Ghibli" by a Japanese newspaper (*Anime News Network*, 2014b), even though he remains a relatively unknown quantity outside Japan. As recently as a special feature documentary titled "The Birth Story of Studio Ghibli," which was provided as part of the *Nausicaa of the Valley of the Wind* US DVD release (2005), the American voice over narrator asks "who is that guy with Hayao Miyazaki?" The answer: Suzuki. Suzuki has been a key member of both the creative process at Studio Ghibli and the key Studio member responsible for Ghibli's growth from anime studio into multinational, multistudio, multimedia brand entity.

Suzuki's memoirs, his Studio histories and his testimonials about the production of Ghibli films reveal his desire to be seen as part of the Studio's creative systems. For example, Suzuki claims responsibility for suggesting books for adaptation and has agreed the content of the Studio's most successful films. He recounts being persuaded into agreeing to produce *Pom Poko*, with Takahata and Miyazaki launching a seemingly planned campaign of "nudges" that led to Suzuki's eventual capitulation (Suzuki 1994). However, Suzuki has also brought ideas to the Studio and to Miyazaki. For instance, he recounts in an interview in the *Yomiuri Newspaper* that *Tales from Earthsea* (written by Ursula LeGuin) had a complex history at Studio Ghibli:

> Originally, it was a work that Miya-san [Hayao Miyzaki] enthusiastically read. I read it too and it had the same impact, and I thought that I wanted to make a film adaptation of it even before we made *Nausicaa of the Valley of the Wind* (1984).... we did negotiate for it one time, but it did not go well.... But, if we had made "Earthsea" at that time, there probably wouldn't be a "Nausicaa." However, around 3 years ago, a Japanese translation was put out by Masako Shimizu and, after that, Ms Le Guin saw Miyazaki's work and she said to him that she wanted him to adapt her story. (Quoted in Yoda, 2005)

Timeliness, greater cultural contact between authors and missed opportunities are listed as reasons for the delay in producing *Tales from Earthsea* (2006) at Studio Ghibli, but Suzuki's role in mediating between creative personnel is significant to the process in both of these examples.

Suzuki's involvement in creative and branding production processes goes even further than this, according to his memoirs and Studio Ghibli personnel's reflections on the processes at the Studio. In his biography *My Film Hobby* (2005), Suzuki relates how he developed his own collaborative and creative working practices while acting as Chief Producer at the Studio. Suzuki claims to have brought his experiences as the Editor-in-Chief at anime magazine *Animage* to bear at Ghibli. He states that "From the first time I did serious film promotion, I took a care over the three-piece visual copy set: the title, along with the title logo and the copy (the advertising catchphrase). I was thinking, 'What do I tell people about those three things?'" (122). His response has often been to think about how to suggest, rather than straightforwardly push, the content of Studio Ghibli's films.

A good example of this can be found in the marketing for *Kiki's Delivery Service* (*Majō no Takyūbin*, Hayao Miyazaki, 1989) in Japan. According to Suzuki, he worked with Ghibli's regular copywriter to produce the marketing campaign. He had Miyazaki draw an image of *shōjo* witch protagonist Kiki staring whistfully out of the window of a bakery. Suzuki reflects that:

> I chose this visual because of the title and counter. To be a witch we know you fly in the air. So what other things should we show instead? This is the story of a lone girl, who has reached puberty. I thought that this would be useless without a picture of it…. Then, Itoi's tagline was born: "I was blue for a time, but I'm happy now." The [marketing] trinity is this kind of thing. I only had one thing I wanted to communicate in the poster for *Kiki's Delivery Service*. This was that "This film is the story of one normal girl." I was convinced that when they learned the orientation was a story of an adolescent girl, we could get audiences to come. (2005, 135–136)

Suzuki's off-center approach to advertising *Kiki's Delivery Service* has been typical of the way he has approached the wider branding and merchandising of Ghibli's films and the Studio itself. As a consequence, the marketing "look" of Studio Ghibli films, and their reliance on pre-sold "book" texts, aligned with a "hook" or marketing concept, are all designed by Suzuki in a manner that aligns with the marketing practices outlined for blockbuster Hollywood filmmaking by Justin Wyatt (1994). *Except* for the fact that the content of Suzuki's marketing campaigns rarely focuses on the most obvious routes that could be taken to achieve success, as this example from *Kiki's Delivery Service* shows.

Suzuki has also worked across the 1990s to differentiate Studio Ghibli's brand associations from those popularized by other kinds of texts. For example, Suzuki claims that he themed the catchphrases for Ghibli's films around the idea of "living" in order to differentiate them from Hollywood films, whose major theme was "love." As evidence he recounts that:

> *Princess Mononoke*'s copy was "Live." *Spirited Away*'s was "Crying out for the strength to live," and *The Cat Returns'* was "The kingdom of cats. It is a place people go when they cannot live in their times." Then, for *Howl's Moving Castle* we used, "The joy of living, the delight in loving." For the films and the period, the expression "live" was changing. (2005, 138)

This copy was also intended to be distinct from the darker image of anime of the time, marked by apocalypse and marketing campaigns that presaged death and destruction, as with *Neon Genesis Evangelion* (Napier 2005; Suzuki 2005). In these ways, Suzuki was responsible for carving out a niche in the Japanese mediascape that Ghibli's film products could uniquely fit, helping to create a brand foundation that could be exploited later in spaces like the Art Museum and Studio Ghibli's many merchandising licenses.

The idea of Ghibli's special status within marketing circles is affirmed in a book of staff reflections on twenty years of Ghibli's marketing history. Therein, staff from outside the Studio recall Suzuki's "foresight" in marketing, particularly regarding the use of the Ghibli logo. Masaya Tokuyama, one of the marketing team for *Porco Rosso* (*Kurenai no Buta*, 1992), remembers that Suzuki insisted on the Totoro logo being used in *Porco Rosso*'s newspaper advertising:

> It did not stand out very much. It didn't stand out in the advertisement of 2nd May because it was a white outline of a Totoro. Suzuki said "Put it on the poster anyway, and in the newspaper advertisements," because this is a film. (2002, 249)

Other partners in the marketing process include Noriko Yoinara, who confirms that this "Ghibli mark" came to affirm the quality of the works being released, while Masaru Yabe notes that the popular *Pokémon* franchise soon followed suit, simply replacing Totoro with an image of Pikachu in their own logo (249–250). Together, these commentators assert that Ghibli was at the forefront of a new push in Japanese film marketing under Suzuki's leadership. Even with the notable pro-Ghibli bias of these kinds of commemorative sources, Suzuki's creative and strategic roles in building the Studio Ghibli brand remain significant.

Suzuki's prominence within Studio Ghibli has been further heightened in recent years, as Miyazaki and Takahata have lessened their promotional activities. Suzuki's emergence as the "face of Ghibli" is a consequence of his being deployed as a symbol of creative continuity and legitimacy for Ghibli films, even when they lack the involvement of the Studio's two main animators. Even more so, for *Tales from Earthsea*, when Hayao Miyazaki publicly denounced his son's installation as a Studio Ghibli director. As Suzuki attempts to explain in the official Studio brochure sold at cinemas screening *Tales from Earthsea*, Gorō Miyazaki was Suzuki's own choice for director:

> When I spoke to his father, Hayao, he said he had expected it, but he was very against it. Making a film all of a sudden is absurd for a guy with no experience. He said, Suzuki, you are not thinking straight. That was his opinion. (2006)

In order to counter the (debatably) bad publicity generated by Hayao Miyazaki's comments, Suzuki refers to other famous Japanese animators' judgments of Gorō's filmmaking. For example, he relates the response of two animators to Gorō Miyazaki's storyboards for *Earthsea* in an interview with *Yomuri Newspaper*:

> more than me, I think I should introduce the words of others: famous animator Yasuo Ōtsuka has praised them saying, "As a film it's great." And, when he asked who drew them, and I said it was Gorō, he was sincerely surprised saying, "It's like his father's." Also, when I showed it to [Hideaki] Anno I told him Gorō's age was 38 years old, and he was astonished, saying "Why wasn't he doing this earlier?" Then he said, "This is totally a Miyazaki-anime." (Quoted in Yano 2005)

The legitimacy conferred by both Ōtsuka and Anno compounds Suzuki's own collaborative agency and works to justify his leadership decisions. While the arch-publicist in Suzuki may have fanned the flames of dispute between father and son for promotional reasons, he is nonetheless careful to manage expectations for the film by drawing comparisons between the generations of Miyazakis working for Studio Ghibli.

Conclusion

The animation brand that Suzuki has created around Hayao Miyazaki and others' films for Studio Ghibli reveals a series of slippages between notions of branding and genres. In the tensions between generations at Studio Ghibli we can see the difficulty inherent in trying to detach a personal brand from an aesthetic or industrial one, moving in this case from a Hayao Miyazaki-centric brand to a more generalized understanding of "Studio Ghibli" filmmaking as a propriety, yet depersonalized, style of filmmaking. Hayao Miyazaki's name value is clear from this debate, and even more so from the US instance of Studio Ghibli as a brand entity.

However, by decentering Hayao Miyazaki from the debates, it becomes possible to see just how much of Studio Ghibli's creative work, industrial power and cultural presence in Japan have gone unregarded within academia and global popular culture. The lack of a consistent style of animation in Japan's version of Studio Ghibli works against an understanding of an aesthetics-based Studio Ghibli brand there. This is compounded by the multiple Studio Ghibli logos and sub-brands in Japan, which promise continuing growth in the Studio's local cultural meanings. As a brand of filmmaking, then, in Japan Studio Ghibli's meanings require a wider understanding of the Studio's political, cultural and economic meanings.

Outside Japan, reception of Studio Ghibli's "house style" does suggest that it has come to take on the kinds of proprietary-yet-generic meanings that cohere around US animation studios. As with other kinds of animation, therefore, Studio Ghibli's transnational meanings may lie in a hybridized ground of genre and branding that reveal a closeness, rather than separation, of these two terms. In part, what is at stake in this debate is the question of whether anime can ever become "mainstream animation" in the USA; but, additionally, there is an important question about the status of animation as a genre in that culture. As an umbrella term for the majority of animated filmmaking in the USA, "animation" is necessarily a broad category, and I argue, one that holds many proprietary branded subgenres within it. As a branded subgenre hybrid, therefore, Studio Ghibli has become just one among many mainstream American proprietary subgenres of "animation." In so doing, Ghibli is becoming a genre, even while it remains a brand.

8

Experiencing Japan's Anime: Genres at the Tokyo International Anime Fair

In earlier chapters of this book, I have claimed that Japan's is a dense and complex animation marketplace. Within Japan's mediascape (Appadurai 1990, 9), anime spans across television, film and online texts and can be watched on a wide variety of old and new media platforms. But the experience of anime does not end with the consumption of its texts. Beyond this, Japan has been exploiting anime, turning into a country described by one recent art exhibition as a *Kingdom of Characters* (2010), and Anne Allison (2006) and Marc Steinberg (2012) both point to the importance of toy, figure and model kit collecting as key means of extending the experience of anime into the everyday lives of children. Steinberg writes that beginning with Osamu Tezuka's *Astro Boy* in 1963 "children were taught to consume characters in all of their material likenesses and across their particular transmedia networks" (111). The experience of anime is thereby extended beyond the practice of watching into the play of children and, as anime cultures have developed in Japan, this playful consumption has expanded into collecting hobbies undertaken by adult fans. Therefore, this chapter investigates the possibilities for experiencing anime in Japan, focusing in particular on the Tokyo International Anime Fair. In doing so, the aim is to further contextualize our understanding of anime, thinking about what it means for anime to be a complex, densely populated market in Japan.

Experiencing anime: From texts to contexts

Anime texts can be found scattered across the television schedules in Japan from early in the morning to late-night broadcasts. Many of these texts are subsequently repurposed—recycled across regional and syndicated television stations before being released on video, and now DVD and Blu-ray, or before being streamed online. As suggested earlier, this means that anime is a significant part of Japan's visual culture, perhaps especially as part of Japan's collecting subcultures, where fans work to collate material archives of anime texts and objects. These collecting subcultures have in turn created subcultural hubs, districts or retail spaces specialized for the amassing of anime texts and merchandise. Such places are scattered throughout Japan, but most famously can be found in Tokyo's Akihabara and Ikebukuro districts, and also in Nakano Broadway's second-hand shopping mall (Macias and Machiyama 2004); anime has become a profitable part of local retail and consumption cultures across Japan. The experience of anime in Japan is consequently unique: it is defined by the ways anime has developed and over time in its home country, forming part of rich transmedia networks of texts and specialized contexts for their consumption.

Out of these constellations of anime-related texts and merchandise, a growing cultural geography of anime has emerged in Japan. Don Mitchell argues that all forms of culture are spatial, and that they are a part of the geography of countries:

> No matter how it is approached, "culture" *is* spatial … it insinuates itself into our daily worlds as part of the spaces and spatial practices that define our lives …. New cultural theory, as it is developing in geography, cultural studies, and many allied disciplines, stresses *space*, understanding culture to be constituted through space and *as* a space. (Mitchell 2000, 63; for further explanations of cultural geography, see Crang 1998 and Harvey 2000)

If culture is spatial, if it is performed and consumed within specific places and at particular times, then understanding the lived experiences of anime in Japan can tell us much about how anime's genres form and are continually reshaped. As evidence for this cultural geography, consider how anime's spaces within Japan are multiple and growing. In addition to the retail spaces mentioned a moment ago, anime can be experienced through a wide range of branded spaces, such as the Studio Ghibli Art Museum discussed in the previous chapter. This is just one example of a growing number of manga and anime museums that have been established in recent times, which include the Kyoto International Manga Museum, the Suginami Animation Museum in Tokyo and a range of museums dedicated to particular texts and authors, such as the Yokohama Anpanman Children's Museum or the Fujiko F Fujio Museum in Kawasaki City. Other themed spaces have also started to become popular over the past two decades, especially in Tokyo where a growing chain of Gundam Cafes are proliferating, providing fans of the *Gundam* anime franchise with themed foods and drinks named for characters, or through the many uses of anime characters in cross-promotional campaigns. The expansion of anime's cultural meanings within Japan's geographic spaces consequently goes beyond straightforward acts of consumption, with anime's spatial presence in Japan necessitating a reconsideration of both its cultural significance and its meanings in its home nation.

For example, licensing practices work to commingle the meanings of characters with specific geographic places, as when signage and statues of Astro Boy came to adorn signs at the Kyoto train station, advertising a small museum dedicated to Astro Boy's creator, Osamu Tezuka, which could be found within the station itself (see Figure 8.1, though the Kyoto museum has now been largely replaced by a larger museum to Tezuka in Takarazuka, outside Osaka). Likewise, whole prefectures have now adopted

FIGURE 8.1 *Astro Boy shows the way to the Osamu Tezuka museum in Kyoto's train station (personal photograph).*

this model of licensing, with manga and anime characters coming to act as ambassadors for the hometowns and regions that their creators hail from. This is causing competition between regions to lay claim to being the home or birthplace of manga and anime. In one relatively recent example, Tottori prefecture has held a "manga summit," adopting Gosho Aoyama's Detective Conan character and Shigeru Mizuki's famous monster hero, Kitarō, as local mascots. Michael Dylan Foster has placed such efforts within attempts by rural locations to "reenergise their economies through processes known as *mura okoshi* (village revitalization) or *furusato zukuri* (hometown making). Such revitalization efforts often exploit or develop a particular cultural resource or local industry" (2009b, 165–166). In Foster's example, Sakaiminato village's installation of over sixty bronze statues borrowed from Mizuki's *Ge ge ge no Kitarō* franchise (which contains both manga and anime iterations) invests the local space with manga characters and meanings, rebranding the village as a site of manga pilgrimage and, as a result, creating manga tourism. This growing cultural geography of manga and anime-related places in Japan is generating new and ever-more elaborate ways to experience anime, remaking Japan itself into a global site of anime tourism.

This is a claim made repeatedly on Japan's National Tourism Organization (JNTO) website. The website promotes the idea of "Anime Pilgrimage" claiming that "These 'sacred sites' have become incredibly popular among fans and the object of 'pilgrimages' by many eager to visit them" (Japan National Tourism Organization, n.d.). In their map of suggested anime pilgrimage locations, the JNTO interweave spaces represented in anime texts with the real Japanese locations they represent—for example, interconnecting the locations represented in *Lucky Star!* (2007) with real-world town of Washinomiya, investing locations such as Washinomiya's Takanomiya Shrine with anime meanings (discussed further in Yamamura 2009). This overt conflation of religious sites and anime subcultural tourist destinations indicates high levels of perceived investment in tourism by anime fans, and their reverential treatment of the places represented within their favorite texts (for more on fandom and pilgrimage, see Geraghty 2014).

However, within these spaces, anime is rarely the sole media being represented or given reverence. Many of these tourist destinations focus on creators who have worked across different kinds of media, or focus on the characters who appear across transmedia franchises, rather than specifically focusing on anime. Even the retail spaces like Japan's popular Animate, Tora no Ana and Mandarake chains tend to mix and match different media, replicating the "media mix" at the heart of Japan's complex mediascape (Steinberg 2012). Consequently, this chapter turns to an event at which anime was continually given primacy: the Tokyo International Anime Fair (TAF) in order to analyze the links between anime's cultural geography and genres.

The Tokyo International Anime Fair: From Expo space to controversial space

The Tokyo International Anime Fair used to be the most significant event in Japan's anime calendar, offering fans and industry alike the opportunity to sample previews of the anime that would shortly appear on Japan's, and later the world's, screens. TAF was held annually in Tokyo, and was organized by the Tokyo Metropolitan Government working with Japan's anime industry to put on an exposition-style, four-day event offering separate business and public announcements about, and celebrations of, Japan's anime industry. TAF began in 2002, at which time there were just over 100 exhibitors and a little over 50,000 attendees. The event used to take place in March, in order to preview the spring television schedule for anime, which normally begins in Japan in April. Like many conventions, TAF was held in a large hall at a convention center, and was structured around rows of booths of differing sizes allowing industry representatives (from television channels, production houses, museums, merchandisers and others) to promote their anime and goods to attendees. In the case of TAF, attendees were split between anime industry, international media distribution professionals and fans, the last of whom were only allowed into the event in the final two days of its four-day event each year. TAF's success is visible in the growth in both attendance and exhibitor numbers over its first decade, at least until controversy struck the event in 2011 (Tokyo International Anime Fair, n.d.).

Leading up to the 2011 event, a strident note of discord was struck between the Tokyo Metropolitan Government and Japan's manga publishing houses (calling themselves the *Manga Jūsshakai*), many of whom are also responsible for anime production. The disagreement emerged from the local government's attempts to halt the sales of pornographic manga in Tokyo's convenience stores, which caused some of the major contributors to TAF, led by Kadokawa Publishing, to form a breakaway event for fans called the Anime Contents Expo, planned for 2011 (Anime News Network 2011). In a further blow for TAF, just weeks before their planned event in March 2011, an earthquake and tsunami struck the Eastern coast of Japan on the 11th of March. This caused widespread devastation and a huge loss of life in the northeastern portion of Japan's main island. As a result, both of the planned anime events were cancelled, with Shintarō Ishihara, then the governor of Tokyo and chair of TAF's organizing committee, proclaiming that his rivals "deserved" the cancellation of the Anime Contents Expo (Furukawa and Denison, 2014). Both events then ran in competition with one another in March 2012, causing attendance figures at TAF to drop by nearly 40,000. Latterly, then, TAF became embroiled in controversy and has subsequently been rebranded and relaunched as Anime

Japan, which started in 2014. This chapter examines TAF's importance up to 2013, primarily through examples drawn from 2008 and 2013, the former being the year which marked the high point of the anime industry's investment in the event (with 289 exhibitors represented) and the latter, the end of TAF's cultural geographic significance to anime in Japan.

Over the period between 2008 and 2013, I repeatedly attended TAF's business and public days, and the remainder of this chapter contains my reflections on TAF's organization in relation to the myriad generic juxtapositions inscribed in its event space. I attended TAF in 2008, 2011 and 2013 (when I also attended Anime Contents Expo), and had assistance from Sachiko Shikoda who attended the event in my stead in 2009. In order to record and understand TAF, we used participant observation techniques, described by Kathleen M. DeWalt and Billie R. DeWalt in the following manner:

> participant observation is a method in which a researcher takes part in the daily activities, rituals, interactions, and events of a group of people as one means of learning the explicit and tacit aspects of their life routines and their culture. (2011, 1)

In our research, Shikoda and I focused on the event and the way it was used to present a range of animated texts to international industry distributors (during the business days) and the public (in the latter days of the event). We focused on understanding how genres functioned within TAF's event space at Tokyo Bay's Big Sight convention halls (also home to manga's largest fan event, ComiKet) and how their close proximity to one another generated surprising examples of connection, collisions and even confusions between different kinds of anime texts and subcultures. In the sections that follow, I show how TAF, as a significant part of anime's cultural geography, presented an intensified experience of the complexities of Japan's contemporary anime mediascape.

Anime collisions: Contrastive genre juxtapositions at the Tokyo International Anime Fair

In its heyday, TAF was a place where most kinds of anime texts commingled—from those made for television to those made for theaters and for internet distribution. The notable exception being Japan's *ero* (erotic or pornographic) anime genres, whose explicit content does not appear to have been welcome at the event, although the business days in 2013 contained panels with representatives from that side of the industry. In addition, the range of productions featured at TAF consistently ran the gamut from short anime television series (like the five-minute episodes of *Chi's Sweet Home* featured at TAF in 2008, or the shorts and installations offered in TAF's Creator's World) through to high-profile *geikijōban* (theatrical film versions of popular series) and also included standalone films by high-profile directors, including those of Studio Ghibli and Production IG. The range of different types of texts generated often surprising collisions between anime's markets and genres.

The space of TAF—a cavernous hall filled with hundreds of booths, additional film viewing spaces, retail (including food) booths and large stages for announcements—at first glance looked like a chaotic jumble of texts vying for attention. The additions of large, floating character balloons, a plethora of screens with blaring trailer reels, colorful posters and billboards, museum-style exhibitions, life-sized character models and games for fans to play as they walk around the event (see Figure 8.2) compounded this impression. However, TAF was, in fact, a carefully crafted set of interconnected spaces. The main grid of the Fair contained a circular route beginning from a single entrance, with powerful production studios, major television channels and the biggest new releases showcased around the outer rim of the event space, with international animation booths, university student work, smaller producers and booths promoting licensed tie-ups filling the central aisles and corners of the Fair. In this way, fans and distributors were encouraged to keep to a path that featured already-successful anime producers and texts, before seeking out more specialist vendors. Nevertheless, this circuit-pattern produced some surprising textual juxtapositions that have the potential to impact upon how we contextualize anime texts within genres.

Popular characters from radically differing genres were frequently associated by proximity at TAF, creating the potential for new and outlandish generic recontextualizations. Consider, for example, the image provided in Figure 8.2, where death god Ryuk from thriller-horror hybrid franchise *Death Note* (2006–2007, here advertising the forthcoming *Death Note Relight* (2007) DVD release) is captured in the same visual frame as action-fantasy *Pokémon's* (1997– in anime) star character, Pikachu.[1] This juxtapositioning indicates the generic and audience fluidity that TAF created, with children's texts in close visual proximity to those, like *Death Note*, aimed at older age groups. The image also makes plain the importance of star characters to a wide range of anime in Japan, even those aimed at disparate age groups. It demonstrates the elasticity of anime's generic landscape, with a wide range of genres and audiences capable of raising characters up to star status. In this example, furthermore, both characters are used as a shorthand for the larger franchises within which they form a linchpin of meanings, or what Hiroki Azuma calls the "common world of the work and characters, or, in extreme

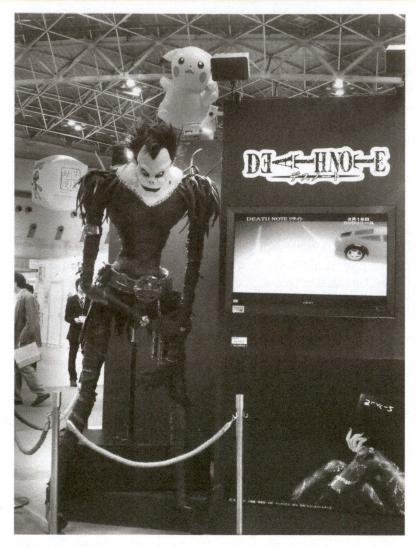

FIGURE 8.2 Pokémon's *Pikachu looks over the shoulder of* Death Note's shinigami *(death god) Ryuk (personal photograph).*

cases, characters alone" (2001, 48). As such, characters like Pikachu and Ryuk are overburdened with meanings—not just generic, but also those of their wider media mix network of texts. On yet another level, the presence of such star characters also highlights the celebratory and promotional aims of TAF, showcasing already-popular texts in order to expand the reach of popular franchises within and beyond Japan.

It was not just contrasting characters that collided in the space of the Fair. Different kinds of anime texts also routinely sat side-by-side. Figure 8.3 provides a radical example—the literal attaching of the booths for *Case Closed: Full Score of Fear* (*Meitantei Conan: Senritsu no Furu Sukoa*, Yasuichiro Yamamoto, 2008) and *Detroit Metal City* (2008). The former is part of one of Japan's most successful and long-running manga-anime franchises. The text being promoted, *Full Score of Fear*, is the twelfth *gekijōban* film in the *Case Closed* anime subfranchise that takes in both film and television. *Case Closed* is one of the most regularly featured texts at TAF. It boasts near-annual *gekijōban* film releases and intervening television series, which have allowed it to achieve a near-continual presence in the anime market in Japan. By comparison, *Detroit Metal City* was a shorter-lived franchise, and its booth was being used to promote a series of OVA, which were due to be released as a box-set shortly after TAF. This collision between the family-friendly *Case Closed* and the adult-oriented *Detroit Metal City* signals the breadth of the anime market in Japan, but also the kinds of collisions that took place between anime's markets during TAF.

Though both texts were linked by a musical theme, emphasized by Krauser's guitar and Conan's violin in Figure 8.3, they were generically

FIGURE 8.3 Case Closed *booth literally attached to one for* Detroit Metal City *(personal photograph).*

distinct—*Full Score of Fear* being a mystery and *Detroit Metal City* a comedic parody of the Japanese music scene. However, the conjoining of these two promotional spaces is easily explainable through their shared Japanese distributor—Tōhō Co. Ltd—the sponsor of their exhibition spaces at TAF in 2008. Tōhō were backing the production of a live-action film version of *Detroit Metal City*, and used TAF as a venue to heighten awareness of the franchise (TAF program 2008, 81). They situated *Detroit Metal City* near *Case Closed* because of the latter's greater profile, thereby maximizing the *Detroit Metal City* franchise's chances of finding an audience as attendees were drawn into its space via the geographic orbit of the *Case Closed gekijōban*. In these sorts of ways, the seeming cacophony of TAF's textual positioning begins to take on more calculated, pragmatic notes. Rather than chaos, TAF offers a wide range of examples wherein seemingly disparate texts and genres were brought together for calculated economic reasons.

The result is a set of collisions between genres born out of a highly saturated marketspace. The mediascape for anime in Japan, therefore, needs to be understood industrially as well as textually, because the seemingly strange juxtapositions of genre texts can be a consequence of calculated crossovers, alternative programming or even about the space of TAF itself. By not grouping texts generically, but rather providing a space in which freer constellations of texts could be decided upon by industry, TAF enabled new forms of generic hierarchy and popularity to emerge. The large floating Pikachu balloon, for example, could thus become associated with a wide range of other possible texts, dominating them and floating above them, while the positioning of the Ryuk statue by the entrance to TAF in 2008 worked to signal the success of the *Death Note* franchise and consequently the prominence of its producers and distributors.

Anime conflations: Anniversaries and TV channel booths at the Tokyo International Anime Fair

Other combinations of texts at TAF were more obviously purposeful. For example, in 2013, in anticipation of the fiftieth anniversary of anime's television advent in Japan, an exhibition charting anime's television history was placed in one of the Fair's central booth spaces. It brought together a range of historical anime texts deemed important, many of which had franchises still represented at the Fair. *Astro Boy* was the highest profile example, proclaimed as the first anime made for television, according to the exhibition and a fiftieth anniversary display adorned the top of that year's Tezuka Productions booth. This worked to unite two anniversaries—one for anime in general and the other for one of its still most high-profile characters—celebrating *Astro Boy* and reasserting Tezuka's primacy within the hierarchy of anime creators. Moreover, the fiftieth anniversary displays, positioned near the event stages of the Fair in 2013, also functioned as a space of nostalgia for bygone anime. A nostalgia for past anime feeds into one of the secondary business aims of the Fair. It functioned as a platform not just for new anime, but for showcasing the anime catalogs owned by many of Japan's larger animation studios. Nostalgia, as a consequence, was a recurring theme at TAF between 2008 and 2013, with a continual flow of anniversaries celebrated by producers, television channels and directors represented in the booths at TAF.

It is difficult to overstate the amount of anniversary celebrations taking place at TAF. In 2013 alone, Astro Boy celebrated turning 50, Isao Takahata and Hayao Miyazaki's *Panda Go Panda* (*Panda Kopanda* 1972 and 1973) turned 40 and was granted a special booth and there was also an exhibition celebrating 60 years of Leiji Matsumoto's artwork, including paintings based on his famous *Galaxy Express 999* (1978–1981) manga and anime. Nor was this unusual. In 2008, too, there were also a number of anniversary celebrations, including the fortieth anniversary of *Lupin Sansei* (*Lupin III*), whose manga by Monkey Punch was first published in the late 1960s. Beyond these sorts of character and artist-oriented anniversary celebrations, TAF has also celebrated more nebulous industry anniversaries. For example, in 2008, anime producer Pierrot celebrated its thirtieth anniversary. Pierrot's official website proclaims that it was founded in 1979, making anime "series and films of diverse genres ranging from action to comedy, thriller to romance, sports to edutainment and more" (Nunokawa n.d.). Their anniversary booth at TAF, however, suggests that two anime texts have been key to their current success: *Naruto* (2002–2007) and *Bleach* (2004–2012) (see Figure 8.4).

However, Pierrot acts as both an anime production studio and a character merchandising licensor and, consequently, their anniversary booth at TAF was laden with character goods, including *gatchapon* (toy vending machines) that attendees could use, and a special line of anniversary merchandise, used to nostalgically showcase even their most recent anime hits. This nostalgia was apparent in the way Pierrot encased recent merchandise in display cabinets, giving them the aura of museum displays. They also provided anniversary merchandise with a "traditional" Japanese orientation. An image of *Bleach*'s protagonists Ichigo and Rukiya, for instance, was reproduced on a traditionally styled *mini irogami* (a small square painting on Japanese colored paper, usually for mounting on scrolls), emblazoned twice with Pierrot's anniversary logo. While the booth favored new releases more heavily than Pierrot's historically

FIGURE 8.4 *Pierrot's anniversary booth at TAF 2008 (personal photograph).*

significant texts, its presentation of collectable goods that mimicked older Japanese art forms encapsulates the kinds of manufactured nostalgia such anniversary celebrations worked to evoke at TAF.

Nostalgia and cataloging therefore played important roles for anime companies at TAF. Perhaps the most overt examples of these sorts of practices were the showcasing of deceased anime creators' work. Again, Osamu Tezuka's two representative companies—Tezuka Productions and Mushi Pro—offer instructive examples of "catalog" promotions. Each year that I attended the Fair, Tezuka Productions had a large booth near the entrance, usually showcasing Astro Boy and other core Tezuka creations. By comparison, Mushi Pro, which handles anime rights always had smaller, more compact booths, replete with brochures but lacking the investment in character balloons, cosplaying booth representatives and other markers of high investment seen in the Tezuka Productions stands. These differences can be read either as a means to avoid competition or as a nod to the more sober sales agenda of the Fair versus its showier promotional facets. The combined presence of Tezuka's businesses at TAF, however, act as a restatement of his position as *the* key authorial figure within manga and anime culture, dominating the event space and reminding audiences of his characters' foundational and deep integration with Japan's visual culture.

This split between the business agenda of the Fair and its promotional aspects is most starkly drawn at the level of studio booths. It was in these instances that TAF's role as tastemaker became most apparent, and the conflations of genre under studio brands became most noticeable. The booth used by anime industry giant Gainax (Condry 2013) to promote its forthcoming *gekijōban* for popular anime series *Gurren Lagann* (2007) placed the imagery and title of the series above the studio's brand. With Gainax's brand subordinated to the text, and *Gurren Lagann* promoted over any other previous Gainax anime, the importance of promotion and TAF's role as a gatekeeping tastemaker become apparent (Figure 8.5). With trailers, information boards, production information and, in the case of high-profile titles like *Gurren Lagann*, sometimes even the provision of huge back-lit billboards, anime television series become encapsulated in a relay of promotional imagery designed to entice potential viewers into the interior spaces of the booths for more information. On the one hand, texts can come to overwhelm the meaning of the brands to which they are attached. In the case of *Gurren Lagann*, the meanings of the brand become conflated with the meanings of the text in a cross-promotional move designed to encourage a relay of meanings between the two.

FIGURE 8.5 *Gainax's booth for the launch* of Gurren Lagann *at TAF 2008 (personal photograph).*

On the other hand, however, studio booths were also often used to brand a cross-section of productions from disparate genres. Madhouse Animation's booth at the 2008 TAF offers a good example of this trend (Figure 8.6). It featured, among other texts, everything from traditional 2D anime features, to Madhouse's first CG-animated film, to television series. These texts were carefully grouped underneath the Madhouse logo banner, with films and television shows grouped together, and extra information about the animators of the films and their forthcoming projects provided on the outer walls of the booth. This allowed a grouping of anime based not on genre, but on media platforms to be developed. On the left of Figure 8.6, for example, are displays for *Redline* (Takeshi Koike, 2009) and Madhouse's adaptation of *Highlander* (Yoshiaki Kawajiri and Hiroshi Hamasaki, 2007), presenting a combination of stylized car racing in the former case and imported transnational fantasy genre franchising in the latter case. On the right, by contrast, are two anime television shows, *Chi's Sweet Home* and *Kaiba* (2008). Neither of these is genre anime in a straightforward way. The former consists of short episodes, of under five minutes each, about the adventures of a kitten, Chi, who struggles to find a home. The latter is made by experimental animator Masaaki Yuasa and was labeled a science

FIGURE 8.6 *Madhouse's booth at TAF 2008 (personal photograph).*

fiction-romance hybrid, but became more celebrated as an artistic award-winning animation than as a genre anime (Anime News Network 2008b).

Torn between a nostalgic impulse to look back at past successes and the future thrust of experimental film and television production, anime's meanings began to shift, thanks to the cultural geographic space of TAF. From examples like *Gurren Lagann*'s, we can see that popular anime rarely stay on one platform, constantly moving between television, film and DVD. Likewise, studios are shown to be using a variety of techniques to anchor their brands—in the case of Pierrot, using merchandising to exploit their biggest hits; while Gainax relied on a blockbuster-style hit; and, different again, Mushi Pro relied on a largely unchanging "classic" back catalog of works. By contrast, Madhouse presents a film-led anime culture that relies on named directors and experimental animation to alter understandings of "anime" itself. Each in its own fashion pushes the boundaries of anime culture in Japan. Under the auspices of studio brands, therefore, we can see companies playing with genres, often conflating their meanings and texts, in order to build a coherent brand identity. These conflations are significant because each producer-brand has the potential to change thinking about what might be included under the rubric of "anime."

Anime confusions: Commerce and art "anime" at the Tokyo International Anime Fair

If the studio booths push the boundaries of what we might think of as "traditional" anime, other examples from TAF break with textual definitions of anime entirely. For one, the Fair assembled animation from around the world, including representatives from the Chinese and South Korean animation industries. This gave the Fair a regional identity, as a way of bringing together and celebrating animation cultures from across Asia under the auspices of an ostensibly "anime" focused event. This transnational perspective also extended to US animation companies. At the 2008 Fair, a range of US animation companies with a stake in Japanese broadcasting had booths promoting localizations and dubbed versions of their popular US products. For example, Cartoon Network and Nickelodeon had small booths at TAF in 2008. Their localized US texts were bookended by displays from local anime producers Animax and Kids Station, the latter promoting *Pokémon*. This display brought together US and Japanese animation, emphasizing their shared market and meanings in Japan. This juxtaposition worked to naturalize the imported US texts within Japan's anime marketplace, including high-profile animation series like *Ben 10* (2005–) and *Spongebob Squarepants* (1999–). The resultant spatial proximity was thereby used to suggest cultural similarities. In these transnational industrial meetings, anime became blended with other kinds of animation from other places, generating a shared sense of TAF as a space in which the entirety of global animation culture could be subsumed under the Japanese rubric of "anime."

This is not especially surprising, given that it is normal in Japan to refer to animation as anime. However, the anime appellation hides, or confuses, the wide variety of texts found at TAF. In the example above, imported animation texts became localized as anime, but in other instances it was not just texts but whole animation production cultures that became subsumed under the term "anime." The Creators' World area of TAF provides one such example in which young, independent animators were given space at the Fair in a kind of artistic animation ghetto. Shintarō Ishihara's introduction to this aspect of the Fair reads: "As in previous years the 'Creators' World,'" is "a place for young up-and-coming creators to display their works and gain valuable business opportunities" (2008, 3). However, the Creators' World was normally off to one side of the main circuit of the Fair, in a smaller alleyway lined with tiny booths that allowed industry initiates to propose their wares, signaling their outsider status by comparison to their industrial surroundings. For some, like Gaku Kinoshita, the aim was not to enter the anime industry per se, but to find outlets for his personal animation and animated art installations—international gallery exhibitions in particular (personal interview, 2012, Kinoshita's showreel is available on YouTube). Kinoshita's presence at TAF, therefore, was outward-looking and transnational in focus, and far more specialized in form than Ishihara's notion of "business opportunities" suggests. Although just a single example, Kinoshita's approach to animation-as-art shows the variability of TAF's cultural geography of anime, and the confusions that can emerge when considering the whole of Japanese animation culture as "anime."

Pushing the boundaries of "anime" in other directions were commercial interests whose uses of TAF were often very different from one another. For example, in 2013, Studio 4°C (who most famously made the film *Tekkonkinkreet*, Michael Arias, 2006) used the Fair to announce their advertising collaboration with car manufacturer Toyota. Titled *PES—Peace Eco Smile*—the work began as webisodes that acted in part as advertisements for Toyota's Vios vehicle. Studio 4°C's advertisement work, and the high-profile promotion of *PES* at TAF 2013, is not all that unusual within the anime industry (see Chapter 7). What is significant in the collaboration between Toyota and Studio 4°C was the cross-promotional space of TAF, which involved a game that attendees could take part in as a means to win character merchandise from the advertisement. In this way, the advertisement was extended into character goods merchandising, creating a nascent franchise out of an otherwise ephemeral set of productions.

In a less overtly commercial example, Tōei Animation also announced an anime titled *Kyōsō Giga* (*Capital Craze Comic*) at TAF in 2013. Like *PES*, this was a relatively unusual anime "release" in that *Kyōsō Giga* had begun as an online-only web anime available through Nico Nico Dōga, a major online distributor in Japan. *Kyōsō Giga*'s introduction as a "new" text at TAF, therefore, was a misnomer (Figure 8.7). In this case, the use of TAF to promote *Kyōsō Giga* implied their desire to move across distribution platforms—to create a hit television show out of something that began as a free online anime giveaway. While *Kyōsō Giga* had previously been previewed at 2012's Tokyo Anime Festival in Akihabara, it was only at TAF that exclusive merchandise began to be made available for purchase, showing the show's slow progress toward the kinds of commodification desired by anime media mix strategies.

In these examples of commercial imperatives driving booths at TAF, the importance of TAF as a launching-space for anime becomes clear. Moreover, with Japan's biggest advertiser, Dentsu, taking out booth-space at TAF, the importance of anime to advertising cultures in Japan is also made explicit through the Fair's cultural geography. In 2008, for example, Dentsu was involved in the *seisaku iinkai* (production committees) for several high-profile anime, including Studio Bones' *Soul Eater* (2008). Notably, *Soul Eater* became

FIGURE 8.7 Kyōsō Giga *booth, new media anime with exclusive merchandise (personal photograph).*

the most intensively promoted new series at TAF in 2008, enjoying its own booth, artwork in the Fair's programs and a replication of its promotion within Dentsu's own booth. These multiple tactics suggest that Dentsu's advertising power was a major influence in helping *Soul Eater* to gain traction within the crowded space of the Fair and beyond. Through such collaborations and promotional outlets, the understanding of anime as the product of Japan's animation studios is complicated, challenging not just what "anime" is, but also who is responsible for its progress through Japanese culture. While it might seem that these examples straightforwardly link to the business side of the Fair, they also suggest alternative ways of understanding what anime is and how it begins to flow through Japanese culture.

Conclusion

The breadth of the collisions, conflations and confusions around anime that emerge through an examination of even a limited number of years at the Tokyo International Anime Fair is a testament to the fact that anime simply is not the same in Japan as it is outside it. Within Japan, for instance, it would not be strange to consider advertising as anime, or to see short webisodes and trailers for unfinished "projects" as anime. Anime also becomes a description of a mode of production—standing in for the whole of animation culture—and not just the genre-rich landscape of "mainstream" anime television production. In Japan, therefore, anime is a rather more fluid concept than it is outside its home nation.

In TAF's cultural geography, many of these complexities emerge as undeniably important phenomena. Studio brands vie for attention with the broadcasters that feature their products. Some anime are raised up as "star texts" within booths, and can be spread across the space of the Fair and its ancillary products as a means of saturating the space with promotional information. These star texts and characters vie for attention with well-established star characters, whose images are being repetitiously included in the Fair's space in order to maintain their status within anime's cultural hierarchy. New and old texts collide, therefore, just as genres, authors and characters crash together within the Fair's limited space. These collisions offer a useful way of beginning to reconsider the bounded nature of anime texts, seeing them instead as more porous and easily conflated within ever-expanding contexts. In this, the web of the anime intertexts becomes rather tangled. Anime's meanings become dependent on how their texts (and intertexts) are framed in ever-new situations like TAF. Therefore, the example of TAF tells us that spatial proximity has the ability to shape genres, to alter textual meanings and to reconceptualize characters.

This helps explain why anime studios and distributors at TAF seek alternative ways to make sense of anime. As seen through the examples of US imports and Madhouse Animation, technologies of distribution often underpin the organization of texts at the Fair. The differential status of film versus television versus OVA or web forms of anime is generating an alternative hierarchy of anime, and one quite distinct from the way anime is understood and organized by questions of genre. Moreover, as technological possibilities for anime are changing—as the web becomes an ever-greater presence at fairs like TAF—the cultural geography of anime is expanding still further, moving from the real space of the Fair to a more dispersed online world of promotion.

As a consequence of these technological shifts, the previous conflations of anime under studio brands and channels is also shifting, and the borders of what is, and is not, considered anime are becoming more porous. This is evidenced by examples like that of Gaku Kinoshita, a relative industry "outsider" whose work, nonetheless, is now available to all via YouTube. In this shifting market for anime, and in TAF's rebranding as Anime Japan in 2014, we can see the need to continually reinvent what we consider to be "anime." In the next chapter, I follow one particular genre of anime, horror, from its promotion in Japan to its promotion in the USA and UK in order to better map how these sorts of shifting contexts alter the mediascape of "anime." For TAF, the controversies about its organization meant a tarnishing of its brand that required an entire reconceptualization of its meanings in order for it to survive. As it used to operate, TAF's ever-changing cultural geography of anime was a major influence on how anime came to prominence, and its significance lies in the way it acted as a space in which new anime stars could be born.

9

Anime Horror and Genrification

While the horror genre has a long and abiding presence in film history, its manifestations in animation, and in anime, are far less routinely recounted. While preceding chapters have sought to uncover the dominant histories and genres of anime, and their relationships to key industry personnel, this final chapter investigates a genre whose importance is ordinarily sidelined, but whose presence in anime is becoming increasingly difficult to ignore. Subjugated to dominant genre paradigms at various stages in its discursive life, horror has been lurking at the margins of anime from at least its earliest distribution on home video: from *hentai* pornography through to the action and romance ends of the *shōjo* and *shōnen* genres, horror haunts anime. Consequently, this final chapter argues that horror tropes and languages are regularly being used to understand contemporary anime. Moreover, this chapter uses the idea of horror as a subordinated or mixed generic presence in anime to find out what can be learned from treating anime's meanings as contextually dependent, generically complex, always already hybridized. Therefore, this chapter brings together a wide range of discourses about horror in anime, in order to challenge the idea that the only important genres in film and television are those which are most apparent and dominant.

In examining anime horror, what Rick Altman (1999) identifies as the process of its "genrification," this chapter tests two of Altman's findings about film genres:

The early history of film genres is characterized, it would seem, not by purposeful borrowing from a single pre-existing non-film parent genre, but by apparently incidental borrowing from several unrelated genres. (34)

How "incidental" this borrowing is perceived to be by industrial, mediating and audience groups may have much to tell us about perceptions of the horror genre within anime and, what is more, about perceptions of anime horror as culturally specific "Japanese" horror. However, alone, this does not help to indicate the complexity of the discourses on anime texts as they shift between Japan, the USA and the UK, as I propose to do in this chapter. To that end, a second observation from Altman is useful:

> Even when a genre already exists in other media, the film genre of the same name cannot simply be borrowed from non-film sources, it must be created. Not surprisingly, this recreation process may very well produce a genre that is decidedly not, in spite of the shared name, identical to the non-film genre. (35)

In beginning this research, then, the hypothesis was that anime horror would take on unexpected forms that contrast with established film definitions of horror, be they American or Japanese in origin. Consequently, this chapter revisits these two claims by Altman, in an effort to unpack how horror manifests and means in anime texts.

In this chapter, I have examined coverage of anime horror in specialist magazines from Japan, the USA and the UK because these sources offer a meeting point between industrial (advertising and promotion) and reception (review) discourses. These three nations have been selected on the basis that understanding the anime horror genre from its domestic inception (Japan), through to what is frequently its first (legal) international distribution point (USA), to a tertiary market with close links to that international distribution point (UK) allows us to think about how the meanings of horror anime shift within different markets for both anime and horror. Three sets of magazine texts were therefore selected including: *Animage* (*Animēju*) and *Newtype* (*Nyūtaipu*) from Japan; from the USA, *Anime Insider* and *NewtypeUSA*[1] and *OtakuUSA*, the latter to close gaps when both of the former ceased publication; and, from the UK, *Neo*. For practical reasons, the time period covered in most depth in the study was late 2005 to the summer 2010 (with the greatest overlap in texts being found between 2005–2006 publications in Japan and 2007–2010 publications in America and the UK), but outlying examples have been selected where relevant, in order to compare like-with-like wherever possible and keeping in mind the time lag that often occurs between Japanese and US or UK releases of titles.

Delineating the anime horror "canon": English-language academic and fan assessments of anime horror

Although there are not many academic analyses of anime as horror, what work has been undertaken provides some provocative insights into the conceptualization of the genre. First, the commingling of pornography and horror has received a degree of attention by authors including Susan Pointon (1997), Ian Buruma (1995) and Susan J. Napier (2001 and 2005). Pointon cites *Urotsukidōji: The Legend of the Overfiend* as a precursor to other violent horror anime, and as the progenitor of these debates. Pointon's analysis of this OVA series is pertinent here for the way she insists upon hybridity within its imagery and characterization (50). Anime horror, by extension, is described as hybridized, as tempered by other well-established anime genres and linked to traditions within Japanese culture, as a means of explaining the overt sense of cultural difference apparent in this high-profile text.

Broadening out the debates about bodily transformation and their links to horror and pornography, Napier's analysis of *Akira* is framed via "a comparatively recently defined subset of the horror genre, a subgenre that has been identified as 'Body Horror.'" She applies this genre to *Akira*, continuing, "the film's last fifteen minutes or so contain an extraordinary vision of almost unwatchable excess as Tetsuo's mutations become increasingly grotesque" (2005, 43). In these instances, then, notions of exaggeration and extremity dominate the language used by both of these academic critics, offering a doubled generic landscape that sees the inclusion of horror elements in animated texts as a new form of "extreme" horror.

Napier also cites the gothic as an integral part of the pornographic horror landscape of anime. She writes that "[t]he gothic is a clearly nostalgic mode and it is perhaps not surprising that ... this other world is explicitly identified with traditional Japan" (2001, 348). Once again, here, Japanese tradition haunts the appreciation of a perceived "international" genre of horror (for more on international horror, see Schneider and Williams 2005). The recognition of international hybridization within "gothic" anime texts is taken further by other commentators. Wayne Stein and John Edgar Browning, for example, offer perhaps the most detailed understanding of the hybridization of gothic traditions in anime, in their analysis of *Vampire Hunter D* (1985). They claim that the vampire itself is a "trans/national figure" and that *Vampire Hunter D* has "become a global cult text amalgamating various genres (action/horror/fantasy/sci-fi/western/animation)" (2008, 211). They claim that they are:

decoding *Vampire Hunter D*'s Japanicity in order to cultivate a new form of spirituality that helps define what we call "CyberZen Gothic," a product that merges Eastern and Western Gothic constructs which transcends convention and identity, as well as the forces of hybridity that surface from such a union. (212)

In these examples, generic traditions and origins are understood as crucial. The national origins of gothic traditions, and the naming of new hybridized constructions of the gothic (be it a mode of production or genre), are treated as being of paramount importance in assigning meaning and value to these anime texts. This importance is particularly clear from this last example where, in straining to account for the hybridity of horror in anime, the authors create a new category of CyberZen Gothic that is solely their own.

Another of the ways that anime's hybridity causes problems for academic commentators is when horror characters are transplanted into texts that are otherwise disengaged from the generic norms of the horror genre. Thus, D from *Vampire Hunter D* is recognized by Stein and Browning as a samurai-cowboy-vampire hybrid rather than a straightforward vampire. In a different discussion of *Blood: The Last Vampire* (Hiroyuki Kitakubo, 2000), Christopher Bolton produces an excellent reading of the film's use of CGI and of the ambivalent nationalism to be found in Japan's adoption of the vampire mythos, which he argues has periodically viewed the vampire as self and other (2007, 129). Bolton makes the ambiguous national identity of *Blood: The Last Vampire*'s characters an integral part of his discussion of the film's generic content. Academic criticism, thus, is dominated by a perceived need to discuss what is Japanese about these anime texts, and how character types, modes of production and genres link to national discourses. It is for these reasons that the next section asks whether this is a preoccupation that can also be found in non-academic writing, in the languages used by those promoting anime in Japan and America.

The nation and horror: National discourses in the promotion of anime horror in Japanese anime magazines

One of the most notable results of examining the Japanese discourses on horror anime is how infrequently the term "horror" is overtly used. The only overt reference to horror in Japan that I found referred to *Vampire Knight* (*Vampaia Kishi* 2008) as follows: "When people see them, all vampires uniformly seem to be horrifying [*kyūfu*] entities" (*Animage* 2008, 74). Interestingly, this language is used to suggest a contrast between *Vampire Knight* and other kinds of anime horror, with its romance and teen drama detracting from its "horrifying" aspects. Focusing on the composite text of Japanese anime magazine articles,[2] clear languages relating to the horror genre are legible nonetheless; but, these languages of horror tend to be dispersed under broad generic rubrics like the mysterious (*fushigi*), or are dissipated into elements of *mise-en-scène* and character types such as vampires and demons. These are ambiguous generic markers, but taken together they indicate emergent understandings of anime texts as horror that are defined through language and context as alternately nationally specific and internationally, if not globally, informed.

The dominant generic languages within discussions of anime texts as horror tend to be ones of action and mystery. For example, one article on a series featuring two types of vampire (both alien in origin), called *Trinity Blood* (2005), blends action language with romance, discussing central character Abel Nightroad's action intrigues with a spy from a rival court of Eastern vampires. It describes the agent, Ion Fortuna, in the following terms: "But, even if his outward appearance is beautiful, he is a vampire [*kyūketsuki*] how many hundreds of years old?" (*Animage* 2005, 60). In another example, *D.Gray-Man* (2006–2008), about a team of exorcists fighting a villain called the Millennium Earl, the central text describes the plot as both quest and action narrative: "Alan, while pursuing traces of General Cross, who is a teacher whose whereabouts are unknown, encounters demons [*akuma*] he has to deal with in various places" (*Animage* 2007, 62). In these two examples, which are similar to the plot descriptions of many other texts, action forms the dominant organizational category, but characters like vampires and demons provide subgeneric logics that give shape to these broader generic frameworks.

A slightly more unusual generic framework can also be found in the concept of *fushigi*, or the mysterious, which appears in relation to multiple texts. Michael Dylan Foster outlines the links between this term and Japanese folklore in his book *Pandemonium and Parade* (2009), explaining how:

On one level, *fushigi*, and by extension, *mysterious*, refers simply to the unexplainable. But its meaning with regard to yōkai is deeper than this— for there are many things beyond explanation .... Indeed, creatively translated, *fushigi* might be rendered as "that which cannot be grasped in thought." ...The distinct yōkai that emerge at different times are signs of this deference, metaphors for the impossibility of knowing. (17)

Linked to Japanese folklore through *yōkai*, which Foster notes is "variously translated as monster, spirit, goblin, ghost, demon, phantom, specter, fantastic being, lower-order deity, or, more amorphously, as any unexplainable experience or numinous occurrence" (2), *fushigi* can be linked to the horror genre through its relationship to *yōkai* cultures.

Perhaps unsurprisingly, then, the term *fushigi* is deployed in relation to anime that might easily be classified as horror texts. "In Yuko's mysterious [*fushigi*] shop, a bitter fate awaits ..." (*Animage*, 2006, 12) proclaims the title of *Animage*'s promotional coverage for the first season of *xxxHolic*. The article then goes on, in a sidebar, to discuss the staging of the series, and its "mysterious [*fushigi*] atmosphere," while characters, especially central character Kimihiro Watanuki, are described as having bitter experiences of working with the shop's wish-granting owner, Yuko Ichihara (12–13). Similarly, a promotional interview for the *xxxHolic* film, *xxxHolic: A Misummer Night's Dream* (Tsutomu Mizushima, 2007), with the title "Welcome to the World of Spirits [*Ayakashi*]" prefaces its interview with one of the character designers, Kazuchika Kise, by asking, "As for this mysterious [*fushigi*] story ... what kind of imagery has been done for it?" (*Animage*, 2005, 58). In this example, as littered throughout *xxxHolic*'s coverage, the notion of the *fushigi* is allied closely to the series' supernatural elements including its *ayakashi* or supernatural characters. In these ways, then, the supernatural aspects of the series are not overtly aligned with the horror genre, but juxtaposed with it, creating an ambiguous relationship that relies heavily on notions of traditional Japanese folklore. The alliance of the *fushigi* in the last instance with *ayakashi* may also indicate how the two are used to reinforce a national sense of horror content that is different to more globalized versions of the genre.

A similar tension lurks in the naming of vampires, despite Stein and Browning's (2008) claims for these creatures as "transnational" horror characters. The language used to describe vampire characters is particularly complex. The coverage of *Vampire Knight* reports on an internal class system of vampires within the text. The title imports its term for vampires (*bampaia* or *vampaia*) without translating it into Japanese, but then goes on to use local language associated with vampires (*kyūketsuki*, which is a Japanese myth featuring a blood-drinking demon), to discuss a hierarchy of "blood sucking classes" (*kyūketsushu*) (*Animage* 2008, 74–75). This example mixes the linguistic registers of the vampire, seeing them overall as a foreign import (*vampaia*), but one with local importance. This class system is used to mimic the differences between popular and unpopular cliques within the Japanese school system, with the *vampaia* characters acting as a social elite.

In an earlier example from 2001, *Hellsing* features the central character Alucard (*Ākādo* in Japanese, Dracula spelt backwards), who is borrowed directly from the Dracula mythos. However, the language used to describe

Alucard is uniformly that of the local *kyūketsuki*. The title of one article comes closest to mixing linguistic registers, when it refers to Alucard, "Under a Sky that seems like Blood—Enter 'Undead' [*Andeddo*] Alucard!!" (*Animage* 2001, 192). Here, then, it would seem that familiarity with the Dracula mythos is significant enough to require localization by reference to traditional blood-drinking demons.

However, other, and particularly more recent, examples of vampire series frequently double their vampire characters, offering vampire-hunting vampire heroes in addition to vampire villains. Alucard from *Hellsing* is an early example, but *Trinity Blood, Blood: The Last Vampire* and *Black Blood Brothers* (2006) have enthusiastically taken up this theme in recent years. This means that, in fact, the language surrounding vampires has become increasingly complex in recent times, commingling a variety of generic tropes, as well as cultural registers. As the quote from *Trinity Blood* provided earlier shows, sometimes the antagonist vampires, like Ion Fortuna (who later becomes an ally), are the ones who take on the traditional *kyūketsuki* mantel. Abel Nightroad, the protagonist of the series, is described quite differently as a "Kresnik," overtly as an alien race come to Earth whose behaviors mimic those of traditional vampires (*Animage* 2005, 62). As the regular oscillation between *vampaia* and *kyūketsuki* suggests, there remains a tension in the vampire figure, between local and global, between understandings of vampires as heroic or villainous and between the desire to blend genres as disparate as high school stories and science fiction with the horror genre characters that vampires represent.

Nation and the language of the supernatural in US coverage of anime horror

The same ambivalence around the naming of monsters can also be found in US coverage of anime. *Anime Insider* delimits *D.Gray-Man*'s henchmen as: "evil Akuma, a legion of demons created by the villainous Millennium Earl, whose goal is to destroy humanity (naturally)" (*Anime Insider* 2009, 36). By not translating the name of these monsters, the American reproducers, filtered through mediating press, create a horror-based patois that mixes the horror language of Japan with descriptions that enable viewers to make sense of these foreign characters by reference to local monster typologies. In other examples, more dominant genres seem to edge out the urge to produce new monster language. For example, Kimihiro Watanuki's "ability to see and attract spirits" in *xxxHolic* is explained little further than to assert, "When he's not out buying sake for Yuko, he's usually helping her assist her customers with their spiritual conundrums or solving other supernatural dilemmas, which have nearly killed him on more than a few occasions" (Bricken 2008, 46). This, despite the series featuring named Japanese *yōkai*, and the same magazine featuring articles on *yōkai* in manga and anime culture (Fowlkes 2008, 38–42).

Akuma, then, seems to have been left in Japanese because of the generic way in which they are utilized in *D.Gray-Man*, as generic characters whose appellation does not necessarily signify their cultural otherness beyond the fact that they are appearing in a Japanese anime series. The same is perhaps less true for other recurring character types like death gods, or *shinigami*, who seem to have entered the lexicon of transnational anime fandom in full. For example, Ryuk and the other death gods of the *Death Note* series are often referred to as *shinigami* (for example, Chan 2008, 51) without translation. This may have something to do with the large numbers of *shinigami* appearing in Japanese anime from *Bleach* (who translate the term as Soul Reapers and give it to their heroic characters) to *Soul Eater* (2008–2009, whose *shinigami* character runs a supernaturally inclined school). Alternatively, it is tempting to conclude that promotion of these characters as Japanese-originated *shinigami*, rather than as death gods, has been done to maintain the cultural specificity, and thereby the unique otherness, of Japanese anime. In any case, the patois being created by the adoption of such terms suggests that the spread of horror is not simply a West to East exportation, but a more complex exchange of characters, narratives and genres.

Much the same could be said for the vampires coming from Japan to America. Daryl Surat, in a Blu-ray review, writes, "Anything containing vampires is almost always terrible. That the biggest complaint about *Blood: The Last Vampire* is 'I wish it was longer' puts it in the top echelons of vampire anime" (2010, 92–93). Surat acknowledges that there has been a steady stream of vampire-related anime gaining distribution in America in recent years, with their lack of perceived quality indicating a mismatch between his expectations for the wider horror genre and their incarnations in anime. Similarly, a *NewtypeUSA* article on *Trinity Blood* remarks that "Fascinating characters and powerful drama are only two of the many attractions of this elaborate tale. Whether you're a die-hard goth or just like your anime with bite, this is the vampire show for you" (*NewtypeUSA* 2005, 79). These US comments suggest a new hybrid has formed in the horror genre, and that horror anime are now a recognizable category (Altman 1999). In this way, the vampire anime (sub)genre is perhaps easier to identify than a more generalized horror anime genre and, furthermore, it offers an example that confirms Altman's third point: that genres in one medium are not always constituted as they are in others.

Becoming horror: Horror anime reception in the USA and UK

As the use of Surat's comments earlier indicate, reviewers in America and the UK are often writing some time after the initial release of anime in Japan, at which point the difference between reviews and promotion can become quite blurred. This time lag can affect readings of genres in sometimes unexpected ways. For example, the choice of comparison texts can be instructive. These range widely and are not always texts contemporary with the release of the anime in question. For instance, Mike Toole writes for the *Ghost Hound* series that

> If you rattled off a list of anime's greatest horror stories, that list would be a pretty short one. Something about the medium's penchant for wide eyes, vibrant colours, and lots of explosive motion just doesn't lend itself that well to tales of horror. There are exceptions—*Pet Shop of Horrors*, *Boogiepop Phantom*, and *Requiem from the Darkness* will all give their viewer a nice charge with their atmospheric creepiness, but darker shows tend to lean toward suspense—*Mushi-shi's* atmospheric but contains few scares, as does the deliciously paranoid *Serial Experiments Lain*…. See, *Ghost Hound* is kind of like the *Goonies*, only instead of pirate treasure, the kids discover half-forgotten childhood trauma. (2010, 18–19)

In this example, everything from other anime to live-action American family films are cited in order to canonize and explain the content of *Ghost Hound*, with its meanings definitely relying on previous anime horror hits. Other examples, though, make reference to the J-horror cycle of live-action Japanese films (Smith 2007, 91), and even American crime television, as when Tom Smith from *Neo* contextualizes *Death Note* as "kind of like Hitchcock meets Columbo—minus the cigars and bushy eyebrows" (2009a, 60). Again the sheer breadth of texts cited in these examples hints at the range of genre mixing taking place in horror-aligned anime, but also that there are many sources and origin points for the genre, making its borders seem all the more porous.

Genre mixing is often centrally placed within critical discourses, with praise for series that smoothly shift between genres. *Anime Insider* hedges around generic mixing in describing its "Best Suspense" series winner in 2008: *Hell Girl* (*Jigoku Shōjo*, 2006–2007). One portion of the overview reads,

> This dark series chronicles a mysterious girl named Ai Enma, who runs a very unusual internet-based service, and the harrowing tales of her patrons.

Ai's habit of sending souls to Hell for their misdeeds makes for very dark but extremely compelling viewing. (*AI* Staff 2008, 40)

The repetition of "dark" in this quote, along with references to Hell, could be read as locating the series within the horror genre, but the emphasis on suspense and plotting, and the way in which the series is described, all work to reinforce the mystery elements of *Hell Girl*. This is a much more subtle description of genre mixing than found in many other articles, especially around popular vampire-based series. "*Hellsing* wouldn't be *Hellsing* without the sprinkling of bodily fluids to lighten things up, and what better way to keep things flowing than with the blood and entrails of Alucard's foes?" So writes Tom Smith, before going on to summarize the series as "Ultimate vampire action—that's not so heavy on the action for once" (2009b, 63). Unlike the previous American examples, then, by the time *Hellsing* comes to the UK, the show's genre has regressed from simply being vampire to now being "vampire action" anime, whose horror is heavily dependent on the kinds of viscera associated with body horror.

While the solidification of generic associations will be dealt with in the next section, Matt Kamen's coverage of *Ghost Hunt* (2006–2007) for UK magazine *Neo* offers insight into the way generic attributes are often simultaneously broadened out, while recognizing the importance of genre mixing. Kamen writes,

closer inspection confirms our suspicions—this is one fine show, a truly engrossing paranormal series that can prove genuinely unsettling at times. A perfect blend of pacing, lighting, music and tension will have you leaping out of your skin repeatedly through the 13 episodes, and you'll think twice before sleeping straight after …. *Ghost Hunt* isn't all doom, gloom and angry spirits though, as it provides just enough comic moments to make the characters seem like real, grounded people caught in bizarre, otherworldly situations. (2009, 64)

Frightening, but also funny, *Ghost Hunt* is here demonstrated to belong firmly to the horror, or perhaps "paranormal," genre, while also entertaining generic elements far removed from that genre. The genre mixing is described as episodic, rather than hybridized in nature, enabling the reviewer to cite specific "moments" of generic shift. In this way, then, genre mixing is made a narratively significant aspect of *Ghost Hunt*'s success, all the while insisting upon its dominant horror mode of storytelling. In other words, it is the juxtaposition of two dissimilar genres that enables the success of *Ghost Hunt* for this reviewer, but not its generic hybridization.

Seeing genres: Advertising and promotional imagery in horror anime

Genre mixing, reinforcement and even the addition of new generic meanings can often be seen in anime coverage, even when the ability to read genre from that coverage is less certain. Pictures carry a wealth of additional meaning into discussions of anime texts. For example, the discussion of Ion Fortuna in *Trinity Blood*, cited earlier, was accompanied by a group shot with Abel Nightroad and Esther Blanchett toting guns at its center, while the young, blond, large-eyed Ion Fortuna is picture naked to the waist in profile off to the right as bandages trail around his form like smoke. Positioned near the coverage about his beauty, the image reinforces not only the action elements of the storyline, but also the romantic and vulnerable role played by Ion Fortuna within the series.

The sepia-toned color scheme for this image is mimicked in later UK advertising for the series, as when the complete series box-set was advertised in *Neo* in a composite one-page spread. Teenzone.net is quoted in the advertisement as saying *Trinity Blood* is "a fascinating series that will hook horror and sci-fi lovers with its rich storyline," atop of a composite image of the series' main characters reproduced in the same sepia tones as seen in the Japanese example (*Neo* 2009, 37). Action is eschewed in this second image in favor of focus on character design, with nine central characters framed by an image of Abel Nightroad that takes up the left and top of the image. Gold crosses are highlighted throughout this imagery, emphasizing the series' links to the gothic, while science fiction, in this example at least, is mentioned only in the quotation. Gothic and religious iconography, action and science fiction are all played with in the promotional language and imagery for *Trinity Blood*, hinting at this anime's highly complex genre hybridity, while creating an appealing, angular, gothic horror-infused "look" for it (Wyatt 1994, see: Figure 9.1).

By contrast, sometimes imagery is provided for anime that plays up elements not fully explored within the texts themselves. This is a particularly frequent occurrence in Japanese coverage, as when *Black Butler*, or *Kuroshitsuji* (2008–), garnered the cover of *Animage* in December 2008 showing its young male protagonist, Ciel Phantomhive, cross-dressing as a girl and being held in an embrace of his demonic butler, Sebastian. The text around the image lays out the content of the magazine, but adds little information about the show other than its title, the fact that the magazine is giving away free merchandising for it, and that it contains a special discussion between two of its voice actors, Jun Fukuyama and Daisuke Ono.

FIGURE 9.1 *Abel Nightroad activates the Kresnik and embraces his inner, gothic vampire.*

While the lack of generic text makes this image difficult to locate, it is reminiscent of *shōnen ai*, or boys' love, genre texts (Levi et al. 2008). Creating a performance of homosexual romance (both characters' gazes "to camera" suggest a knowingness in the imagery), the cover does not correspond to images reproduced inside the magazine, nor with the central premise of the text (Manry 2008, 63) and thus offers an expansion of the series' generic content. The appeals to audiences of *shōnen ai* texts, gothic-Lolita texts and other forms of popular subcultures in Japan may also imply a local identity for this anime text and its promotion.[3] In this example, then, promotional imagery positions "extra" images alongside those grounded in the text in order to naturalize a greater number of readings and generic associations for the series.

Sometimes, however, promotional giveaway imagery is used to reinforce dominant generic textual attributes of series. A promotional, double-sided poster for *Elfen Lied*, given away in *NewtypeUSA*, for instance, is comprised of two central images used in the packaging of the series on DVD in the USA (July 2005). The poster has an image of central character Lucy/Nyu with one image on either side. Nyu is shown against a cherry blossom background, her large pink eyes gazing directly at the viewer, mouth open and suggestively drawn wearing only a man's white shirt open down her front. On the reverse, Lucy is shown against a blood-drenched black backdrop, her right hand covered in dripping blood to the elbow, eyes closed as the left side of a mask breaks revealing her face. She is again naked, and again only the artful cropping of the image prevents the revelation of her vagina, while her bloody hand is drawn covering her breasts. The sexual nature of this imagery is somewhat misleading in that while Lucy/Nyu is drawn naked in the series at times, it is not a pornographic show, though this imagery does seem to suggest as much proffering fanservice over an accurate representation of content.

These images, and particularly the latter, were reproduced throughout the marketing campaign for *Elfen Lied*. Lucy's blood-spattered form appears in advertising for DVD and television broadcasts of the series (*NewtypeUSA* 2005, 178 and 189), on the front cover of the first volume of the series on DVD and on the front of its boxed set. The consistent use of the image of Lucy signals attempts by the American reproducer-distributors to create an image of the show that incorporates the perceived generic split at its core, what the tagline calls "A vicious killer mutant...a helpless girl unable to speak...both trapped in a single mind!" (*NewtypeUSA* 2005, 189). While the imagery presents *Elfen Lied* as a science fiction-horror hybrid, this text makes no mention of the bloody imagery, aligning the series instead with psychological thrillers and science fiction. Without the image of Lucy's bloody hand, and the blood-spattered background, there would be no reason to believe that this was a horror series, making the inclusion of imagery crucial to understanding the whole gamut of genres activated by promotional discourses.

Sometimes, too, the inclusion of advertising imagery as well as discourses is necessary to understanding how the generic meanings of a text can become honed and simplified over time. *Ghost Hunt*'s advertising campaigns in the USA and UK demonstrate this point well. In the USA, FUNimation's advertisements carried the tagline "the dead have something to say/can you hear them?" overlaid on top of an image of a school classroom, with a girl's shadowy figure in the background and a ghostly hand reaching out of a desk in the foreground. While the text personalizes links to the ghost story, and associations with currently popular ghost-hunting reality television series, the imagery suggests further associations to the *shōjo* meta-genre, with its depiction of the mysterious female figure and school setting. Moreover, the logo for the show combines text and image with the words *Gōsuto Hanto* written in Japanese combined with a splash of blood and the title written in English underneath. In total, this image provides a melange of different nationally oriented generic markers and thereby makes appeals to cross-cultural audiences and Japanophiles. The generic nature of this imagery and text: a girl, a classroom, blood and a ghostly hand is important precisely because it evokes numerous possible national and global generic possibilities.

When *Ghost Hunt* was released in the UK, by Manga in association with FUNimation, they split it into two halves and produced separate image campaigns for both. The tagline was shortened to "the dead have something to say" and a wider variety of images were used, including an action shot of central parapsychologist character Kazuya "Naru" Shibuya holding on to his jacket as walls warp behind him and a large ghostly face screams over his left shoulder (*Neo* 2009, 83). In addition, the advertisement carries a quotation from the AnimeNewsNetwork.com that calls the show "genuinely intense and horrifying." More succinct and more centered on an attractive male character, this advertisement begins a process whereby the generic meanings of the series are clarified, and even standardized.

The "Part 02" advertisement from the UK demonstrates just how important notions of horror genre tropes became to *Ghost Hunt*'s advertising. This second image repeats the tagline, logo and even inverts the color scheme of the first US advertisement, which washes the image in red and green (the original reversed the order but used the same colors). However, the central image is different, with a large group of school children standing outside a school, their backs to "camera" and drawn as if through a fish-eye lens, creating warping around the edges of the image. Like the first school-room image, this image seems linked to the popular vein of Japanese live-action horror films set in schools, from the *Gakkō no Kaidan* (*School Ghost Story*, Toru Tsumitsu, 1995) series to films like *Battle Royale* (Kinji Fukusaku, 2000). Again, further text provides more generic information, and Eyeonanime are quoted as saying, "Spooky shenanigans haven't been so good…the banter of Ghostbusters mixed with the scepticism of Most Haunted"(*Neo* 2009, 39). New and old texts from the USA and UK are brought to bear in making sense of the generic content of *Ghost Hunt* here, texts from different countries, times and media. In these ways, the meanings of *Ghost Hunt* are increasingly localized, but the generic nature of the imagery (only one advertising image features a character from the show) and language used to sell the series on DVD is suggestive of the importance of genre to the success of anime as it travels between different countries.

Conclusions

This chapter has endeavored to produce a reading of horror in anime that is just as open-ended and mixed as the texts themselves. The point was not to declare that horror anime exist and fulfill certain generic and subgeneric types, but, rather more importantly, the aim was to investigate the breadth of horror's manifestations in relation to anime. These manifestations have been shown to range from the creation of new subgenres (like the "vampire anime" subgenre), to the adoption of transnational and local horror styles (like the gothic and *yōkai*) and horror characters (like Dracula), into generically hybridized texts otherwise remote from any "pure" notion of the horror genre.

Additionally, the places in which horror discourses can be found range from the texts themselves through epiphenomenal advertising and promotion. They appear in the discourses found in advertising, promotion and reception, through to the images used to add further meanings to those written discourses. Consequently, horror in anime serves a variety of different masters. It is at once used to contextualize new texts, implying strategies for reading them. At the same time, genre is used to sell anime texts, through giveaways like posters and in direct advertising imagery and text designed to attract the widest possible sets of genre audiences. Horror anime is not, then, one simple entity, but almost innumerable different things to different groups.

The transnational borrowing of horror tropes is not incidental. Instead, horror in anime has been aligned to dominant generic types, with action, romance and mystery all playing important roles in horror's shifts toward more and more mainstream productions. Science fiction has also played a major role in the recognition of horror in anime with everyone from academics like Susan J. Napier to the industry acknowledging links between the two forms. This is something that Steve Neale has pointed to: "As has often been noted, it is sometimes very difficult to distinguish between horror and science fiction. Not only that, it can at times be difficult to distinguish between horror and crime film, and science fiction, adventure and fantasy as well" (2000, 92). If horror is difficult to distinguish, this chapter has suggested that the reason may be that horror is often mixed, hybridized or even synthesized within these, and other, genres.

Furthermore, its recognition as such depends on local knowledge of the multiple, culturally specific origins and manifestations of "horror," in addition to a reading of horror as encompassing everything from long-established subgenres from fiction, such as the gothic, to newer forms, such as body horror, or even "gorenography." The discursive practices analyzed here suggest that commentators draw from wide cultural and historical arena for horror, citing contemporary textual influences alongside those decades past. None of this is "incidental," though; rather it is a complex process through which the dominant forms of generic production are worked through. By looking for horror discourses, the genres that are dominant in anime production become clearer, but so do those genres that are routinely mixed with them in order to produce new and exciting genre texts for audiences.

Finally, the national specificity of horror in anime has been included in this discussion because it plays a vital role in how commentators have assessed the presence of horror in anime texts. Peter Hutchings has rightly asserted about British horror that:

> Thinking about the similarities and differences between British and American horror films leads to another difficulty in our attempt to locate horror within a specifically national cinema: namely that the operations of the horror genre are not restricted to any one country or culture but rather are spread across much of the filmmaking world. (1993, 15)

While this is true for much of the horror that appears in anime, we have also seen how local horror cultures can also influence the promotion and reception of texts. Within Japan, the language of the *fushigi* and *kyūketsuki* provide examples of Japanese localization of horror; and in American and British examples, the adoption of the *shinigami* likewise indicates an exchange of horror genres rather than any simple understanding of "global" horror.

This seems a good place to conclude: with a context-based understanding of genre in anime, and anime as a genre, that represents an increasingly fluid and complex exchange of cultures and ideas between national industries. By opening up the discussion of anime and genre to a series of voices that are not normally privileged either by fans or academics, I have attempted to show that anime's genrification takes places continually, even after production and reception in the originating Japanese context. Moreover, I have demonstrated repeatedly that our understandings of anime have been built upon continual shifts in our understandings of the context through which anime have flowed. Anime and genre thereby provide an exciting means by which to think through the influences, meanings and content of contemporary media cultures as they travel across the globe.

Notes

Introduction

1 For similar statements about pronunciation, see Antonia Levi, *Samurai from Outer Space: Understanding Japanese Animation* (1996). Translations throughout this volume are my own, unless otherwise stated, and Japanese names are given in Anglophone order, written with surname second. Given the huge "worlds" of texts made around intellectual properties in Japan, and the multimedia nature of anime texts, providing a filmography would require most of this book. Therefore, all film and other media titles are given with their common English and Japanese versions (where different), and the date ranges indicate the initial years that they aired in Japan.

2 I am, inevitably, limited by my linguistic expertise and by my ability to access discourses from around the world. Consequently, English and Japanese language coverage dominates the discourses analyzed in this book. Similarly, the sources analyzed have a particular bias toward Japanese, US and UK sources, reflecting my own position as a UK-based researcher. Other discursive studies based in other locales would doubtless reveal different and exciting alternative debates around the meanings of anime, but they are beyond the scope of this book.

3 The studio was named Tōei Dōga in its early period (see Chapter 4)—one of Japan's first major animation studios, and one initially concerned with feature filmmaking, not television.

Chapter 1

1 Jim Kitses' *Horizons West* was first published in 1969, with a second revised edition published in 2007.

Chapter 4

1 *Journey to the West* was released in the USA as *Alakzam the Great*, and had one of the first star-studded US voice casts in anime's US history. Frankie Avalon sang the songs and popular voice actors including Jonathan Winters, Stirling Holloway and Arnold Stang provided voices.

Chapter 7

1 GKIDS has held the license to theatrically distribute Studio Ghibli's films since 2011, but Disney retains the copyright for home entertainment distribution (Marechal 2011).

2 The spelling of *Ghiblies 2* as *Giburīsu* instead of *Jiburīsu* as the Studio's name would normally be Romanized from Japanese was a brand distinction that came with a new reworking of the Studio Ghibli logo, transforming the white outline of Totoro into a black outline of one of the central characters from the short films, which all focus on fictionalized representations of the working life at Studio Ghibli. In this way, the text reflexively acknowledges the importance of the Studio's brand and the growing interest in its animators within Japanese culture.

3 The latter borrowed from a character name in *Laputa: Castle in the Sky, Tenkū no Shiro Lapyuta*, Miyazaki, 1986.

Chapter 8

1 It is worth noting that these generic labels are sourced from the Anime New Network—I use them here as a means of shorthand to enable a wider consideration of the differences between texts in TAF's event space, but I do so full in the knowledge of genre's flexible, discursive and contextually dependent meanings.

Chapter 9

1 Produced by the ADV distribution company as a translation of the Japanese magazine with added reviews and segments.

2 Japanese promotional articles are, in some ways, distinct from those found in American and UK publications. They tend to be image heavy, often with a central background image around which text and further graphic elements are grouped, and they are often arranged across two-page (or longer) spreads. Such articles tend to be anonymously authored, with large titles and subordinate paragraphs outlining a central concept or plotline. They almost always contain standardized information about official websites and broadcast schedules and, in addition to introductory paragraphs and short character biographies, they usually also feature a longer interview with cast or crew members.

3 This cover image was also reproduced in a set of free promotional playing cards given away in a later issue of *Animage* (April 2009). In this epiphenomenal set of playing cards, images from the text itself were reproduced, but the box that holds them featured the same image as seen above.

Bibliography

"20% Less Booths at Tokyo Anime Fair as Talks Continue," *Anime News Network*, January 26, http://www.animenewsnetwork.co.uk/news/2011-01-26/20-percent-less-booths-at-tokyo-anime-fair-as-talks-continue (2011) (accessed March 14, 2014).

"A Girl Between," [*Hazama no Shōjo*] *Animage*, August: 96–97. (2005)

"AMV Contest," *AnimeExpo AX 2015*, http://www.anime-expo.org/schedule/amv-contest/ (n.d.) (accessed September 21, 2014).

"An Angel Descends to the Desert Stage," [*Tenshi wa Sabaku ni Mai Oriru*] *Animage* 326, August: 60–61. (2005)

H. Furukawa (trans.) "An Investigation of Nichijōkei with a Bookstore Staff Member," [*Honya-san to issho ni saguru "nichijōkei"*] *Screen Plus* 29: 18–19. (2011)

Animage [*Animēju*], 374(8). (2009)

"Black Blood Brothers," *Animage*, May: 145. (2006)

"Bubblegum Crisis," *Anime UK* 2: 24–39. (1992)

"Concerning the Establishment of 'Ghibli West,' Studio Ghibli's New Studio," [*Sutajio Jiburi Shinstajio "Nishi Jiburi" Setsuritsu ni Tsuite*] *Studio Ghibli Official Website*, http://www.ghibli.jp/10info/005681.html (2009) (accessed June 10, 2014).

"Congratulations: *Spirited Away*," *Variety* (March 31–April 6): 5. (2003)

"Crimson Night," *Animage* 361, July: 74–75. (2008)

"Crunchyroll Reports 200,000+ Paid Subscribers," *Anime News Network*, March 23, https://www.animenewsnetwork.co.uk/news/2013-03-23/crunchyroll-reports-200000+paid-subscribers/2 (2013) (accessed April 14, 2014).

"D. Gray-Man," *Anime Insider* 64, January: 36. (2009)

"Elfin Lied Advertisement," *NewtypeUSA* 4.7, July: 178. (2005)

"Elfin Lied Advertisement," *NewtypeUSA* 4.7, July: 189. (2005)

"Elfin Lied Poster," *NewtypeUSA* 4.7, July. (2005)

"Eternal Anime," *Anime UK* 2, June–July: 30. (1992)

"Full Season of the Best Anime from FUNimation Channel Launch on JumpInMobile.TV," *Anime News Network*, August 9, http://www.animenewsnetwork.com/press-release/2008-07-09/full-seasons-of-the-best-anime-from-funimation-channel-launch-on-jumpinmobile.tv-the-new-mobile-video-on-demand-service-from-red-planet-media (2008a) (accessed September 9, 2014).

"Funimation Cancels One Piece Simulcast (Update 2)," *Anime News Network*, May 30, http://www.animenewsnetwork.com/news/2009-05-30/funimation-cancels-one-piece-simulcast (2009) (accessed September 9, 2014).

"Funimation Channel Launches on AT&T U-Verse in High Definition," *Anime News Network*, September 30, http://www.animenewsnetwork.com/

press-release/2010-09-30/funimation-channel-launches-on-at&t-u-verse-in-high-definition (2010) (accessed September 9, 2014).

"Funimation Channel Launches Website," *Anime News Network*, November 24, http://www.animenewsnetwork.com/news/2005-11-24/funimation-channel-launches-website (2005) (accessed September 9, 2014).

"Ghibli Co-Founder Suzuki: Studio Considers Dismantling Production Department," *Anime News Network*, April 8, http://www.animenewsnetwork.com/news/2014-08-04/ghibli-co-founder-suzuki-studio-considers-dismantling-production-department/.77263 (2014a) (accessed September 26, 2014).

"Ghibli Co-Founder Toshio Suzuki Retires as Producer," *Anime News Network*, March 9, http://www.animenewsnetwork.co.uk/news/2014-03-09/ghibli-co-founder-toshio-suzuki-retires-as-producer (2014b) (accessed June 10, 2014).

"Ghost Hunt Advertisement," *Neo* 58, May: 83. (2009)

"In Yuko's Mysterious Shop, a Bitter Fate Awaits…," *Animage*: 12–13. (2006)

"Japan Anime Map: Sacred Places Pilgrimages," *Japan National Tourism Organization*, http://www.jnto.go.jp/eng/animemap/ANIMEmap_back.pdf (n.d.) (accessed March 23, 2014).

Japan: Kingdom of Characters, http://www.jpf.go.jp/j/culture/exhibit/oversea/traveling/pdf/Characters.pdf (2010) (accessed March 23, 2014).

"Manga Entertainment," *Anime News Network*, https://www.animenewsnetwork.co.uk/encyclopedia/company.php?id=10 (n.d.) (accessed September 12, 2014).

"Matters of Life," *Observer*, January 1: 10. (1995)

"Mobile Police Patlabor," *Anime UK* 1, Winter: 4–11. (1991–1992)

"Otaking77077," *YouTube*, http://www.youtube.com/user/OtaKing77077 (n.d.) (accessed June 6, 2014).

"Past Data of TAF," *Tokyo International Anime Fair*, http://www.tokyoanime.jp/en/info/archive/ (n.d.) (accessed March 14, 2014).

Right Stuf!.com, http://www.rightstuf.com/rssite/main/ (n.d.) (accessed September 1, 2014).

"Slam Dunk: Crunchyroll Teams Up with Toei Animation," *Anime News Network*, October 27, https://www.animenewsnetwork.co.uk/press-release/2008-10-27/slam-dunk-crunchyroll-teams-up-with-toei-animation (2008) (accessed December 1, 2012).

"The Actors Are Placed," [*Yakusha wa Sorotta*] *Animage* 348, June: 62–63. (2007)

"The Elites of Manga and Anime Talk Enthusiastically About 'Nichijōkei'!" [*Genjō no Seiei "Nichijōkei" o Atsuku Kataru!*] *Screen Plus* 29: 20–22. (2011)

"The History of Studio Ghibli," [*Sutajio Jiburi no Rekishi*] *Studio Ghibli Official Website*, http://www.ghibli.jp/30profile/000152.html (n.d.) (accessed June 10, 2014).

"This Month in Anime History: June 1961," *NewtypeUSA* 2.6, June: 54. (2003)

"Those Who Hunt Vampires," *NewtypeUSA* 4.7, July: 78–79. (2005)

"*Trinity Blood* Advertisement," *Neo* 56, April: 37. (2009)

"Tsumiki no Ie, Piano Forest, Kaiba Win Media Arts Awards," *Anime News Network*, December 10, http://www.animenewsnetwork.com/news/2008-12-10/tsumiki-no-ie-piano-forest-kaiba-win-media-arts-awards (2008b) (accessed March 14, 2014).

"Under a Sky that Seems like Blood—Enter 'Undead' [*Andeddo*] Alucard!!" [*Chi no you na Sorano Shita ni: "Andeddo" Ākādo Tōjō*] *Animage* 282, December: 192. (2001)

"Video Notes," *Video Week*, September 20, n.p. (1993)
"Welcome to the World of Spirits," [*Ayakashi no Sekai ni Yōkoso*] *Animage* 326: 58–59. (2005)
xxxHolic DVD sleeve. Series 1, Volume 2. Manga Entertainment UK. (2009)

Allen, R.C. (1989) "Bursting Bubbles: 'Soap Opera,' Audiences, and the Limits of Genre," in E. Seiter, H. Borchers, G. Kreutzner and E. Warth (eds) *Remote Control: Television, Audiences and Cultural Power*, New York: Routledge, pp. 44–55.
Allison, A. (2000) "Sailor Moon: Japanese Superheroes for Global Girls," in T.J. Craig (ed.) *Japan Pop!: Inside the World of Japanese Popular Culture*, Armonk, NY: M.E. Sharp, pp. 259–278.
Allison, A. (2006) *Millennial Monsters: Japanese Toys and the Global Imagination*, Berkeley: University of California Press.
Alloway, L. (1963) "On the Iconography of the Movies," *Movie* 7: 4–6.
Altman, R. (1984) "A Semantic/Syntactic Approach to Film Genre," *Cinema Journal* 23.3, Spring: 6–18.
Altman, R. (1999) *Film/Genre*, London: BFI Publishing.
Anime Insider Staff (2008) "Best by Genre: Other Honorable Mentions of 2008," *Anime Insider* 63, December: 36–44.
Azuma, H. ([2001] 2009) J.E. Abel and S. Kono (trans.), *Otaku: Japan's Database Animals*, Minneapolis: University of Minnesota Press.
Bertschy, Z. (2008a) "Interview with the Fansubber," *Anime News Network*, March 11, https://www.animenewsnetwork.co.uk/feature/2008-03-11 (accessed July 11, 2010).
Bertschy, Z. (2008b) "Interview: Crunchyroll's Vu Nguyen," *Anime News Network*, March 25, https://www.animenewsnetwork.co.uk/interview/2008-03-25/vu-nguyen (accessed September 13, 2014).
Bolton, C. (2007) "The Quick and the Undead: Visual and Political Dynamics in *Blood: The Last Vampire*," in F. Lunning (ed.) *Mechademia 2: Networks of Desire*, Minneapolis: University of Minnesota Press, pp. 125–142.
Bolton, C., I. Csicsery-Ronay, Jr. and T. Tatsumi (eds) (2007) *Robot Ghosts and Wired Dreams: Japanese Science Fiction from Origins to Anime*, Minneapolis: University of Minnesota Press.
Bordwell, D. (1985) *Narration in the Fiction Film*, London: Methuen.
Bowman, M.R. (2011) "Beyond Maids and *Meganekko*: Examining the *Moe* Phenomenon," *Cinephile* 7.1, Spring: 15–19.
Brendt, J. (2010) *Comic Worlds and the World of Comics: Towards Scholarship on a Global Scale, Global Manga Studies* 1. Kyoto Seika Daigaku, http://imrc.jp/2010/09/26/20100924Comics%20Worlds%20and%20the%20World%20of%20Comics.pdf (accessed December 1, 2011).
Bricken, R. (2008) "The Cost of Living," *Anime Insider* 57, June: 42–46.
British Board of Film Classification (2013) "Podcast Episode 17: Anime," *BBFC Website*, http://www.bbfc.co.uk/case-studies/podcasts/bbfc-podcast-episode-17-classifying-anime (accessed January 5, 2014).
Broder, J.M. and S. Shane (2013) "For Snowden, a Life of Ambition, Despite the Drifting," *New York Times*, June 16: A20.
Brophy, P. (2005) *100 Anime*, London: BFI Publishing.
Bull, B. (2007) "Evolving Anime Films Follow New Inspirations," *Variety*, October 22–28: A3.

Buruma, I. (1984) *Behind the Mask: On Sexual Demons, Sacred Mothers, Transvestites, Gangsters and Other Japanese Cultural Heroes*, New York: First Meridian Publishing.

Buscombe, E. (1970) "The Idea of Genre in the American Cinema," *Screen* 11.2: 33–45.

Cavallaro, D. (2006) *The Art of Hayao Miyazaki*, Jefferson: McFarland & Co.

Cavallaro, D. (2007) *Anime Intersections: Tradition and Innovation in Theme and Technique*, Jefferson: McFarland & Co.

Cavallaro, D. (2009) *The Art of Studio Gainax: Experimentation, Style and Innovation at the Leading Edge of Anime*, Jefferson: McFarland.

Chan, J. (2008) "Unusual Suspects," *Anime Insider* 56, May: 51.

Cherry, B. and M. Mellins (2011) "Negotiating the Punk in Steampunk: Subculture, Fashion and Performative Identity," *Punk and Post Punk* 1.1: 5–25.

Chun, J.M. (2007) *A Nation of a Hundred Million Idiots?: A Social History of Japanese Television 1953–1973*, New York: Routledge.

Cintas, J.D. and P. Muñoz Sánchez (2006) "Fansubs: Audiovisual Translation in an Amateur Environment," *Journal of Specialised Translation* 6, http://www.jostrans.org/issue06/art_diaz_munoz.pdf (accessed April 1, 2015).

Clements, J. (2013a) *Anime: A History*, London: BFI Publishing.

Clements, J. (2013b) "Tezuka's Anime Revolution in Context," in F. Lunning (ed.) *Mechademia 8: Tezuka's Manga Life*, Minneapolis: University of Minnesota Press, pp. 214–226.

Clements, J. and M. Tamamuro (2003) *The Dorama Encyclopedia: A Guide to Japanese TV Drama since 1953*, Berkeley, CA: Stone Bridge Press.

Condry, I. (2010) "Dark Energy: What Fansubs Reveal about the Copyright Wars," in F. Lunning (ed.) *Mechademia 5: Fanthropologies*, Minneapolis: University of Minnesota Press, pp. 193–208.

Condry, I. (2013) *The Soul of Anime: Collaborative Creativity and Japan's Media Success Story*, Durham: Duke University Press.

Corbett, A. (2009) "Beyond *Ghost in the (Human) Shell*," *Journal of Evolution and Technology* 20.1: 43–50.

Corliss, R. (2002) "High Spirits," *Time,* September 22, http://content.time.com/time/magazine/article/0,9171,1101020930-353577,00.html (accessed June 10, 2014).

Crafton, D. (2005) "Planes Crazy: Transformations of Pictorial Space in 1930s Cartoons," *Cinémas: Journal of Film Studies* 15.2–3: 147–180.

Crang, M. (1998) *Cultural Geography*, London and New York: Routledge.

Crawford, B. (1996) "Emperor Tomato-Ketchup: Cartoon Properties from Japan," in M. Broderick (ed.), *Hibakusha Cinema: Hiroshima, Nagasaki and the Nuclear Image in Japanese Film*, London: Kegan Paul International, pp. 75–90.

Crunchyroll (n.d.) Crunchyroll.com, http://www.crunchyroll.com/about (accessed August 9, 2009).

Cubbison, L. (2005) "Anime Fans, DVDs, and the Authentic Text," *Velvet Light Trap* 56, Fall: 45–57.

Davis, J. (2002) *Animerica: Gundam Official Guide*, San Francisco, CA: Viz Publications.

deCordorva, R. (1994) "The Mickey in Macy's Window: Childhood, Consumerism, and Disney Animation," in E. Smoodin (ed.), *Disney Discourse: Producing the Magic Kingdom*, New York: Routledge, pp. 203–213.

Denison, R. (2007) "The Global Markets for Anime: Hayao Miyazaki's *Spirited Away* (2001)", in A. Philips and J. Stringer (eds) *Japanese Cinema: Texts and Contexts*, Abingdon: Routledge, 308–321.

Denison, R. (2010) "Anime Tourism: Discursive Construction and Reception of the Studio Ghibli Art Museum," *Japan Forum* 22.3–4: 545–563.

Denison, R. (2011) "Anime Fandom and the Liminal Spaces between Fan Creativity and Piracy," *International Journal of Cultural Studies* 14.5, September: 449–466.

Denison, R. (2014) "Franchising and Failure: Discourses of Failure within the Japanese-American *Speed Racer* Franchise," *Mechademia 9: Origins*, Minneapolis: University of Minnesota Press, pp. 269–281.

Denison, R. (2015) *American Superheroes in Japanese Hands: Superhero Genre Hybridity as Superhero Systems Collide in Supaidāman*, Jackson: University of Mississippi Press, pp. 53–72.

Denslow, P.K. (1997) "What Is Animation and Who Needs to Know? An Essay on Definitions," in J. Pilling (ed.) *A Reader in Animation Studies*, London: John Libbey, pp. 1–4.

Desser, D. (1992) "Toward a Structural Analysis of the Postwar Samurai Film," in A. Nolletti, Jr. and D. Desser (eds) *Reframing Japanese Cinema: Authorship, Genre, History*, Bloomington: Indiana University Press, pp. 145–164.

DeWalt, K.M. and B.R. DeWalt (2011) *Participant Observation: A Guide for Fieldworkers*, 2nd ed., Lanham: AltaMira Press.

Diaz Cintas, J. and P. Muñoz Sánchez (2006) "Fansubs: Audiovisual Translation in an Amateur Environment," *The Journal of Specialised Translation* 6, July: 37–52.

Dyar, D.N. (1992) "A Decade of the Dirty Pair," *Anime UK* 2: 4–14.

Dyar, D.N. (1992–1993) "Mobile Suit Gundam Century," *Anime UK* 5, December–January: 6–17.

Dyar, D.N. (1993a) "Mobile Suit Gundam, Part 2," *Anime UK* 6, February–March: 12–24.

Dyar, D.N. (1993b) "Mobile Suit Gundam, Part 3," *Anime UK* 7, April–May: 6–18.

Ebert, R. (2005) "Steamboy," *RogerEbert.com*, March 17, http://www.rogerebert.com/reviews/steamboy-2005, (accessed September 1, 2014).

Egan, K. (2007) *Trash or Treasure?: Censorship and the Changing Meanings of the Video Nasties*, Manchester: Manchester University Press.

Elley, D. (2008) "The Sky Crawlers," *Variety*, September 15–21, n.p.

Evans, P. (1993) "The Beautiful and the Terrible," *Anime UK* 9: 27–31.

Evenson, L. (1996) "Cyberbabe Takes on Tokyo in 'Ghost,'" *San Francisco Chronicle*, April 12, http://www.sfgate.com/movies/article/Cyberbabe-Takes-On-Tokyo-in-Ghost-Tough-2986873.php (accessed August 27, 2014).

Featherstone, M. and R. Burrows (eds) (1995) *Cyberspace/Cyberbodies/Cyberpunk: Cultures of Technological Embodiment*, London: Sage.

Felperin, L. (2004) "Steamboy," *Variety*, November 15–21: 56.

Foster, M.D. (2009a) *Pandemonium and Parade: Japanese Monsters and the Culture of Yōkai*, Berkeley: University of California Press.

Foster, M.D. (2009b) "Haunted Travelogue: Hometowns, Ghost Towns, and Memories of War," in F. Lunning (ed.), *Mechademia 4: War/Time*, Minneapolis: University of Minnesota Press, pp. 164–181.

Fowlkes, C. (2008) "The Monster Maker," *Anime Insider* 62, November: 38–42.

Fowlkes, C. (2009) "Kingdom Come," *Anime Insider* 67, April: 63.

Fukuda, J. (2012), Hiroko Furukawa (trans.), "*Nichijōkei* Manga Is Getting Popular—An Unrealistic Wonderful World," *Yomiuri Newspaper*, November 30, http://www.yomiuri.co.jp/book/news/20111129-OYT8T00833.htm

Furniss, M. (1998) *Art in Motion: Animation Aesthetics*, London: John Libbey.

Furukawa, H. with R. Denison (2014) "Disaster and Relief: The 3.11 Tohoku and Fukushima Disasters and Japan's Media Industries," *International Journal of Cultural Studies,* http://ics.sagepub.com/content/18/2/225.abstract (accessed July 6, 2015).

Galbraith, P. (2009) "Moe: Exploring Virtual Potential in Post-Millennial Japan," *Electonic Journal of Contemporary Japanese Studies,* http://www.japanesestudies.org.uk/articles/2009/Galbraith.html (accessed April 1, 2015).

Galt, R. and K. Schoonover (eds) (2010) *Global Art Cinema*. Oxford: Oxford University Press.

General Headquarters, SCAP, CI&E, "The Fundamental Law of Education," *Education in the New Japan* 2, Tokyo, pp. 109–111, http://ad9.org/pegasus/Education/law-of-educationE.html (accessed September 21, 2014).

Geraghty, L. (2014) *Cult Collections: Nostalgia, Fandom and collecting Popular Culture*, Abingdon: Routledge.

Gerow, A. (2010) *Visions of Japanese Modernity: Articulations of Cinema, Nation, and Spectatorship 1895–1925*, Berkeley: University of California Press.

Gledhill, C. (2000) "Rethinking Genre," in C. Gledhill and L. Williams (eds), *Reinventing Film Studies*, London: Arnold, pp. 221–243.

Goldberg, W. (2009) "Transcending the Victim's History: Takahata Isao's Grave of the Fireflies," in F. Lunning (ed.), *Mechademia 4: War/Time*, Minneapolis: University of Minnesota Press, pp. 39–52.

Goodridge, M. (2008) "Awards Countdown: Animation Oscar Preview," *Screen International*, November 21, n.p.

Graham, J. (2014) "*The King and the Mockingbird*," *Total Film* 219, May: 59.

Grainge, P. (2008) *Brand Hollywood: Selling Entertainment in a Global Media Age*, Abingdon: Routledge.

Gravett, P. (2004) *Manga: Sixty Years of Japanese Comics*, London: Lawrence King Publishing.

Gray, J. (2008) "Rinko Kikuchi, Ryo Kase to voice Sky Crawlers," *Screen Daily*, April 16, http://www.screendaily.com/rinko-kikuchi-ryo-kase-to-voice-sky-crawlers/4038264.article (accessed July 17, 2015).

Haider, A. (2005) "Steamboy," *Times* (London), December 3: 11.

Hancock, D. (1995) "Manga Mania Rises in West," *Daily Mirror*, October 19: 7.

Harada, A. (2008) *Hell Girl Illustrations: Mirrored Flowers, Moonlight in Water* [*Jigoku Shōjo Irasutorēshonzu: Kyōka Suigetsu*], Tokyo: Ichijinsha.

Harrington, R. (1993) "Movies; 'Overfiend': Cyber Sadism," *Washington Post*, April 26: D7.

Harrington, R. (1996) "'Ghost': Virtually Vivid," *Washington Post*, March 29: B07.

Harrison, S. (2004) Posting to Rec.arts.anime, June 19, https://groups.google.com/forum/#!searchin/rec.arts.anime.misc/first$20anime$20on$20dvd$20ever/rec.arts.anime.misc/Mf4G10tbUDg/Eq7_6ZuOeAcJ (accessed September 14, 2014).

Hartlaub, P. (2010) "Action Aplenty in Animated Fantasy 'Earthsea'," *SF Gate*, http://www.sfgate.com/movies/article/Action-aplenty-in-animated-fantasy-Earthsea-3178389.php (accessed June 10, 2014).

Harvey. D. (2000) *Spaces of Hope*, Edinburgh: Edinburgh University Press.

Hayakawa, K. (2008) *Tokyo International Anime Fair 2008* [*Tokyo Kokusai Anime Fea 2008*], Tokyo: Tokyo International Anime Fair Executive Committee.

Hesmondhalgh, D. (2007) *The Cultural Industries*, 2nd ed, London: Sage.

Hikawa (2001) "In Animation Director Hirotoshi Sano's Eyes," [*Sano Hirotoshi no Shisen*] *Animage* 282: 122–124.

Hoberman, J. (2005) "London Fog," *Village Voice*, March 8, http://www.villagevoice.com/2005-03-08/film/london-fog/ (accessed September 3, 2014).

Honeycutt, K. (2010) "*Tales from Earthsea*—Film Review," *The Hollywood Reporter*, October 14, http://www.hollywoodreporter.com/review/tales-earthsea-film-review-29875 (accessed June 10, 2014).

Horbinski, A. (2011) "War for Entertainment," in F. Lunning (ed.), *Mechademia 6: User Enhanced*, Minneapolis: University of Minnesota Press, pp. 304–306.

Hornaday, A. (2008) "'Speed Racer' Is Stuck on a Fast Track to Nowhere," *Washington Post*, May 9: C01.

Hornaday, A. (2014) "A Final Flight of Fancy," *The Washington Post*, February 21: T30.

Hosoda, M. (2006) "Interview," in *The Girl Who Leapt through Time: Notebook* [*Toki o Kakeru Shōjo: Notebook*], Tokyo: Kadokawa, pp. 82–87.

Howe, D. (1993) "Film Capsules," *Washington Post*, April 23: N33.

Howell, P. (2008) "World Cinema Lines Up for Festival," *Toronto Star*, August 7: E01.

Hu, T.Y.G. (2010) *Frames of Anime: Culture and Image Building*, Hong Kong: Hong Kong University Press. E-book.

Hunter, S. (1990) "Extraordinary Animation, Powerful Vision Breathe Life into 'Akira's' Violent Future," *Baltimore Sun*, September 13, http://articles.baltimoresun.com/1990-09-13/features/1990256006_1_akira-otomo-neo-tokyo (accessed September 3, 2014).

Hunter, S. (2005) "'Steamboy': Anime Powered by Hot Air," *Washington Post*, March 25: C01.

Hutchings, P. (1993) *Hammer and Beyond: The British Horror Film*, Manchester: Manchester University Press.

Ishihara, S. (2008) "Greeting from the Governor of Tokyo," [*Goaisatsu*] in K. Hayakawa (ed) *Tokyo International Anime Fair 2008* [*Tokyo Kokusai Anime Fea 2008*], Tokyo: Tokyo International Anime Fair Executive Committee, pp. 2–3.

Ito, M. (2003) "Technologies of Childhood Imagination: Media Mixes, Hypersociality, and Recombinant Cultural Form," *Items and Issues: Social Sciences Research Council* 4.4, Winter: 31–34.

Ito, M. (2008) "Manga in Japanese History," in M.W. MacWilliams (ed.), *Japanese Visual Culture: Explorations in the World of Manga and Anime*, London: ME Sharp, pp. 3–25.

Iwabuchi, K. (2002) *Recentering Globalization: Popular Culture and Japanese Transnationalism*, Durham: Duke University Press.

James, N. (2008) "A Few Choice Triumphs Keep the Lido Afloat [Venice Film Festival]," *Observer*, September 7, 15.

Jameson, F. (1983) "Postmodernism and the Consumer Society," in Hal Foster (ed.), *The Anti-Aesthetic, Essays on Postmodern Culture*, Port Townsend: Bay Press.

Jancovich, M. (2000) "'A Real Shocker': Authenticity, Genre and the Struggle for Distinction," *Continuum: Journal of Media and Cultural Studies* 14.1: 23–35.

Jancovich, M. (2010) "Two Ways of Looking: The Critical Reception of 1940s Horror," *Cinema Journal* 49.3, Spring: 45–66.

Jenkins, H. (2006a) *Fans, Bloggers, and Gamers: Exploring Participatory Culture*, New York: New York University Press.

Jenkins, H. (2006b) *Convergence Culture: Where Old and New Media Collide*, New York: New York University Press.

Johns, I. (2005) "Unlike a Dignified Samurai, Everyone Else Seems to Be Blowing Off Steam," *Times* (London), December 1: 17.

Johnson, S. (1995) "Good Things in Soft Packages," *Independent*, December 7: 8.

Johnston, S. (1991) "Film," *Independent* (London), January 25, p.16.

Joo, W., R. Denison and H. Furukawa (2013) *Manga Movies Project Report 1: Transmedia Japanese Franchising*, http://www.mangamoviesproject.com/publications.html (accessed September 3, 2014).

Kamen, M. (2009) "Ghost Hunt Season 1, Part 1 ('multiformat')," *Neo* 57, April: 64.

Kamen, M. (2014) "2014: What You'll Be Watching!" *Neo* 119, January: 9–21.

Kanai, M. (2011) " '*K'On!*': Solution to a Phenomenon," ["*Keion!*" *Genshō no "Kai*"] *Nikkei Entertainment* 177: 16–18.

Kemps, H. and L. Lamb (2013) "Interview: BONES Studio President Masahiko Minami," *Anime News Network*, October 25, http://www.animenewsnetwork.com/interview/2013-10-25/interview-bones-studio-president-masahiko-minami (accessed March 15, 2014).

Kinder, M. (1993) *Playing with Power in Movies, Television and Video Games*, Berkeley: University of California Press.

Kinema Junpo Research Office (2011) H. Furukawa (trans.) "*Nichijōkei Anime*": *The Law of Hits* ("*Nichijōkei Anime*": *Hitto no Hōsoku*), Tokyo: Watermark Publishers.

Kinsella, S. (1995) "Cuties in Japan," in L. Skov and B. Moeran (eds), *Women, Media and Consumption in Japan*, Honolulu: University of Hawaii Press, pp. 220–254.

Kitses, J. (2007) *Horizons West: The Western from John Ford to Clint Eastwood*, London: BFI Publishing, first published 1969.

Klinger, B. (1984) "'Cinema/Ideology/Criticism' Revisited: The Progressive Text," *Screen* 25.1: 30–44.

Klinger, B. (1994) *Melodrama and Meaning: History, Culture, and the Films of Douglas Sirk*, Bloomington: University of Indiana Press.

Klinger, B. (1997) "Film History Terminable and Interminable: Recovering the Past in Reception Studies," *Screen* 38.2: 107–128.

Klinger, B. (2006) *Beyond the Multiplex: Cinema, New Technologies, and the Home*, Berkeley: University of California Press.

Koulikov, M. (2008) "Anime Expo 2008: Industry Roundtable: Fansubs— The Death of Anime?" *Anime News Network*, August 3, http://www.animenewsnetwork.com/convention/2008/anime-expo/industry-roundtable (accessed September 8, 2008).

Kusanagi, S. (2003) *How did Japanese Anime Come to Be Watched in America? [Amerika de Nihon no Anime wa, Dōu Miraredekitaka?]*, Tokyo: Studio Ghibli Publishing.

Ladd, F. with H. Deneroff (2009) *Astro Boy and Anime Come to the Americas*, Jefferson: McFarland.

LaMarre, T. (2002) "From Animation to Anime: Drawing Movements and Moving Drawings," *Japan Forum* 14.2: 329–367.

LaMarre, T. (2006a) "The Multiplanar Image," in F. Lunning (ed.), *Mechademia 1: Emerging Worlds of Anime and Manga*, Minneapolis: University of Minnesota Press, pp. 120–143.

LaMarre, T. (2006b) "Platonic Sex: Perversion and Shōjo Anime (Part One)," *Animation: An Interdisciplinary Journal* 1.1: 45–59.

LaMarre, T. (2008) "Speciesism, Part 1: Translating Races into Animals in Wartime Animation," in F. Lunning (ed.), *Mechademia 3: Limits of the Human*, Minneapolis: University of Minnesota Press, pp. 75–95.

LaMarre, T. (2009) *The Anime Machine: A Media Theory of Animation*, Minneapolis: University of Minnesota Press.

Langer, M. (1992) "The Disney-Fleischer Dilemma: Product Differentiation and Technological Innovation," *Screen* 33.4: 343–360.

Lee, W. (2000) "From *Sazae-san* to *Crayon Shin-chan*: Family Anime, Social Change and Nostalgia in Japan," in T. Craig (ed.), *Japan Pop!: Inside the World of Japanese Popular Culture*, Armonk, NY: ME Sharp, pp. 186–203.

Lee, H. (2009) "Between Fan Culture and Copyright Infringement: Manga Scanlation," *Media, Culture and Society* 31.6: 1011–1022.

Leonard, S. (2005) "Progress Against the Law: Anime and Fandom, with the Key to the Globalization of Culture," *International Journal of Cultural Studies* 8.3: 281–305.

Lerman, L. (1996) "Anime Vids Get Euro-Friendly," *Variety*, 24–30 June: 103.

Levi, A. (1996) *Samurai from Outer Space: Understanding Japanese Animation*, Chicago, IL: Open Court.

Levi, A. (2006) "The Americanization of Anime and Manga: Negotiating Popular Culture," in C. Bolton (ed.), *Cinema Anime*, New York: Palgrave Macmillan, pp. 43–63.

Levi, A., M. McHarry and D. Paggliassotti (eds), (2008) *Boys' Love Manga: Essays on the Sexual Ambiguity and Cross-Cultural Fandom of the Genre*, Jefferson: McFarland.

Leydon, J. (1996) "Ghost in the Shell," *Variety*, 1–7 April: 57.

Lister, D. (1993) "Cartoon Cult with an Increasing Appetite for Sex and Violence," *Independent*, October 15: 10.

Litten, F.S. (2014) "On the Earliest (Foreign) Animation Films Shown in Japanese Cinemas," http://litten.de/fulltext/nipper.pdf (accessed September 20, 2014).

Lobato, R. (2012) *Shadow Economies of Cinema: Mapping Informal Film Distribution*, London: BFI Publishing.

Lowing, R. (1991) "Sophisticated, but there's a bit too much," *Sun Herald* (Australia), January 13: 112.

Lunning, F. (2009) *Mechademia 4: War/Time*, Minneapolis: University of Minnesota Press.

Lunning, F. (2011) "Under the Ruffles: *Shōjo* and the Morphology of Power," in F. Lunning (ed.), *Mechademia 6: User Enhanced*, Minneapolis: University of Minnesota Press, pp. 3–19.

Lury, C. (2004) *Brands: The Logos of the Global Economy*, London: Routledge.

Lyman, E.J. (2008) "Venice Film Festival Unveils Lineup," *Hollywoodreporter.com*, July 29, n.p.

McArthur, C. (1972) *Underworld USA*, London: Secker and Warburg.

McCarthy, H. (1991–1992) "Anime and How to Get It," *Anime UK* 1, Winter: 15–19.

McCarthy, H. (1992a) "Project A-Ko," *Anime UK* 3, August–September: 5–10.

McCarthy, H. (1992b) "Porco Rosso," *Anime UK* 4, October–November: 30.

McCarthy, H. (1999) *Hayao Miyazaki: Master of Japanese Animation*, Berkeley, CA: Stone Bridge Press.

McCarthy, H. and J. Clements (1998) *The Erotic Anime Movie Guide*, London: Titan Books.

McCrea, C. (2008) "Explosive, Expulsive, Extraordinary: The Dimensional Excess of Animated Bodies," *Animation: An Interdisciplinary Journal* 3.1: 9–24.

McGray, D. (2002) "Japan's Gross National Cool," *Foreign Policy*, June: 44–54.

Macias, P. and T. Machiyama (2004) *Cruising the Anime City: An Otaku Guide to Neo Tokyo*. Berkeley, CA: Stone Bridge Press.

McKnight, A. (2010) "Frenchness and Transformation in Japanese Subculture, 1972–2004," in F. Lunning (ed.), *Mechademia 5: Fanthropologies*, Minneapolis: University of Minnesota Press, pp. 118–137.

McLelland, M. (2006) *"A Short History of 'Hentai',"* Intersections: Gender, History and Culture in an Asian Context, no.12, http://intersections.anu.edu. au/issue12/mclelland.html (last accessed 20/07/2015).

Malcolm, D. (1992) "Film: Manga! Manga! Manga! Season of Japanese Animations," *Guardian*, October 22: 6.

Manovich, L. (2009) "The Practice of Everyday (Media) Life: From Mass Consumption to Mass Cultural Production?" *Critical Inquiry* 35, Winter: 319–331.

Manry, G. (2008) "Tune In Tokyo," *Anime Insider* 63, December: 63.

Marechal, A.J. (2011) "GKids to Release Miyazaki Toons in U.S." *Variety,* http:// variety.com/2011/film/news/gkids-to-release-miyazaki-toons-in-u-s-1118042372/ (accessed June 10, 2014).

Marin, R., with T.T. Gegax, S. Jones, A. Rogers and H. Takayama (1995) "Holy Akira! It's Aeon Flux," *Newsweek*, August 14: 68.

Markoff, J. (1990) "Ideas & Trends; Art Invents a Jarring New World from Technology," *New York Times*, November 25, http://www.nytimes. com/1990/11/25/weekinreview/ideas-trends-art-invents-a-jarring-new-world-from-technology.html (accessed September 1, 2014).

Marshall, L. (2008) "The Sky Crawlers," *Screen International*, September 3, http:// www.screendaily.com/the-sky-crawlers/4040517.article, (accessed August 28, 2014).

Maslin, J. (1990) "Akira: A Tokyo of the Future in Vibrant Animation," *New York Times*, October 19, http://www.nytimes.com/movie/review?res=9C0CE1DF1 13CF93AA25753C1A966958260&partner=Rotten%2520Tomatoes (accessed August 26, 2014).

Mastrangelo, T. (n.d.) "The Pros and Cons of Being a Female Anime Fan," Mania. com, http://www.mania.com/pros-cons-being-female-anime-fan_article_84138. html (accessed September 12, 2014).

Masuda, H. (2007) *Understanding the Anime Business* [*Anime Bijinesu ga Wakaru*], Tokyo: NTT Shuppan.

Masuda H. (2011) *A Better Understanding of the Anime Business* [*Motto Wakaru Anime Bijinesu*], Tokyo: NTT Publishing.

Masuda H. and the Japanese Animation Association Database Working Group (2011) *Anime Industry Report 2011* [*Anime Sangyō Repōto 2011*], Tokyo: Japanese Animation Association Database Working Group.

Melville, I. (1999) *Marketing in Japan*. Oxford: Butterworth-Heinemann.

Mikami, K. (2011) "The Skill and Techniques of Anime Production," [*Anime no Seisaku Shuhō to Gijutsu*], in M. Takahashi and N. Tsugata (eds), *Anime Studies* [*Anime Gaku*], Tokyo: NTT Publishing, pp. 70–112.

Minamida, M. (2000a) "The Ultimate 'Anime Masterpiece' that Proves Anime Can Be High Quality Experiences that Are Superior to the Readers', [*Anime ga Dokusha ni Masaru Ryōshitsuna Tsuitaiken tarieru toiu koto o shōmei shita kyūkyoku no 'meisaku anime'*]," in Inoue Takeo (ed.), *Encyclopaedia of 20th Century Animation* [*Nijū Seiki Anime Daizen*], Tokyo: Futabashi, pp. 34–37.

Minamida, M. (2000b) "Introduction to the Recent History of Anime" [*Saikin Animeshi Gairon*], in Inoue Takeo (ed.), *Encyclopaedia of 20th Century Animation* [*Nijū Seiki Anime Daizen*], Tokyo: Futabashi, pp. 6–13.

Ministry for Economics Trade and Industry (METI) (2012) *Cool Japan Strategy*, September, http://www.meti.go.jp/english/policy/mono_info_service/creative_industries/pdf/121016_01a.pdf (accessed December 14, 2013).

Mitchell, D. (2000) *Cultural Geography: A Critical Introduction*, Oxford: Blackwells.

Mittell, J. (2001) "A Cultural Approach to Television Genre Theory," *Cinema Journal* 40.3 (Spring): 3–24.

Mittell, J. (2004) *Genre and Television: From Cop Shows to Cartoons in American Culture*, New York: Routledge.

Miyao, D. (2002) "Before Anime: Animation and the Pure Film Movement in Pre-war Japan". *Japan Forum* 14.2: 191–209.

Morely, D. and K. Robins (1995) *Spaces of Identity: Global Media, Electronic Landscapes and Cultural Boundaries*, London: Routledge.

Morgenstern, J. (2002) "A Dazzling 'Spirited Away' Is More Vivid than Reality," *Wall Street Journal*, September 20, http://online.wsj.com/news/articles/SB1032476245649812195 (accessed June 10, 2014).

Mori, T. (1995) "Interview: Producer Toshio Suzuki: One More Ghibli History—1983–1995, An On-site Report," [*Suzuki Toshio Purodyūsā – Intabyū: Mō Hitotsu no Jiburishi – '83-'95 Genba kara no Hōkoku*] *Kinema Junpo* 1166, November: 46–52.

Munson-Siter, P. (1993) "RG Veda," *Anime UK* 9: 21–26.

Murakami, Takashi (2000) *Supāfuratto* [*Superflat*], Tokyo: Madora Shuppan.

Napier, S.J. (1996) "Panic Sites: The Japanese Imagination of Disaster from Godzilla to Akira," in J. Whittier Treat (ed) *Contemporary Japan and Popular Culture*, Richmond, VA: Curzon, pp. 235–262.

Napier, S.J. (1998) "Vampires, Psychic Girls, Flying Women and Sailor Scouts: Four Faces of the Young Female in Japanese Popular Culture," in D.P. Martinez (ed) *The Worlds of Japanese Popular Culture: Gender, Shifting Boundaries and Global Cultures*, Cambridge: Cambridge University Press, pp. 91–109.

Napier, S.J. (2001) *Anime from Akira to Princess Mononoke: Experiencing Contemporary Japanese Animation*, New York: Palgrave.

Napier, S.J. (2002) "When the Machines Stop: Fantasy, Reality, and the Terminal Identity in 'Neon Genesis Evangelion' and 'Serial Experiments Lain'," *Science Fiction Studies* 29.3, November: 418–235.

Napier, S.J. (2005) *Anime from Akira to Howl's Moving Castle: Experiencing Contemporary Japanese Animation*, New York: Palgrave.

Napier, S.J. (2006) "Matter Out of Place: Carnival, Containment, and Cultural Recovery in Miyazaki's 'Spirited Away'," *Journal of Japanese Studies* 32.2, Summer: 287–310.

Neale, S. (1993) "Melo Talk: On the Meaning and Use of the Term 'Melodrama' in the American Trade Press," *Velvet Light Trap* 32, Fall: 66–89.

Neale, S. (2000) *Genre and Hollywood*. New York: Routledge.

Nesselson, L. (2003) "Review: 'The Cat Returns'," *Variety* (August 29), http://variety.com/2003/film/reviews/the-cat-returns-1200539688/ (accessed June 10, 2014).

Newitz, A. (1995) "Magical Girls and Atomic Bomb Sperm: Japanese Animation in America," *Film Quarterly* 49.1, Autumn: 2–15.

Nunokawa, Y. "Message from Chairman Yuji Nunokawa," *Pierrot Official Website*, http://en.pierrot.jp/company.html#co_001 (accessed March 13, 2014).

O'Connell, M. (1996) "Ghost in the Shell: A Gem in the Video Store," *Washington Post*, May 29: R15.

Odell, C. and M. Le Blanc (2009) *Studio Ghibli: The Films of Hayao Miyazaki and Isao Takahata*, Harpenden: Kamera Books.

Onoue, I., K. Makuta and N. Kimura (2012) "It All Started with Ultraman," [*Subete wa Urutoraman kara Hajimatta*] *Nikkei Entertainment!* 181, April: 28–30.

Orbaugh, S. (2002) "*Sex* and the Single Cyborg: Japanese Popular Culture Experiments in Subjectivity," *Science Fiction Studies* 2.3: 436–452.

Orbaugh, S. (2012) "*Kamishibai* and the Art of the Interval," in F. Lunning (ed.), *Mechademia 7: Lines of Sight*, Minneapolis: University of Minnesota Press, pp. 78–100.

Osmond, A. (2014) "*The King and the Mockingbird*," *Empire* 299, May: 56.

O'Sullivan, M. (2005) "'Steamboy': So Cool It's Cold," *Washington Post*, March 25, http://www.washingtonpost.com/wp-dyn/content/article/2005/03/24/AR2005062901013.html (accessed September 3, 2014).

Overton, W. (1992–1993) "Nadia Notes," *Anime UK* 5, December–January: 24.

Patten, F. (2003) "This Month in Anime History—December 1972," *NewtypeUSA* 2.12 (December): 54.

Patten, F. (2004a) *Watching Anime, Reading Manga: 25 Years of Essays and Reviews*, Berkeley, CA: Stone Bridge Press.

Patten, F. (2004b) "The Era of 'Lost' Anime," *NewtypeUSA* 3.1, January: 55.

Patten, F. (2004c) "This Month in Anime History—March 1976," *NewtypeUSA* 3.3, March: 54.

Perren, A. (2012) *Indie, Inc.: Miramax and the Transformation of Hollywood in the 1990s*. Austin: University of Texas Press.

Plumb, A. (2014) "The Lizard Kings," *Empire* 299, May: 74–78.

Pointon, S. (1997) "Transcultural Orgasm as Apocalypse: *Urotsukidoji; The Legend of the Overfiend*," *Wide Angle* 19.3, July: 41–63.

Poitras, G. (1999) *The Anime Companion: What's Japanese in Japanese Animation?* Berkeley, CA: Stone Bridge Press.

Puig, C. (2002) "'Spirited Away' Turns Heads in U.S.," *USA Today*, http://usatoday30.usatoday.com/life/movies/reviews/2002-09-19-spirited-away_x.htm (accessed June 10, 2014).

Richmond, S. (2009) *The Rough Guide to Anime*, London: Rough Guides.

Rickey, C. (1996) "Virtual Reality Takes a Wild Ride," *Philadelphia Inquirer*, May 9: C04.

Ringel, E. (1996) "Review: 'Ghost in the Shell'." *Atlanta Journal and Constitution*, April 19: 11P.

Robertson, J. (1988) "*Furusato* Japan: The Culture and Politics of Nostalgia," *Politics, Culture, and Society* 1.4, Summer: 494–518.

Romney, J. (1995) "Manga for All Seasons," *Guardian*, May 4: T15.

Ruh, B. (2004) *Stray Dog of Anime: The Films of Mamoru Oshii*, New York: Palgrave Macmillan.

Ruh, B. (2005) "The Robots from Takkun's Head: Cyborg Adolescence in *FLCL*," in S.T. Brown (ed.), *Cinema Anime*, New York: Palgrave, pp. 139–160.

Ruh, B. (2010) "Transforming U.S. Anime in the 1980s: Localization and Longevity," in F. Lunning (ed.), *Mechademia 5: Fanthropologies*, Minneapolis: University of Minnesota Press, pp. 31–49.

Saitō, T. ([2000] 2011) J.K. Vincent and D. Lawson (trans.) *Beautiful Fighting Girl*, Minneapollis: University of Minnesota Press.

Sandler, K.S. (ed.) (1998) *Reading the Rabbit: Explorations in Warner Bros. Animation*, New Brunswick, NJ: Rutgers.

Schatz, T. (1981a) *Hollywood Genres*, Austin: University of Texas Press.

Schatz, T. (1981b) *Hollywood Genres: Formulas, Filmmaking and the Studio System*, Boston, MA: McGraw-Hill.

Schatz, T. (2003) "The New Hollywood," in J. Stringer (ed.), *Movie Blockbusters*, London: Routledge, pp. 15–44.

Schaub, J.C. (2001) "Kusanagi's Body: Gender and Technology in Mecha-anime," *Asian Journal of Communication* 11.2: 79–100.

Schodt, F.L. (1983) *Manga! Manga! The World of Japanese Comics*, Tokyo: Kodansha International.

Schodt, F.L. (2007) *The Astro Boy Essays: Osamu Tezuka, Mighty Atom, Manga/Anime Revolution*, Berkeley, CA: Stone Bridge Press.

Schilling, M. (2004) "Steamboy," *Screen International*, June 18, n.p.

Schneider, S.J. and T. Williams (2005) *Horror International*, Detroit, MI: Wayne State University Press.

Shamoon, D. (2007) "Revolutionary Romance: *The Rose of Versailles* and the Transformation of Shojo Manga," in F Lunning (ed.), *Mechademia 2: Networks of Desire*, Minneapolis: University of Minnesota Press, pp. 3–17.

Shannon, J. (2005) "Anime Adventure Picks Up Too Much Steam in the End," *Seattle Times*, April 1, http://seattletimes.com/html/movies/2002226514_steamboy01.html (accessed August 28, 2014).

Silverberg, M. (2006) *Erotic Grotesque Nonsense: The Mass Culture of Modern Japan*, Berkeley: University of California Press.

Simmons, M. (2002) "A Consideration About the Gundam Universe," in M. Simmons, B. Wright and Animerica Magazine (eds), *Gundam Official Guide*, San Franciso, CA: Viz Communications, p. 4.

Smith, A. (1995) "Inside a Society Dominated by Rigid Codes of Conduct, There Is a Parallel Universe where Anything Goes," *Observer*, November 19: 20.

Smith, L. (2007) "Hell Girl Volume 1," *NewtypeUSA* 6.10, October: 91.

Smith, T. (2009a) "Complete Series: Death Note" *Neo* 63, October: 60–61.

Smith, T. (2009b) "Vol. 4: Hellsing Ultimate," *Neo* 57, May: 63.

Solomon, C. (1990) "Movie Review: 'Akira': High-Tech Hokum from Japan." *Los Angeles Times*, March 14. http://articles.latimes.com/1990-03-14/entertainment/ca-113_1_akira-comics (accessed September 11, 2014).

Span, P. (1997) "Cross-Cultural Cartoon Cult," *Washington Post*, May 15: B01.

Spangler, T. (2013) "Chernin Group Takes Majority Stake in Anime Website Crunchyroll," *Variety*, December 2, http://variety.com/2013/digital/news/chernin-group-takes-majority-stake-in-anime-website-crunchyroll-1200910515/ (accessed August 9, 2014).

Staiger, J. (1992) *Interpreting Films: Studies in the Historical Reception of American Cinema*, Princeton, NJ: Princeton University Press.

Staiger, J. (2000) *Perverse Spectators: The Practices of Film Reception*. New York: New York University Press.

Staiger, J. (2005) *Media Reception Studies*. New York: New York University Press.

Standish, I. (1998) "*Akira*, Postmodernism and Resistance," in D.P. Martinez (ed.), *The Worlds of Japanese Popular Culture: Gender, Shifting Boundaries and Global Cultures*, Cambridge: Cambridge University Press, pp. 56–74.

Stein, W. and J. E. Browning (2008) "The Western Eastern: De-Coding Hybridity and CyberZen Gothic and *Vampire Hunter D* (1985)," in A.H.S. Ng (ed.), *Asian Gothic: Essays on Literature, Film and Anime*, Jefferson: McFarland, pp. 210–223.

Steinberg, M. (2012) *Anime's Media Mix: Franchising Toys and Characters in Japan*, Minneapolis: University of Minnesota Press.

Street, R. (1995) "Take Your Pick from Big List of Pic Projects," *Daily Variety*, September 20: a.p.

Studio Ghibli Advertising Editors (2002) *Have You Seen the Newspaper Advertisements for Nausicaa?—An 18 Year History of Ghibli's Newspaper Advertisements* [*Naushika no "Shimbun Kōkoku"tte Mita Koto Arimasuka?—Jiburi no Shimbun Kōkoku 18nenshi*], Tokyo: Tokuma Publishing Studio Ghibli Section.

Sugawa Shimada, A. (2011) *Representations of Girls in Japanese Magical Girl TV Animation Programmes from 1966 to 2003 and Japanese Female Audiences' Understanding of Them*, PhD Thesis, University of Warwick.

Surat, D. (2010) "High Stakes!: *Blood: The Last Vampire* Debuts on Blu-Ray," *OtakuUSA*, 3.4, February: 92–93.

Suzuki, T. (1994) "Producer Toshio Suzuki Speaks About '*Pom Poko*': From the Planning to the Star of the Scenario." [*Suzuki Toshio Purodyūsā ga Kataru "Heisei Tanuki Gassen Pom Poko": Kikaku kara Shinario Chakushu Made*] *Pom Poko* [*Heisei Tanuki Gassen Pom Poko* Official Brochure], Tokyo: Toho, pp. 27–28.

Suzuki, T. (2005) *My Film Hobby*. [*Eiga Dōraku*], Tokyo: Pia.

Suzuki, T. (2006) "Message: 'Is It Experience, or Is It Inspiration?'," [*Message: Keiken ka, Soretomo Insupirēshonka"*] *Tales from Earthsea* [*Gedo Senki*, Official Brochure], Tokyo: Toho Stellar, 6.

Takahashi, M. and N. Tsugata (eds), (2010) *Anime Studies* [*Anime Gaku*], Tokyo: NTT Publishing.

Takamae, E. (2002) Robert Ricketts and Sebastian Swan (trans.) *The Allied Occupation of Japan*, New York: Continuum.

Tanaka, M. (2014) "Trends of Fiction in 2000s Japanese Pop Culture," *Electronic Journal of Contemporary Japanese Studies* 14.2, http://www.japanesestudies.org.uk/ejcjs/vol14/iss2/tanaka.html (accessed April 1, 2015).

Tartaglione-Vialatte, N. (2008) "Elle Driver Picks Up Japanese Title the Sky Crawlers," *Screen International*, May 16: n.p.

Tezuka, O. (1997) *My Manga Life* [*Boku no Manga Jinsei*], Tokyo: Iwanami Publishing.

Tobin, J. (ed) (2004) *Pikachu's Global Adventure: The Rise and Fall of Pokémon*, Durham: Duke University Press.

Toguchi, K. (2011) "Thinking About the Reasons for the Popularity of 'Hidamari Sketch'." ['*Hidamari suketchi': Ninki no Riyū o Kangaetemita*], *Screen Plus* 29: 24–26.

Toku, M. (2007) "Shojo Manga! Girls' Comics! A Mirror of Girls' Dreams," in F. Lunning (ed.), *Mechademia 2: Networks of Desire*, Minneapolis: University of Minnesota Press, pp. 19–32.

Tokugi, Y. (1999) *Complete Book of TV Animation: Illustrated* [*Zusetsu Terebi Anime Zensho*], in Misono, M. (ed.), *Fifteen Years of Original Video Animation* [*OVA no Jūgonen*], Tokyo: Hara Shobō, pp. 305–330.

Toole, M. (2010) "Ghost Hound: Complete Collection 1: The Dream-Quest of Unknown Suiten," *OtakuUSA* 3.4, February: 18–19.

Tsugata, N. (2005) *Introduction to Animation Studies* [*Animēshon Gaku Nyūmon*], Tokoyo: Heibonsha.

Tsugata, N. (2011a) "What Is Anime?" [*Anime to wa Nanika?*], in Takahashi, M. and N. Tsugata (ed.), *Anime Studies* [*Anime Gaku*], Tokyo: NTT Publishing, pp. 3–23.

Tsugata, N. (2011b) "Animation History," [*Anime no Rekishi*], in M. Takahashi and N. Tsugata (ed.), *Anime Studies* [*Anime Gaku*], Tokyo: NTT Publishing, pp. 24–44.

Tsukue, C. and C. Tamura (eds), (2007 [2001]) R. Izutsu-Vajirasarn (trans.) *Ghibli Museum, Mitaka*, Tokyo: Tokuma Memorial Cultural Foundation for Animation.

Tudor, A. (1974) *Theories of Film*, London: Secker and Walburg.

Wasko, J. (2002) *Understanding Disney*. Cambridge: Polity Press.

Wasser, F. (2001) *Veni, Vidi, Video: The Hollywood Empire and the VCR*. Austen: University of Texas Press.

Wells, P. (1997) "Hayao Miyazaki, Floating Worlds, Floating Signifiers," *Art and Design* 53: 22–25.

Wells, P. (2003) "Smarter than the Average Art Form: Animation in the Television Era," in C.A. Stabile and M. Harrison (eds), *Prime Time Animation: Television Animation and American Culture*, London: Routledge.

Winge, T. (2006) "Costuming the Imagination: Origins of Anime and Manga Cosplay," in F. Lunning (ed.), *Mechademia 1: Emerging Worlds of Anime and Manga*. Minneapolis, University of Minnesota Press, pp. 65–76.

Wright, B. (2002) "Mobile Suit Gundam: Production History," in J. Davis (ed.), *Animerica: Gundam Official Guide*, San Francisco, CA: Viz Publications, pp. 5–16.

Wyatt, J. (1994) *High Concept: Movies and Marketing in Hollywood*, Austin: University of Texas Press.

Yamaguchi, Yasuo (2004) *Complete History of Japanese Animation* [*Nihon no Anime Zenshi*], Tokyo: Ten Books.

Yamamura, T. (2009) "Anime Pilgrimage and Local Tourism Promotion: An Experience of Washinomiya Town, the Sacred Place for Anime '*Lucky Star*' Fans," *Hokkaido University Collection of Scholarly and Academic Papers*, http://hdl.handle.net/2115/38541 (accessed March 14, 2014).

Yasumoto, S. (2011) "Impact on Soft Power of Cultural Mobility: Japan to East Asia," (Winter), http://www.tft.ucla.edu/mediascape/Winter2011_SoftPower.html (accessed December 14, 2013).

Yoda, K. (2005) "The World's Earliest 'Tales from Earthsea' Interview (Full Version)," [Sekai Ichi Hayai 'Gedo Senki' Intabyū] Yomiuri Online, December 15, [Reproduced on Studio Ghibli Official Website], http://www.ghibli.jp/20special/000283.html (accessed June 10, 2014).

Yoshioka, S. (2008) "Heart of Japaneseness: History and Nostalgia in Hayao Miyazaki's Spirited Away," in Mark MacWilliams (ed.), Japanese Visual Culture: Explorations in the World of Manga and Anime, Armonk, NY: M.E. Sharp, pp. 256–273.

Zahlten, A. (2007) The Role of Genre in Film from Japan: Transformations 1960s–2000s, PhD Thesis, Johannes Gutenberg University, Mainz.

Zanghellini, A. (2009) "Underage Sex and Romance in Japanese Homoerotic Manga and Anime," Social Legal Studies 18.2, June: 159–177.

Index

5 Centimeters Per Second (Byōsoku Go Senchimētoru) 31
AD Vision 87
Adventures of Hutch the Honey Bee (Konchū Monogatari: Minashigo Hatchi) 89
Aim for the Ace! (Ēsu o Nerau!) 90
Akira 31–43, 67, 87, 155
Allison, Anne 57–58, 133
Altman, Rick 17–20, 40, 118, 153
anime
    aesthetics 8–9, 55, 67, 79–80
    bodies 34, 51–68, 155
    canon 11, 15, 155–156
    and children 18, 31, 57, 66, 69–76, 78, 81–83, 89–90, 133
    controversies 3–4, 27, 63–66, 73–74, 137–38
    cultural phenomenon 2, 12, 16, 24, 27, 114
    industry 4, 7–8, 23, 25, 60, 72, 75–80, 83, 136–38, 142–47
    genres 3–4, 12, 16, 22–29, 88, 90, 102
    globalization 6, 23, 35–37, 62, 80–83, 85–88, 94–99, 102–10, 118–22, 159–63
    localization 4, 25–26, 28, 52, 80–83, 85–88, 97–98, 147–48, 159, 168
    music videos (amvs) 107–8
    nation 10–14, 111
    nationalism 10–11, 74–75
    pilgrimage 18, 134–36
Anime Contents Expo 17, 137–38
Anime UK fanzine 86, 94–98
Anne of Green Gables (Akage no An) 54
Arabian Nights: Sinbad the Sailor (Arabian Naito: Shinobaddo no Bōken) 77, 81

Arias, Michael 148
Astro Boy (Tetsuwan Atomu) 5–6, 31, 52, 78–83, 85, 87, 88, 91–92, 99, 133, 135, 142–44
Attack No.1 (Atakku No.1) 90
Azuma, Hiroki 7
Azumanga Daioh 112, 114

Ben 10 147
Bishōnen 56
Black Blood Brothers 159
Black Butler (Kuroshitsuji) 163
Blade Runner 41–42
Bleach 94, 143, 160
Blood: The Last Vampire 156, 159–60
Blossoms of Tomorrow (Hanasaku Iroha) 104
Boogiepop Phantom 161
Bones (studio) 61, 149
Brave Exkaiser (Yūsha Ekusukaizā) 92
Brave Raideen (Yusha Raideen) 85
Bubblegum Crisis 96

Candy Candy 89
Case Closed (Meitantei Konan) 28, 141–42
Cat Returns, The (Neko no ongaeshi) 121, 124, 129
Cavallaro, Dani 7–9
Chevallier D'Eon 90–91
Chibi 57
Chibi Maruko-chan 92, 112
Chi's Sweet Home 110, 139, 146
Chobits 59
Clements, Jonathan 2, 4–5, 59–66, 70–71, 75, 77–79, 88, 90, 113
ComiKet 17, 138
Condry, Ian 1–2, 93–94, 107
Cowboy Bebop 17, 28
Crayon Shin-chan 112, 114
Cream Lemon 61–62

Crunchyroll 109–110
cyberpunk 32, 35, 38, 40–43
cyborgs 34–35, 41, 43, 45, 58–59, 67

Dangaioh 87
Death Note 139, 142, 160, 161
Dekobō Shingajō (Kid Deko, Kid
    Deko's New Picture Book) 71
Detroit Metal City 29, 141–42
D.Gray-Man 157, 159–60
Dirty Pair 62, 96, 99
discourse analysis 6, 12, 20–22
Doggie March (Wanwan
    Chūshingura) 77
Dōjinshi (amateur manga artists) 17, 53
Dōseiai (same-sex love) 90
Dragon Ball 91
Dragon Crisis (Doragun
    Kuraishisu!) 109

Elfen Lied 164–65
erotic (ero) anime 4, 25, 62–64, 65,
    138

Fables of the Green Forest (Yama
    Nezumi Rokkichakku) 89
fans
    creativity 3, 103–107
    distribution 87, 105–6
    fansubbing 87, 101, 105–7, 109
    fanzines 86
    otaku 7, 53, 99, 113
FLCL 58
Free! – Iwatobi Swim Club (Furī) 110
Freedom 60
Fullmetal Alchemist (Hagane no
    Renkinjutsushi) 25, 60–61
FUNimation 60, 101, 105, 108–9, 165

Gainax 79, 91, 108, 145, 147
Galaxy Express 999 143
Garden of Sinners (Kara no Kyōkai) 60
genre method 20–22
genre theory 15–22
Ghiblies 2 (Ghiburīsu 2) 124
Ghost Hound 161
Ghost Hunt 162, 165–6
Ghost in the Shell (Kōkaku kidōtai)
    31–43, 48, 58, 79, 104
Ghost in the Shell: Innocence 67

Ghost in the Shell: Standalone
    Complex 34
Girl Who Leapt Through Time, The
    (Toki o Kakeru Shōjo) 27
Grave of the Fireflies (Hotaru no
    Haka) 11
Graveyard Kitarō (Hakaba no Kitarō;
    Gegege no Kitarō) 11, 136
GunBuster (Toppu o Nerae!) 87
Gundam 92–93, 97, 99, 135
Gurren Lagann (Tengen Toppa Guren
    Ragan) 145, 147
Guyver (Kyōshoku Sōkō Gaibā) 59

Hakujaden (Panda and the Magic
    Serpent) 77
Hayate the Combat Butler (Hayate no
    Gotoku!) 110
Hell Girl (Jigoku Shōjo) 161–62
Hellsing 158–59
Hentai (perverse, "ecchi" or "h") 26,
    62–64, 66, 109, 153
Highlander 146
horror anime 52, 58, 63, 66, 155–168
Hosoda, Mamoru 27–28,
Howl's Moving Castle (Haoru no
    ugoku shiro) 120, 122, 129
Hurricane Polymar (Hariken Porimā) 89

Ikeda, Ryoko 90
intertextuality 7–8, 150
Ishihara, Shintarō 137, 148
Iwabuchi, Koichi 10, 111

Japanese culture
    folklore 4, 28–29, 157–58
    myths 4, 72, 122, 158
Japanese manga animation 39
Japanimation 38–39, 43, 62

Kaasan—Mom's Life (Mainichi
    Kaasan) 110
Kagaku Ninjatai Gatchman (Battle of
    the Planets, G-Force) 81, 83, 89
Kaiba 146
Kamishibai 70–71, 76
Kiki's Delivery Service (Majō no Takyū
    bin) 122, 128–29
Kimba the White Lion (Jangaru Taitei)
    82–83

King and the Mockingbird, The (Le Roi et l'oiseau) 122–23
Kinoshita, Gaku 148, 151
Kitayama, Seitarō 72–73
K'On! (Keion!) 53, 110–114
Kōuchi, Junichi 72–73
Kyara Bijinesu (Character Business) 52–53, 79
Kyōsō Giga (Capital Craze Comic) 149
Kyoto Animation 53, 110, 114

Ladd, Fred 81–83
Lamarre, Thomas 8–9, 11, 59, 74–75
Ledford, John 87
Levi, Antonia 3, 4, 10, 54
Limited animation 9, 80
Little Norse Prince, The (Taiyō no Ōji:Horusu no Daibōken) 81
Little Witch Sally (Mahō Tsukai Sarī) 88
Lucky Star 112, 114, 136
Lupin Sansei (Lupin III) 143

Madhouse Animation 146
Magical Angel Creamy Mami (Mahō no Tenshi Kurīmī Mami) 91
Magical girl 26, 56, 59, 91, 99, 109
Magical Mako (Mahō no Mako-chan) 89
Manga eiga 5
Manga Entertainment UK 23, 25, 39, 66, 94, 105
Marine Boy (Kaitei Shōnen Marin) 82–83
Masaoka, Kenzō 76
Masterpiece Theater 54
Matsumoto, Leiji 143
Mazinger Z 93
McCarthy, Helen 3, 4, 26, 62–66, 94, 98
Mecha 26–27, 33–35, 58, 92–94, 97–98, 109
media mix 78–79, 103–104, 136, 140, 149
Melancholy of Haruhi Suzumiya, The (Suzumiya Haruhi no Yūutsu) 114
meta-genre 22–29, 165
Minami, Masahiko 25
Mittell, Jason 19–22, 23
Miyazaki, Hayao 11, 76, 81, 87, 95, 98, 103, 117–131, 143, 170 n.3
Mobile Police Patlabor (Kidō Keisatsu Patoreibā) 60, 97–98, 99

moe 53, 112–14
Momotarō's Divine Sea Warriors (Momotarō no Umi no Shinpei) 75
Momotarō's Sea Eagles (Momotarō no Umiwashi) 75
Mukuzo Imokawa the Doorman (Imokawa Mukuzo Genkanban no Maki) 72
Murata, Yasuji 76
Mushi Productions (also Tezuka Osamu Productions) 6, 78–79, 81, 144, 147
Mushi-shi 166
MVM 23, 105
My Neighbour Totoro (Tonari no Totoro) 122, 124–125
My Sun Wukong (or My Son Goku, Boku no Songokū) 77, 78
MyM magazine 23

Nadia: The Secret of Blue Water (Fushigi no Umi no Nadia) 95
Napier, Susan J. 10, 11, 16–17, 33–34, 35, 56, 58–59, 62, 99, 111, 155, 167
Naruto 94, 105, 107, 143
Natsume's Book of Friends (Natsume Yūjinchō) 110
Nausicaa of the Valley of the Wind (Kaze no Tani no Naushika) 87, 127, 128
Neo magazine 110, 154, 161, 162, 163
Neo-Human Casshern (Shinzō Ningen Kyashān) 89
Neon Genesis Evangelion 9, 80, 91, 92, 99, 129
Neuromancer 41
Newitz, Annalee 3, 4, 56
Nichijōkei anime 53, 102, 110–115
Night on the Galactic Railroad (Ginga Tetsudō no Yoru) 98
Norakuro, Private Second Class (Norakuro Nitōhei) 74

Ōfuji, Noburō 81
Ōkawa, Hiroshi 77
One Piece 105, 108
Original Animation Video 59–63
Original Video Animation 6, 59–63

Oshii, Mamoru 10, 32, 34, 42, 43–45, 48, 60, 97, 111
Otogi Manga Calendar 78
Otogi Pro 78, 81
Ōtomo, Katsuhiro 32, 34, 36–38, 41, 43, 46–47, 60

Panda Kopanda (*Panda Go Panda*) 143
paper animation 5, 72
Patten, Fred 78, 81, 85–86, 87, 93
Peeping Life 110
Pet Shop of Horrors 161
Pierrot Studio 143–144, 147
Poitras, Gilles 3, 4
Pokémon franchise 22, 103, 130, 139, 147
Pom Poko (*Heisei Tanuki Gassen Pom Poko*) 125, 128
Ponyo (*Gake no ue no Ponyo*) 121, 127
Porco Rosso (*Kurenai no Buta*) 98, 130
pornography 26, 52, 62–68, 153, 155
Prince of Tennis (*Tenisu no Ōjisama*) 110
Princess Knight (*Ribon no Kishi*) 90
Princess Mononoke (*Mononokehime*) 119, 120, 122, 125, 127, 129
Production IG 45, 139
propaganda 11, 74–75
Puella Magi Madoka Magica (*Mahō Shōjo Madoka Magika*) 99

rabu kome (love comedy) 56
Rahxephon 28
Ranma ½ 56, 58, 96
Rascal 54
Redline 146
Requiem from the Darkness 161
RG Veda (*Seiden: Rigu Vēda*) 95
Right Stuf! 104–105
Robotech 26, 27, 83
romance 3, 27, 45, 48, 51, 55, 56, 91, 109, 143, 147, 153, 164, 167
Rose of Versailles (*Berusayu no Bara*) 89, 90

Sailor Moon (*Bishōjo Senshi Sērā Mūn*) 57–58, 80, 88, 89, 90, 99
Saint Seiya (*Seitōshi Seiya*) 91
Sazae-san 112

science fiction (sci fi, SF) 12–13, 26–28, 31, 33–35, 40, 43–46, 48–49, 58, 59, 61, 78, 87, 91–92, 99, 105, 113, 159, 163, 165, 167
Secret of Akko-chan, The (*Himitsu no Akko-chan*) 89
Seinen 24, 109
Serial Experiments Lain 161
Sex 3, 26, 35, 56, 58, 59, 63, 65–66, 90–91, 165
Shimokawa, Ōten 72
shōjo 24–26, 52, 54–59, 67, 86, 88–92, 94, 95–97, 99, 105, 107, 109, 110, 128, 153, 165
shōnen 24–26, 54, 56, 58, 67, 86, 88–98, 99, 105, 107, 109–110, 153
shōnen ai (boys' love) 26, 164
Short Short 60, 125
Sky Crawlers, The 32, 43–45, 48
soft power 14, 23, 103
Soul Eater 149–50
Space Battleship Yamato (*Uchū Senkan Yamato*) 28, 89, 91, 92
Space Brothers (*Uchū Kyōdai*) 110
Space Dandy 28
Speed Racer (*Mahha Go Go Go*) 43, 55, 81, 82, 83, 85
Spice and Wolf (*Ōkami to Kōshinryō*) 28
Spirited Away (*Sen to Chihiro no Kamikakushi*) 11, 120–21, 122, 127, 129
Spongebob Squarepants 146
sports anime 28, 90, 91, 94, 110, 143
Spread of Syphilis, The (*Baidoku no Denpa*) 73
Star of the Giants (*Kyōjin no Hoshi*) 90
Steamboy 32, 43–48
steampunk 32, 43–48
Steinberg, Marc 54, 78–79, 133
Studio 4°C 148
Studio Ghibli 6, 11, 12, 22, 60, 81, 103, 117–132
Suzuki, Toshio 118, 123, 127–132

Tales from Earthsea (*Gedo Senki*) 121, 128, 130
Takahashi, Mitsuteru 5–6
Takahashi, Rumiko 56, 96

Takahata, Isao 11, 54, 76, 81, 118, 123, 125, 128, 130, 143
Tatsunoko Productions (Tatsunoko Pro) 81
terebi manga 5
Tezuka, Osamu 5, 9, 27, 31, 52, 77–80, 81, 82, 90, 133, 135, 143, 144
  Tezuka's Curse 78–79
Tezuka Productions 143, 144
Time Bokan 89
Tōei Dōga (also Toei Animation) 9, 54, 77–78, 81, 88, 89
Tokyo International Anime Fair (TAF) 133, 136–151
Treasure Island Revisited (Shin Takarajima) 81
Trinity Blood 157, 159, 160, 163
Tsugata, Nobuyuki 5–6, 61, 70, 71, 72, 73, 91, 92

Urotsukidōji: Legend of the Overfiend (Chōjin Densetsu Urotsukidōji) 26, 52, 62–68, 155
Utsushi-e 70

Vampire Hunter D 155–56
Vampire Hunter Yōko (Mamono Hantā Yōko) 62
Vampire Knight (Vanpaia Naito) 29, 156–57, 158
violence 39, 62, 65, 66, 67, 82–83
Voltron 26, 87

Wagnaria! (Working!!) 110
Watanabe, Shinichirō 17, 28
Weekly Shōnen Jump 26, 91, 94
Whale, The (Kujira) 81
Wind Rises, The (Kaze Tachinu) 119, 121

xxxHolic 24–25, 158–159
xxxHolic: A Midsummer Night's Dream 158

yaoi 26
Yamamoto, Sanae 73
Yoshida, Tatsuo 81
Young Chame's Airgun (Chame no Kūkijū) 73